AF

D1568179

Hollywood and the Profession of Authorship, 1928-1940

Studies in Cinema, No. 29

Diane M. Kirkpatrick, Series Editor

Professor, History of Art
The University of Michigan

Other Titles in This Series

Hollywood and the Profession of Authorship, 1928-1940

by
Richard Fine
Assistant Professor of English and
Coordinator of American Studies Program
Virginia Commonwealth University
Richmond, Virginia

UMI RESEARCH PRESS
Ann Arbor, Michigan

Produced and distributed by
UMI Research Press
an imprint of
University Microfilms International
A Xerox Information Resources Company
Ann Arbor, Michigan 48106

Library of Congress Cataloging in Publication Data

Fine, Richard.
  Hollywood and the profession of authorship, 1928-1940.

  (Studies in cinema ; 29)
  Revision of thesis (Ph.D.)—University of Pennsylvania,
1979.
  Bibliography: p.
  Includes index.
  1. Screen writers—United States—Biography.
2. Moving-picture industry—United States—History.
I. Title. II. Series: Studies in cinema ; no. 29.
PN1998.A2F536 1985   384'.8'0973   84-28129
ISBN 0-8357-1602-3

Contents

Acknowledgments

I began researching this project in 1973, while a graduate student in the Department of American Civilization at the University of Pennsylvania. In the intervening ten years, I have consulted documentary and manuscript collections at these institutions: Academy of Motion Picture Arts and Sciences Library, Beverly Hills, California; American Film Institute Library, Beverly Hills, California; Berg Collection, New York Public Library, New York, New York; Beinecke Library, Yale University, New Haven, Connecticut; Boston Public Library, Boston, Massachusetts; Houghton Library, Harvard University, Cambridge, Massachusetts; Humanities Research Center, University of Texas, Austin, Texas; Library of Congress, Washington, D.C.; Penn State University Library, State College, Pennsylvania; Princeton University Library, Princeton, New Jersey; UCLA Library, UCLA, Los Angeles, California; and the Van Pelt Library, University of Pennsylvania, Philadelphia, Pennsylvania. My grateful thanks to the staffs of all of these institutions.

In addition, Hesper Anderson, the late W. R. Burnett, Robert Carson, the late George Oppenheimer, Samson Raphaelson, and Budd Schulberg graciously granted interviews to the author. The late S.N. Behrman, Daniel Fuchs, the late Jonathan Latimer and the late Nunnally Johnson all responded to requests for written statements. I appreciate their invaluable assistance.

Several teachers and colleagues read this manuscript at various stages of its development. I would like to thank Professors Robert Lucid and Janice Radway—and especially Neil Leonard—all of the University of Pennsylvania—for their encouragement and counsel while I was at Penn. I would also like to thank John Caughey and Gordon Kelly, both members of the American Studies Program at the University of Maryland, for their advice while I was conceiving the project. Robert Bennett of the Université de Caen in Caen, France, Daniel Aaron of Harvard University and Boyd Berry, Lynn Bloom and James Kinney—all colleagues in the English Department of Virginia Commonwealth University—pointed out many flaws in my argument and many infelicities of style which I have tried to correct. Any which remain, remain my own responsibility.

The secretarial staff of the English Department at VCU—Sharon Call, Norma Middleton, Donna Sabol, and Lucy Fraser—helped in a hundred ways during the production of this book. Jacqueline Giri deserves special mention for mastering the vagaries of the VCU word processing system to complete this manuscript.

I would also like to acknowledge the encouragement of my parents, Ruth and Roy Fine; I could never have begun, much less completed, this work without them. And a final word of thanks to Sara Ferguson, my wife, who helped greatly with this book, not the least of which by reminding me that there are many things more important than books.

Introduction: The Hollywood Legend

For more than fifty years American authors have regularly accepted work in the movie industry, and for more than fifty years they have been warning that there is no territory more dangerous for a talented writer than Hollywood. American writers had been involved with the commercial motion picture as early as the turn of the century, but it was not until the invention of the talkies in the late 1920s that they began to arrive *en masse* to work as screenwriters. The industry's need for experienced writers mushroomed between 1927 and 1930, when the studios converted rapidly from silent to sound production. The desire of serious writers for a studio paycheck reached a peak a few years later when the Depression crippled the publishing industry and the commercial theater. By 1935 hundreds of playwrights, novelists, poets, and newspapermen had left their homes in the East, boarded the Super Chief for the West Coast, and assumed their new identities as screenwriters. Many more would enter the studios in the years to come.

Writers' difficulties with the film industry had been well known in the literary community for years. Few writers returned from Hollywood without at least one eyewitness account of studio mistreatment, neglect, or stupidity. Magazines and newspapers eagerly printed such tales. So many Hollywood articles had appeared by 1930 that Stephen Vincent Benét rejected a suggestion that he draft a magazine piece about his recent term as a screenwriter. "I'd rather be the person who went there and didn't," Benét pointedly informed his agent.[1]

But when controversy over the writer's situation flared in the mid-thirties, it was Eastern critics and intellectuals, more than the writers themselves, who fanned the flames. Two prominent critics of the day, George Jean Nathan and Edmund Wilson, were especially heated in their rages against the film industry and its effect upon American writers and writing. Nathan is best remembered for editing the *American Mercury* with H. L. Mencken. One of the country's most influential theater critics, he epitomized the sophisticated, urbane New Yorker of his day. A self-appointed guardian of the highest standards and ideals of the "serious" theater, Nathan repeatedly charged Hollywood with abducting Broadway's finest talents and most promising newcomers. Nathan also condemned those playwrights who sold their independence and integrity for "the potential of mauve motor cars, marble dunking pools, English butlers, and seven-dollar neckties."[2]

Previewing the coming season on Broadway for *Scribner's Magazine* in 1937, Nathan observed that a surprising number of productions scheduled to open were the work of playwrights last heard from in Hollywood. Nathan accused Ben Hecht, Lawrence Stallings, Zoe Akins, Clifford Odets, Herman Mankiewicz, Vincent Lawrence and Sidney Howard among others of "scampering back to the ship now that they have found it isn't sinking after all."[3] He looked forward with little enthusiasm to the work of those who had succumbed to "Hollywood harlotry." "Playwrights who go to Hollywood for any length of time," he complained, "seldom come back without a fatal *streptococcus septicus.*"[4] The "bowwowism" of dramatists returning to New York full of praise for the film medium and indifference to the theater particularly infuriated Nathan: "One wonders how a sneering contempt for the theater and drama, if it be honest and not merely *apologia pro vita sewer,* may be reconciled with the achievement of sound dramatic writing."[5] In this article and many others of similar tone, Nathan, more than any other critic of his day, popularized the notion that most playwrights who went to Hollywood prostituted their talents and turned their backs on the American theater.

In the early forties, Edmund Wilson reinforced Nathan's verbal barrage against the film industry. *The Boys in the Back Room,* Wilson's slim volume of essays on California writers (which he subtitled "The Playwrights in Paradise: A Legend of Beverly Hills"), begins with this bitter lament:

> What shining phantom folds its wings before us?
> What apparition, smiling yet remote?
> Is this—so portly yet so highly porous—
> The old friend who went west and never wrote?[6]

In a brief postscript to the same volume, and prompted by the sudden deaths a day apart of Scott Fitzgerald and Nathanael West in Southern California, Wilson angrily complained that "both West and Fitzgerald were writers of a conscience and with natural gifts rare enough in America or anywhere and their failure to get the best out of their best years may certainly be laid partly to Hollywood, *with its already appalling record of talent depraved and wasted.*"[7] Nathan and Wilson were not the only, nor even the earliest, critics of Hollywood's effect on the writers in its employ. They were, however, two of its most insistent. And they captured remarkably in these few lines the main thrust of what has been said since about Hollywood's dangers for the writer: that working in the film studios dried up a writer's creativity or absorbed it in the sponge of a decadent and wasteful society.

So was born the Hollywood-as-destroyer legend, nurtured through the years by both writers and their partisans. Novelists and playwrights of acute sensibility and talent, so the legend goes, were lured to Hollywood by offers of huge amounts of money and the promise of challenging assignments; once in the studios they were set to work on mundane, hackneyed scripts; they were treated without respect by the mandarins who ruled the studios; and they were subjected to petty interferences by their intellectual inferiors. In the process, they were destroyed as artists. Hollywood was a loathsome and demeaning place which invariably corrupted writers. Although writers prostituted themselves by accepting Hollywood paychecks, the film industry itelf was the true villain of the tale.

Asked by one interviewer how he remembered his screenwriting experience, S. J. Perelman answered: "With revulsion. The mere mention of Hollywood induces a condition in me like breakbone fever. It was a hideous and untenable place when I dwelt there, populated with few exceptions by Yahoos."[8] Even the usually tight-lipped William Faulkner complained to a friend, "Hollywood is the only place in the world where a man can get stabbed in the back while climbing a ladder."[9] By the 1940s many believed that the talking picture had "done in" the legitimate theater by co-opting the cream of a generation of American playwrights. As Robert E. Sherwood, himself late of the Hollywood wars, argued in 1949:

> There was enough brilliance and even genius in those lists [of playwrights in Hollywood] to have produced a golden age and one is inclined to ask whatever happened to it? The principal answer to that is, I suppose, the talking pictures, which came into being in the later 1920's, thereby saving the movie industy from one of its recurrent appointments with catastrophe. It was not the competition the talkies gave the theater for popular favor that mattered so much as it was the fearful devouring of talent by the insatiable studios. Young playwrights of exceptional promise—and now I am not mentioning names—were whisked away to Hollywood and never heard from again.[10]

Some of the names Sherwood most likely had in mind but would not mention included Herman Mankiewicz, Edward Justice Mayer, Preston Sturges, Vincent Lawrence, Clifford Odets, John Monk Saunders, Lawrence Stallings and Robert Riskin. With scores of other playwrights and novelists, both apprentice and established, their experiences in Hollywood in the decade after the coming of sound provided the foundation upon which the Hollywood-as-destroyer legend was built.

Perhaps the leading character in the legend's narrative remains F. Scott Fitzgerald, whom Samuel Marx, his story editor at MGM in the thirties, considered "Hollywood's most celebrated catastrophe."[11] Fitzgerald first arrived in Los Angeles while still basking in the glow of critical favor and public fame. In 1927, First National Pictures hired him to write a script titled "Lipstick" for its leading star, Constance Talmadge. Fitzgerald was paid a $3500 advance, and promised an additional $12,500 if his script was accepted for filming.[12] Fitzgerald duly performed this task while he dined and danced with Hollywood's elite. His script was rejected by the front office, however, and Fitzgerald left the West Coast shortly thereafter, realizing that he had not made the hoped-for hit with his studio bosses nor the financial windfall he had envisioned. Indeed, Fitzgerald and his wife Zelda had spent far more than his $3500 fee during their three-month stay in Hollywood.[13]

In 1931, Fitzgerald worked briefly for MGM with little more success; he returned to Hollywood again in 1937, this time deeply in debt and out of favor with both the critics and the public. Determined to redeem himself and his career, Fitzgerald spent the last four years of his life working on dozens of assignments for several studios and independent producers, but received only one screen credit for his efforts (for *Three Comrades* 1938). During the first eighteen months of this final stay in Hollywood, Fitzgerald did no "serious" writing. In a letter to his teenage daughter Scottie, dated 7 July 1938, he sadly despaired that "what I am doing here is the last tired effort of a man who once did something finer and better."[14] His reputation as an unreliable drunk grew throughout the years, so that by late 1939 few producers would hire him even though he was more often than not sober and steady. "Isn't Hollywood a dump," Fitzgerald cursed in a letter to his former secretary, "in the human sense of the word. A hideous town, pointed up by the insulting gardens of its rich, full of the human spirit at a new low of debasement."[15] Five months later, Fitzgerald suffered a heart attack and died in Sheilah Graham's Hollywood apartment, a writer unwanted by the movie industry.

Fitzgerald's biographers portray him as depressed and despairing in his last years, increasingly frustrated by studio interference and rejection, and angered by the cavalier attitude with which he and his work were treated. Perhaps no description of Fitzgerald in Hollywood is more pathetic than James M. Cain's memory of meeting him one day in the MGM commmissary: "The poor bastard just sat there and didn't say a word the whole hour. Somebody told me afterwards he was waiting to see if I tried to feel sorry for him. He did that with everybody then."[16]

His affair with Sheilah Graham, one of the industry's leading gossip columnists, provided the sole joy of Fitzgerald's Hollywood existence. In a series of books about her life with Fitzgerald, beginning with *Beloved Infidel* in 1957, Graham portrays Fitzgerald as often sober and hopeful, but frequently devastated by Hollywood's disregard for his talent.[17] Aaron Latham's *Crazy Sundays* (1970), a narrative of Fitzgerald's screenwriting experience and an analysis of the scripts he wrote, follows much the same dramatic line. Latham

F. Scott Fitzgerald in Hollywood, 1937
(Photo: Carl Van Vechten; Courtesy of the Library of Congress)

argues that Fitzgerald's scripts showed real growth through the years and often a great deal of merit, which he contends most of Fitzgerald's studio superiors never recognized. "Hollywood had used him and cheated him and neglected him," Latham concludes, "but it had also taught him."[18] It had provided the author with the material and technique for *The Last Tycoon,* the unfinished novel which confirms to Latham and other Fitzgerald scholars his undiminished power as a writer.

With the exception of Sheilah Graham, no one has written more knowingly of Fitzgerald's tribulations in the studios than Budd Schulberg. The son of one of the most powerful executives in Hollywood, Schulberg was sent east to Dartmouth for his education before returning to Hollywood to work as a reader and junior writer for David Selznick. A year later at MGM, Schulberg was teamed with Fitzgerald on a "college caper" script called "Winter Carnival." Both were ordered to Dartmouth with a film crew in the middle of winter in order to steep themselves in college atmosphere before writing the script.

This trip holds a central place in all accounts of Fitzgerald's career in the movies, and Schulberg has written of it no less than three times.[19] In short, it proved to be an unmitigated disaster for Fitzgerald. A harrowing cross-country plane and train journey left him exhausted, ill and drinking heavily by the time he reached New Hampshire. After repeated embarrassing run-ins with Walter Wanger, the movie's producer, Fitzgerald was summarily fired. He staggered as far as a New York hospital bed, where he spent a month recuperating and drying out. "One of the things that impressed me most in the course of that arctic winter hell," Schulberg reveals, "was the quality of Scott's creative intelligence and the courage (of his humor)."[20] Nonetheless it is the sad picture of a brutalized and abused Fitzgerald which dominates Schulberg's, and most other, accounts of this trip. "The months that followed the Dartmouth episode," writes André LeVot in his recent biography of Fitzgerald, "confirmed the defeat of the man who had set out to conquer Hollywood, the failure of his struggle against alcoholism."[21]

Fitzgerald's career is the siege gun used in most attacks on Hollywood's treatment of writers. The careers of scores of other writers serve as lighter artillery. Critics point to Nathanael West's churning out dreadful "B" movie scripts, William Faulkner's unhappy Mississippi leave-takings, Dashiell Hammett's inability to finish another novel after *The Thin Man* in 1933, and Dorothy Parker's diminished output of stories and poems as examples of Hollywood's waste and neglect of the talent it employed. Hollywood would "doubtless turn Eugene O'Neill loose on 'Rebecca of Sunnybrook Farm'," Robert E. Sherwood lamented in 1929, "if they could get him."[22] The rise of the *auteur* theory in the fifties and early sixties only exacerbated the existing antagonism between the literary community and the film industry. Articulated initially in the 1950s by François Truffaut and other young French movie critics and filmmakers in the pages of *Cahiers du Cinéma,* the *politiques des auteurs* maintains that the director, rather than the writer, was the legitimate author of a film. A director's personal style and visual sense could be identified in each of his movies and hence was the films's creative signature. While on the staff of *Film Culture* in 1963, Andrew Sarris introduced *auteur* theory to American cineastes, and thereby legitimized the serious study of hundreds of previously neglected Hollywood movies. "Suddenly," Sarris later wrote, "the old Hollywood movies were something in which to take pride instead of the Fifth."[23] John Ford, William Wellman, Howard Hawks, Frank Capra, and other directors whose work in the studios during the 1930s had been ignored for years were suddenly elevated to the status of artists, each with his own particular film style. Contemporary movies were referred to as "Preminger pictures" or "Bergman films."

Nothing could have rankled writers more. For years screenwriters had complained that Hollywood had intentionally minimized or neglected their contributions to the movies. Many took issue with the auteurist glorification of the director. Gore Vidal, for one, remembers coming to a far different conclusion about the director's contribution:

> In the Fifties when I came to MGM as a contract writer and took my place at the Writer's Table in the commissary, the Wise Hack used to tell us newcomers, "The director is the brother-in-law." Apparently the ambitious man became a producer (that's where the power was). The talented man became a writer (that's where the creation was). The pretty man became a star . . .

> Even as late as 1950 the star Dick Powell assured the film cutter Robert Parrish that "anybody can direct a movie, even I could do it. I'd rather not because it would take too much time. I can make more money acting, selling real estate, and playing the market." That was pretty much the way the director was viewed in the Thirties and Forties, the so-called classic age of the talking movie. . . .

> With certain exceptions, (Alfred Hitchcock, for one), the directors were, at worst, brothers-in-law; at best, bright technicians. All in all, they were a cheery, unpretentious lot, and if anyone had told them that they were *auteurs du cinéma,* few could have coped with the concept, much less the French. Then out of France came the dreadful news: all those brothers-in-law of the classic era were really autonomous and original artists. Apparently each had his own style that impressed itself on every frame of any film he worked on. Proof? Since the director was the same person from film to film, each image of his OEUVRE must then be stamped with his authorship. The argument was circular but no less overwhelming in its implications. Much quoted was Giraudoux's solemn inanity: "There are no works, there are only auteurs."[24]

Fueled as much by auteurism as by charges of ill-treatment, the conflict between Hollywood and its screenwriters continues. "When you are talking about going Hollywood, you're talking about corruption," one contemporary screenwriter explained to a reporter:

Am I right or am I right? That's what screenwriters know about. You're talking about that mysterious disease which struck down Fitzgerald and Faulkner and James M. Cain and Your Name Here at the height of their powers, destroying their talent with quick money and fast women and palm trees before breakfast. You're talking about screenwriters eternally frustrated by scenes unrealized, character mishandled, subtleties of texture and meaning rudely plowed under the tractor of Commerce, lines that might CHANGE THE WORLD if only Burt Lancaster didn't speak them, the routine mutilation of every significant work of Western literature, the corruption of all drama into the most trivial and disagreeable farina, the march of the culture barbarians, the pigslop of mass opinion—is that about it?[25]

Similarly, when Larry McMurtry, himself a novelist-cum-screenwriter, reviewed James Baldwin's *The Devil Finds Work,* a long essay on the movies, he concluded:

Baldwin knows that he is writing about an American industry, and one, moreover, that has always been entirely controlled by white conservatives. He knows too, that the function of industry is to produce products that make money. That the industry employs artists, and that these artists sometimes manage to slip a work of art past the factory gates, is a result of the fact that artists are tricky. It does not mean that the industry is well-intentioned.[26]

Such characterizations of the writer's plight in Hollywood of course have not gone unchallenged. Many of the writers who worked in Hollywood in the 1930s scoffed at the idea of Hollywood destroying their talent or their lives. James M. Cain, for one, announced in 1933 that he had never worked "any place where courtesy was more in evidence than on movie lots, or where daily contacts were more pleasant. The capacity of a studio to make life agreeable to you, indeed, savors almost of the magical."[27] Irwin Shaw, forty years later, also rejected the view of Hollywood as a mill grinding up writers:

Writers are going to find some way to do it—Hollywood is just another way. They can destroy themselves in the corner saloon, the Beverly Hills Hotel, the back lot of Warners, skiing or whoring. I tell young writers, "Any kind of writing you do—as long as you don't stick at it for more than two years—will help."[28]

"Hollywood only ruins those who want to be ruined," Shaw emphasized to another reporter.[29] Even William Faulkner, whose screenwriting career often sapped his strength, did not believe that Hollywood stifled first-rate writers: "It's not pictures which are at fault. The writer is not accustomed to money. Money goes to his head and destroys him—not pictures. Pictures are trying to pay for what they get. Frequently they overpay. But does that debase the writer?"[30] Many other writers also found ludicrous the charge that writers making as much two thousand dollars a week were exploited. When asked why he went to Hollywood after writing three commercially unsuccessful novels in the thirties, Daniel Fuchs replied:

I *wanted* to, for God's sake. I had been teaching school at $6 a day as a substitute and all that—I knew nothing about working in Hollywood before I came here except that it was written everywhere that it was horrible, degrading and I and every other writer couldn't wait to get here.[31]

Ben Hecht, one of the industry's harshest critics, recalled that during his first years in Hollywood he "looked upon movie writing as an amiable chore." There was little responsibility and it was a source of easy money and pleasant friendships. "For many years Hollywood held this double lure for me," Hecht remembered, "tremendous sums of money, for work that required no more effort than a game of pinochle."[32]

Not all writers, then, felt betrayed by the studios. Hollywood's defenders—including many writers, industry executives, and film historians—have maintained that the film industry during the thirties merely offered much needed employment at a time when authors could not hope to support themselves and their families by the sale of their serious writing; that work in the film industry was not inherently more damaging than selling commercial fiction to middle-brow magazines such as the *Saturday Evening Post;* and that their talents were anything but wasted in Hollywood. It was in large part due to their efforts in producing literate and entertaining scripts, so Hollywood's defenders argue, that films reached maturity in the 1930s. "Hollywood destroyed them," Pauline Kael wrote of George S. Kaufman, Moss Hart, Marc Connelly, and other playwrights of the thirties, "but they did wonders for the movies."[33] Other cineastes, like Robert Kirsch of the *Los Angeles Times,* contend that many of the writers hired by the studios "found in Hollywood and in movies material and techniques which enhanced their [serious] work."[34] John Schultheiss's "The Eastern Writer in Hollywood in the 1930s," surveys the careers of scores of writers, and argues that those of real talent were unaffected by their years in Hollywood; that those writers whose careers were sidetracked from other forms of writing most likely would have derailed in any case; and, finally, that many writers discovered that their talent was more amenable to the screen than to drama or fiction. Robert Riskin, Dudley Nichols, Preston Sturges, Nunnally Johnson, and Herman Mankiewicz are all cited in this regard.[35]

Tom Dardis, a self-confessed movie addict, also disputes the idea of Hollywood-as-destroyer. In his *Some Time in the Sun,* Dardis explores the experiences of five writers—Fitzgerald, Faulkner, Nathanael West, Aldous Huxley, and James Agee—and concludes that their Hollywood years were more productive and less debilitating than is commonly assumed.[36] Dardis examines these writers' careers not for what they gave Hollywood, but for what Hollywood gave to them: Fitzgerald and West found in Hollywood the subject of their finest novels; film producers Henry Hathaway and William Bacher suggested the original idea for Faulkner's *A Fable.*[37] All three writers, moreover, received dearly needed financial support from the movies at a time when their book royalties rarely exceeded advances. What difficulties they encountered in Hollywood, Dardis submits, were usually the result of their lack of mastery of the screenwriter's craft.

Thus there are presently two sides to the Hollywood-as-destroyer controversy, both of which distort history. Even the quickest glance at the historical record left by these writers reveals that the Hollywood as destroyer legend does not always hold true: too many writers enjoyed successful and productive careers in the film industry by any standard. Not all writers were mangled in Hollywood's machinery. Writers may have been treated cavalierly on occasion, and less frequently with outright hostility, but they were not actively persecuted. Indeed, many did their best serious writing after reaching Hollywood.

Yet, working in Hollywood was anything but the sanguine or rewarding experience pictured by many of Hollywood's defenders. Some writers *were* treated shabbily and became embittered foes of the industry. Those who defend Hollywood turn deaf ears consistently to the genuine expressions of bewilderment, anguish, anger, and despair to be found in the testimony of authors about their movie experience. Schultheiss, for one, never comes to grips with these writers' professional and personal unhappiness in the studios, choosing to dismiss it as mere condescension. "It is important to recognize," he asserts, "that this criticism of the Hollywood film formed the background of a general feeling of snobbery against which many Eastern writers made their commitments to movie writing."[38] It is just this same insensitivity which allows Pauline Kael to report that although Hollywood destroyed certain writers, they did great things for the movies.

Other defenders let their enthusiasm for movies blind them to some of the realities of movie making. Tom Dardis, for instance, dubiously equates Faulkner's collaboration with Howard Hawks with that of "Brecht and his Berliner Ensemble or Ingmar Bergman and his regular group of film workers."[39] Dardis's enthusiasm also leads him to accept Anthony Powell's opinion that Fitzgerald was happy and content in Hollywood, even though Powell met Fitzgerald only once, and then in a cocktail lounge when Fitzgerald presumably was feeling little pain. Dardis dismisses, on the other hand, the recollections of Budd Schulberg and Sheilah Graham, who knew Fitzgerald much more intimately.[40]

So much energy has been directed toward proving or refuting the Hollywood-as-destroyer legend, in fact, that many of the actual circumstances surrounding the employment of writers in the film industry in the 1930s remain obscure. It is true that this movement approached being a literal migration of a generation of American writers. Included were the young and the struggling as well as the popular and established; those with a modicum of talent and those with a lion's share. Fitzgerald, Faulkner, Dorothy Parker, Lillian Hellman, and George S. Kaufman are among the best known; Paul Green, Mildred Cram, Joseph Fields, and Niven Busch among the least. Although a great deal is known about the screenwriting careers of the most famous, much less is known about the others. Even the term "Eastern" writer, so often used to describe these authors, contains no small measure of vagueness.[41] Who were Edmund Wilson's "shining phantoms," those who went west presumably never to write again? How many were there? And what is particularly "Eastern" about them?

Hollywood's literary recruiting campaigns are often talked about as if the studios employed every person ever to place pen on paper. In 1932, for example, *Life* magazine reported that "more members of the literati work under Thalberg than it took to produce the King James Bible."[42] The year before, Jim Reilly, a veteran aide to theatrical producer Charles Frohman, echoed others when he lamented the dearth of American plays on Broadway and observed that virtually every American playwright had either "disappeared or gone to Hollywood."[43] Yet many prominent authors never came close to inhabiting a Hollywood Writers' Building office. Eugene O'Neill, Thomas Wolfe, Willa Cather, Philip Barry, and Ernest Hemingway, among many others, never worked in Hollywood. Each was offered at least one screenwriting contract, but all found reason or excuse to decline. Wolfe, for instance, received a substantial offer from MGM while on vacation in California. He turned the studio down in order to finish a novel in progress, but not before he reportedly reassured the studio that "if Hollywood wants to seduce me, I am not only willing but eager."[44] The offer, presumably, was never repeated.

Many other writers were less amenable to Hollywood's entreaties. The film industry's recruitment campaign barely touched whole communities of American writers. Members of the radical-bohemian community centered in the Greenwich Village and Chelsea sections of New York rarely found themselves employed in Hollywood, nor did those authors committed to an expatriate life in Europe, nor those practicing a modernist aesthetic in their writing. The last were believed to lack the commercial appeal and the strong sense of narrative deemed essential to successful screenwriting. Writers with a radical or modernist sensibility, for their part, were rarely less than contemptuous of the film industry's product and methods. But neither the bohemians nor the expatriates were totally immune to Hollywood's inducements; some writers associated with the expatriates—Fitzgerald, for example—have become part and parcel of the Hollywood-as-destroyer legend.[45] John Dos Passos, for another, is a writer of both radical and expatriate sensibility who, if only briefly, found himself working in the studios.

As a rule, though, the film studios passed over the Villagers and expatriates in their search for potential screenwriters.

Where did Hollywood conduct its search for writers, then? The answer lies uptown, in Manhattan's network of publishing houses, newspaper and magazine editorial offices, literary agencies, theatrical production companies, and theaters. The writers hired by Hollywood after 1928 were, by and large, those novelists, playwrights and newspapermen who had gained some measure of notice in New York's literary marketplace. They were professional writers in the sense that they all earned, or aspired to earn, their living through writing. This inevitably brought them to midtown Manhattan. Their "Easternness," then, has much more to do with their involvement with New York's literary businesses than it does with their place of birth or residence. Even writers like Faulkner, who lived in Mississippi but traveled regularly to New York to consult with his editors, publishers and agents, can in this sense be considered Eastern.[46]

It is impossible to say with any certainty just how many such writers arrived in Hollywood in the decade after the introduction of sound. John Schultheiss's list of Eastern writers, for example, totals 157, but it includes many Europeans and many authors who first went to Hollywood much before or after the thirties. I have identified 138 writers as being Eastern; they are listed in Appendix A. Each first arrived in Hollywood between 1927 and 1938. Each had previously established at least the beginnings of a literary career in or through New York.[47] While this number is a very small percentage of the total number of writers working in the country, it includes many of those most active in New York during the 1920s. One indication of this fact is that of the ten advisory editors listed in Harold Ross's prospectus for *The New Yorker*, six would eventually find themselves in Hollywood. More importantly, this number *is* a significant percentage of the 800-1000 writers Leo Rosten estimates worked in Hollywood during the thirties.[48] These few figures suggest that while the stock of writing talent was not totally depleted by the migration to Hollywood, the motion picture companies attracted Eastern writers in large enough numbers to comprise a substantial segment of their writing staffs.

I selected the careers of 40 of these 138 writers upon which to base this study: George Abbott, Zoe Akins, Maxwell Anderson, S. N. Behrman, Robert Benchley, Stephen Vincent Benét, Charles Brackett, Sidney Buchman, W. R. Burnett, James M. Cain, Marc Connelly, Mildred Cram, Rachel Crothers, John Dos Passos, William Faulkner, Scott Fitzgerald, Gene Fowler, Daniel Fuchs, Paul Green, Dashiell Hammett, Ben Hecht, Lillian Hellman, Samuel Hoffenstein, Sidney Howard, Nunnally Johnson, George S. Kaufman, Charles MacArthur, Dudley Nichols, Clifford Odets, John O'Hara, George Oppenheimer, Dorothy Parker, S. J. Perelman, Samson Raphaelson, Budd Schulberg, Robert E. Sherwood, Donald Ogden Stewart, Preston Sturges,

Nathanael West, and Thornton Wilder.[49] The members of this group, in representing the larger number of 138 Eastern authors, lie at the heart of the Hollywood-as-destroyer legend, for it is their experience which initially provoked complaint about the studios' treatment of its imported writing talent.

Even a cursory review of these writers' careers reveals that their confusion and unhappiness in Hollywood, although widespread and very real, had little to do with their success or failure within the studios. Neither side of the Hollywood-as-destroyer controversy adequately explains the curious paradox of this historical situation: that many of the Eastern writers most successful in Hollywood were its harshest critics; others, faring less well in the studio system, complained in far more muted tones. Ben Hecht, S. J. Perelman, Gene Fowler, and Dorothy Parker, for example, all prospered as screenwriters yet persistently denounced the industry. William Faulkner, James M. Cain, Nathanael West, and Thornton Wilder, on the other hand, all struggled in Hollywood, yet were more tight-lipped about their life in the movie studios. Not all writers came to sad ends in Hollywood, then, but virtually *every* writer was disquieted or unnerved by the experience. Any sensible analysis of the Hollywood-as-destroyer legend and the meaning of movie work for these writers must account for this paradox. The legend itself offers no explanation, nor do those who dispute it.

Given this paradox, what can explain these writers' antagonism toward the movie industry? One important clue is provided by an Englishman, the novelist and screenwriter J. B. Priestley. In the mid-thirties Priestley offered this warning to his fellow writers contemplating the move to Los Angeles:

> Here, then, is Hollywood, in the middle of this odd unreality of landscape and atmosphere and remote from anything else. Now in Europe when you agree to work in films, you merely take a certain route every morning from your own front door. But in America, you cross the continent and go to Hollywood. On the way, you will have to say goodbye to most of the realities of our communal life.... The real roaring world will disappear behind the mountains and the deserts. It will not be long before you will feel further from its life than if you were lounging on some South Sea island.[50]

A vast gulf, Priestly suggests here, lay between the worlds writers were leaving and entering, a barrier not only physical but cultural. Writers might just as well have continued west to Tahiti for all the similarities between their lives as writers in the studios and their lives as writers in New York.

When sifting through what became a staggering amount of material— mainly in the form of personal letters, business correspondence, contemporary essays and articles, newspaper features, and interviews—about their Hollywood experience, I was struck by how consistently these forty writers, so unlike in temperament, judged one culture (represented by the movie studios) in terms of another (represented by New York's literary marketplace). The chasm between the world they left and the one they entered separated two distinct cultures, each with its own definition of what the writer was and did.

The word culture is used here advisedly and in the anthropological sense, as a "shared system of standards for perceiving, evaluating, and acting," in Ward Goodenough's simple definition.[51] Above all else, these writers shared their involvement in New York's commercial network of publishing houses, writer's agencies, theatrical production companies, and editorial offices. They may or not have been fathers, mothers, actors, musicians, or any number of other important social identities, but each was a professional writer. Largely within this arena writers came to understand the responsibilities, privileges, hazards and rewards—the status and role—of the professional writer in the United States. Within New York's literary marketplace, in short, they learned the system of rules for perceiving, evaluating, and acting appropriately as "writers." It is this common bond which marked them in Hollywood as "Eastern," and distinguished them from the other writers in the studios.

I wish to suggest, then, that a writer's talent was not under attack in Hollywood so much as the profession of authorship as he had known it. A radical—and for the most part unexpected—change occurred in writers' professional lives when they moved to Hollywood. And their palpable frustration and pain upon arriving in the studios suggests how very important their identities as writers were to their complete self-images. In short, working in Hollywood inevitably challenged, and in some cases shattered, many traditional notions about the nature of the professional writer's trade and life.

Any discussion of Eastern writers in Hollywood in the 1930s must begin with an inspection of the cultural baggage they brought with them. Chapter 1 examines these forty writers' activities in New York during the twenties, particularly in the literary marketplace. It surveys developments in the profession of authorship up to and including the 1920s affecting contracts, copyrights, and royalty arrangements in both publishing and the theater. The relationships of authors and their publishers, editors, and theatrical producers provide vital keys to the attributes and underlying values considered basic to their professional identities: creative autonomy, personal independence, legal control and ownership of their work, and fair compensation. Most writers entered the studios only after the Depression had ended a decade of unparalleled activity and prosperity in the literary marketplace. The twenties were marvellous times for American writers, and their reaction to the film industry cannot be understood outside this context. Chapter 1 provides just such a context.

Chapter 2, "The Writer and the Silent Screen," reviews the development of professional screenwriting, concentrating on the Hollywood experiences of specific novelists and playwrights in the silent era. It examines Sam Goldwyn's "Eminent Authors" project, for instance, Hollywood's first important attempt to retain well-known playwrights and novelists as screenwriters. This chapter also looks at the career of Herman Mankiewicz; as supervisor of story at Paramount and chairman of its unofficial "Fresh Air Fund," Mankiewicz was instrumental in signing writers (including many of the forty I studied closely) to their first studio contract. Writers, of course, came to Hollywood with preconceived notions of what screenwriting and the film community would be like; chapter 2 indicates what those notions were.

Preconceived ideas or not, writers eventually faced the reality of working in the studios. According to the Hollywood-as-destroyer legend, writers were hoodwinked or coerced into signing long-term disadvantageous contracts; they then worked long hours in the shabby offices of studio Writers' Buildings, where they were subjected to constant interference by studio producers and their underlings. They were paid handsomely, and in return were expected to work obediently and without causing problems. Nathanael West's first letter to his friend Josephine Herbst after he arrived in Hollywood in 1933 to go to work for Columbia, for instance, is the food which nourished this legend:

> This stuff about easy work is all wrong. My hours are from ten in the morning to six at night with a full day on Saturday. They gave me a job to do five minutes after I sat down in my office—a scenario about a beauty parlor—and I'm expected to turn out pages and pages a day. There's no fooling here. All the writers sit in cells in a row and the minute a typewriter stops someone pokes his head in the door to see if you are thinking. Otherwise, it's like the hotel business.[52]

Chapter 3 re-examines this industrial and commercial organization which has come to be known as the studio system, and particularly the realities of the writer's studio life. It corrects some of the basic misconceptions about how the system worked: writers' salaries, working conditions, contracts, and assignments all have been distorted in the debate over the Hollywood-as-destroyer legend. In truth, there was very little systematic about the studio system. In this light, chapter 3 also looks at how the major studios differed in matters of policy and attitude toward the writers in their employ.

Chapter 4 uses writers' letters, papers, diaries, and other personal documents to reconstruct their view of Hollywood during the thirties. Here we can see most clearly how all writers regardless of their stature in the film industry, understood Hollywood in terms of the literary marketplace in New York. The comments of these forty writers, taken as a whole, form a coherent description and explanation of the workings of the studio system *from the writer's point-of-view*. The movie producer played the most important role in the screenwriter's professional life in Hollywood, consequently this chapter deals at length with the writer-producer relationship—especially from the writer's perspective.

Many Eastern writers refused to conform to the studio system; many others did so only under the greatest protest; and still others, with little success, sought ways to circumvent the system and re-establish the writer's traditional prerogatives. Ultimately, Eastern screenwriters learned that to succeed they, and not the studios, would have to change. Chapter 5 explores their efforts to modify, defy, circumvent, and eventually accommodate the film industry's practices. Finally, this section explores the implications of these writers' experience for the profession of authorship generally. Their situation in the 1930s often anticipated the fundamental dilemmas which have plagued authors ever since, for in Hollywood Eastern writers faced forces far larger than the film industry itself. In New York during the twenties and thirties, writers primarily dealt with small, privately owned and financed businesses; they often enjoyed cordial, sincere, and loyal support from their publishers and editors. In Hollywood, on the other hand, writers were the employees of multi-million dollar companies which, in turn, were frequently subsidiaries of even larger public corporations. Consequently, writers' dealings with movie producers and front-office executives—the management of the studios—were unaccustomedly guarded, impersonal, and legally complex.

During and after the Depression, mergers and bankruptcies inexorably thinned the ranks of small publishers and theatrical producers. Large entertainment corporations, with investments in the publishing industry as well as movie, theater and later television production and exhibition, came to play a larger role in the literary marketplace. Thus, the Eastern screenwriter's life in the studios in the 1930s anticipated the increasing bureaucratization of the writer in the modern marketplace and the threat it posed to the writer's traditional identity. Writers were not destroyed in Hollywood in the 1930s. But the profession of authorship as they knew it was certainly under attack.

Many dimensions of the writer's experience in Hollywood in the 1930s are unexplored, or touched upon only briefly, in the following pages. There is very little mention, for instance, of writers' specific screenplays, much less their more general contributions to the art of the motion picture: I have not explored the difference between fiction and film in terms of form and technique. These, in any case, are the province of the critic and the aesthetician, many of whom have written extensively in the area of literature-and-film studies.[53] My focus, on the other hand, remains consistently on how writers viewed, in the context of the profession of authorship, the movie industry and the complicated process by which movies reached the screen. I have concentrated on the attitudes *shared* by these writers as they coped with their new professional circumstances.

Nor is there much mention here of the many plays, novels, and short stories Eastern writers published based on their impression of Hollywood and the film industry. Fitzgerald's *The Last Tycoon* (1941), Dos Passos's *The Big*

Money (1936), Nathanael West's *The Day of the Locust* (1936), and Budd Schulberg's *What Makes Sammy Run?* (1939) are perhaps the four most widely read today. So much Hollywood fiction exists, in fact, that three genre studies have already been written on the subject.[54]

This fiction is appetizingly rich in comment about Hollywood and the workings of the film industry, so there is great temptation to use it as documentary evidence of writers' attitudes toward the movies. It is a temptation I have resisted, given the dangers of assuming any character's voice is the author's, and given the vast amount of evidence available in other, more reliable, forms: personal letters; business correspondence; diaries and journals; contemporary magazine articles, newspaper pieces and interviews; and selected trustworthy biographies and autobiographies. I supplemented this historical data by interviewing or corresponding with several of the surviving members of the study group, their relatives, friends, and business associates. My hope was not to examine all facets and consequences of the Eastern writer's existence in Hollywood, but rather to put the Hollywood-as-destroyer controversy within its historical and cultural context by re-examining it in the light of the concerns of the professional author in the 1930s.

1

The Writer in New York in the 1920s

"I can't prove it," Alfred Kazin once remarked, "but I'm sure New York is the single most important factor in American writing."[1] Certainly no city can claim to have offered as many professional opportunities to writers in this century. New York's cosmopolitan vitality and diversity attracted some would-be authors, but most came to the city primarily to be near Manhattan's vast network of publishing houses, editorial rooms, theatrical producers and literary agents.

It had not always been so. Boston had enjoyed preeminence in the colonial publishing trade and the early American world of letters generally. Only in the early nineteenth century did New York achieve any literary prominence, when Washington Irving, James Fenimore Cooper and William Cullen Bryant all actively participated in the city's literary life. As early as 1825 Cooper had established New York's first literary club—known formally as the Bread and Cheese—including as members Bryant, Samuel F. B. Morse, the publisher Charles Wiley, the poet Fitz-Greene Halleck and others concerned with promoting literature and the arts in New York. G. P. Putnam's, Charles Scribner's, Appleton, and Harper Brothers, among other celebrated publishing firms, all opened their doors before the Civil War. After the war, New York's swift growth as the hub of the nation's financial, transportation, and communication networks created a more favorable business climate for publishers than Boston's increasingly provincial economy. Older firms in New York expanded their operations and built new plants; new houses opened on Publisher's Row every year. By the turn of the century, New York's dominance of the publishing industry was so great that no major general house was founded outside of Manhattan for more than fifty years. "New York is a vast mart," William Dean Howells observed in 1902, "and literature is one of the things marketed here."[2]

Moreover, by the Civil War New York already bustled with theatrical activity; the adoption in the 1870s of the combination system of production by which producers cast and rehearsed companies in New York before taking them on extended national tours guaranteed the city's virtual domination of the American stage. Showmen built new theaters in Longacre Square and other advantageous Manhattan locations as fast as they could finance them. After 1890 producers, managers and booking agents in New York effectively controlled theatrical production for the entire country. Broadway became to the American theater what Hollywood would eventually become to the movies.[3]

Add to New York's preeminence in publishing and the theater its many newspapers, a thriving mass magazine industry, dozens of smaller periodicals, and a host of advertising agencies: the result, by 1900, was America's foremost literary marketplace, a magnet attracting both would-be and established writers to Manhattan. Many actually moved to the city; others, unable or unwilling to uproot their lives, longed for a glimpse into Manhattan's literary community. In "First Day in New York," Carl Van Doren captures vividly what New York meant to aspiring writers of his generation:

> In September 1908 I had no experience of cities, except one or two unsatisfying visits to Chicago. Yet since I was old enough to consider it at all I had never had any doubt that I would go to New York. I did not think about it and decide. I seemed to have already made up my mind when the idea occurred to me. It was, somehow, as if not native to New York, I was natural to it, and the accident of my being born in a distant village made no difference. I was conscious of a wish to be near where books were written and published . . . Life would be large and free in New York, and I must go there to find out what largeness and freedom were.[4]

Van Doren was one of thousands of young writers to feel if not native to New York at least natural to it. Of the forty writers whose careers I studied, for instance, only six were New Yorkers by birth or early upbringing: Nathanael West, Daniel Fuchs, George Oppenheimer, and Samson Raphaelson were all born in the city; Lillian Hellman and Clifford Odets moved there as children. Fully twenty-nine of the forty made the decision to move to New York at some point during the first three decades of the century. The remaining five writers lived in other parts of the country, but they too visited New York regularly to consult with publishers, editors, theatrical producers, and agents.

In 1912 Robert Benchley contemplated his imminent graduation from Harvard and the end of his term as president of the *Lampoon,* its satirical magazine. He asked John Reed, who himself had recently made the transition from Cambridge to Manhattan, for a "word of advice from you as to the safest and sanest approach to literary apprenticeship in New York."[5] Reed suggested that Benchley delay moving to Manhattan until the fall to avoid New York's heat. Benchley accepted a job at the Museum of Fine Arts in Boston, but by October he was anxious to leave New England. "After a short but devitalizing stagnation in this extra heavy cream of Boston culture," he announced to Reed on October 12, "I am moving to New York next week to work with the Curtis Publishing Company. Do you know of a place where I could stay?"[6]

George Abbott as a Young Actor in New York, 1920s
(The Billy Rose Theatre Collection, New York Public Library)

George Abbott followed from Cambridge the next year. After four years at the University of Rochester, Abbott spent a year at Harvard in George Baker's celebrated playwriting course, English 47. After serving a brief apprenticeship in a small Boston theater company, Abbott, too, felt Broadway's lure. "It was a sunny morning," when Abbott arrived at Pennsylvania Station in New York, "and the tall buildings, those fingers of hope reaching up toward the sky, thrilled me beyond description. No immigrant coming to the promised land could have had a greater sense of ecstasy than I. I was here at last; the city beckoned me; the world was my oyster; I would succeed. I was exalted."[7]

World War I temporarily diverted the stream of young writers rolling into Manhattan. After the Armistice, returning veterans, fresh from the barracks if not the battle, resumed knocking on the doors of publishers, editors, and producers. They shared Abbott's sense of heightened anticipation. "Everything is possible," a young F. Scott Fitzgerald wired Zelda Sayre on the day he arrived in Manhattan after his Army discharge, "I am in the land of ambition and success."[8] In 1925, six years later, John O'Hara, then a twenty-year-old reporter and columnist on his local Pennsylvania paper, shared Fitzgerald's sense of New York. "My ambition," he confessed openly to his friend Robert Simonds, "is to get a job on the *World*. To be able to say, 'Yes, I worked for the *New York World* is open sesame.' One can go almost anywhere and say, 'Give me a job on your desk; I want $75 hebdomadally.'"[9] Three years later, O'Hara finally reached New York, where he was hired, not by the *World*, but by the rival *Herald-Tribune*. Nonetheless O'Hara was overjoyed. "Next time this year I'll be somebody," he crowed to Simonds.[10].

Ben Hecht had been a successful reporter and prominent literary man in Chicago for ten years before he first came to New York in 1924 for the publication of his first novel, *Eric Dorn*. Although his experience covering Chicago's tenderloin district had jaded Hecht considerably, he still marvelled at the inexhaustible possibilities for the writer in New York:

> The real strangeness of New York for me lay in things you could not see—the fact that there were theatrical seasons and music seasons, and that the skyscrapers were full of magazine offices and publishing houses. There had been only one Covici in Chicago. New York seemed to swarm with Covicis—all clamoring for works of art to launch. At times I felt like I had come to no city at all but to a bazaar in which I and a few thousand like me were for sale under the loose stock label of artists.[11]

Like Hecht, Maxwell Anderson was a bit older than most writers when he arrived in New York. At thirty, and with a wife and children to support, Anderson clearly understood New York's career advantages for the aspiring writer. Anderson had taught for a decade at Stanford University and Whittier College, during which time he had placed occasional feature articles and a few poems with Eastern magazines. In 1918 the editors of the *New Republic* offered Anderson a staff job if he would move to New York. Having wished for years to abandon teaching and devote himself full-time to writing, Anderson rejoiced at this chance to move into New York's "center of publishing, producing, and thinking." "Nowhere else," he wrote historian Alvin Johnson, "do you get *a glimpse of what's required for the kind of success that enables one to support himself by writing.*"[12]

In the fall of 1918, Anderson quit his teaching position, borrowed fifteen hundred dollars from a friend, and relocated his family in New York. He spent six months "as a sort of apprentice editor" at the *New Republic,* then moved to the daily *Globe and Commercial Advertiser* as an editorial writer. "My poetry brings me nothing," he confided to Harold Munro, an English editor who had accepted some of his poems, "whereas editorial writing, which I detest, supports me in fair comfort."[13] Anderson's jump in early 1921 to the prestigious *World*—whose distinction O'Hara trumpeted four years later—raised his income even further, but did little to satisfy his desire to devote more time to poetry. When William Stanley Braithewaite requested permission to use some of his work in a yearly anthology Anderson ruefully replied: "Your letter heartens me greatly, for I have written verse for years without achieving much in the way of recognition. It seems to me that my work is better lately; if I only had more free time I might really do something."[14] Anderson quit journalism for good in September 1924 when *What Price Glory?,* co-written with his colleague Lawrence Stallings, proved to be the hit of the Broadway season. Anderson never worked at a salaried job—outside of Hollywood—again.

As the careers of these writers suggest, few could support themselves without a steady job when first entering New York's literary marketplace. Still fewer enjoyed an immediate success on Broadway or in the bookstores. Like Anderson, most writers accepted salaried positions on editorial staffs or—like F. Scott Fitzgerald—in advertising agencies while waiting for the day when they could afford to quit. Fully thirty of the forty writers I studied, for instance, worked on the staffs of New York's magazines and newspapers. Of these thirty, only George S. Kaufman, who continued as the entertainment editor of the *New York Times* even after his first hit on Broadway, remained in a salaried job once assured of royalty income from a book or play. Editing and reporting jobs served a vital function in the literary marketplace as training grounds for aspiring writers, and they represented security to many writers whose other work did not sell. But given the choice between salaried employment and freelance work, writers with rare exception chose the latter.

Thus aspiring writers flooded into New York in the early twenties, harboring the not-too-unreasonable notion that there was a job for them in the literary marketplace. None, however, could have predicted the remarkable richness and vitality of New York's literary life during the next ten years, a time of unparalleled prosperity in the literary marketplace. One hundred and forty plays opened during the 1919 Broadway season, for instance, the greatest number in a decade; fully 225 productions, however, opened *on average* each season during the twenties. In 1927 Broadway production peaked, with 254 new plays opening in 71 theaters. By comparison, only 55 plays have opened each year on average since 1970.[15] Similarly, between 1920 and 1925 publishers nearly doubled the yearly number of new titles. Retail sales increased during the same period by 70 percent. By 1930, eighteen new publishing houses had opened; only one had failed.[16] "The publishing industry," to quote Malcolm Cowley, was "booming like General Motors."[17]

Moreover, national attention focused for the first time on *American*, rather than British or Continental, writers. When 400,000 readers bought Sinclair Lewis's *Main Street* (1920), writers and publishers alike realized the enormity of the appetite for new American writers. "In the 1920s American writing had come to seem important," Van Wyck Brooks suggested.

> The idea that America was a dependency of England had vanished, with the world war, from the minds of writers, who were now inclined to agree with Melville that the time had come for America "to set, not follow precedents." They were acutely aware of the country, its promise and its weaknesses, and the problems of the writer living in it, and they were concerned especially with the art of writing.[18]

A handful of ambitious, anti-traditionalist young publishers played an important role in nurturing this belief that American literature had finally come of age. These men were as committed to shaking up the publishing establishment as they were to advancing modern writing. New York's older publishing houses—among them Scribner's, Putnam's, Henry Holt, Harper Brothers, and E.P. Dutton—remained wedded to the social, literary, and political conventions of the nineteenth century well into the twentieth. In-bred and clubby, these firms continued to publish according to Victorian tastes and standards of literary propriety. Experimental and radical fiction, and all who championed them, were anathema. Thus it was left to houses without any allegiance to the entrenched Anglo-American literary heritage to publish the latest European fiction considered too avant-garde or controversial by the older firms. Ben Huebsch, for instance, published the first American edition of James Joyce's *Portrait of An Artist* (1915). The next year Huebsch demonstrated his interest in native writing by publishing Sherwood Anderson's *Winesburg, Ohio* (1916).[19]

After World War I ended, many others followed Huebsch's lead. Alfred A. Knopf, Horace Liveright, Charles and Albert Boni, Richard Simon, M.L. Schuster, Bennet Cerf, S.M. Rinehart, Donald Klopfer, and Lincoln McVeigh had all opened their own houses by the end of the twenties. These new firms did not wrest economic control from the older houses, nor did they corner the market on new writing talent; but they did shake the older publishers out of their conservative lethargy. Young editors in old-line firms, like Maxwell Perkins and John Farrar, convinced their superiors to accept new fiction and encourage new writers. Publishing activity increased generally.

Perhaps no publisher made his presence more felt in the literary world in the twenties than Horace Liveright. Born into a prosperous Pennsylvania Jewish family, Liveright went into publishing with Albert Boni in 1917 after having quickly tired of a family-arranged Wall Street job. When his partnership with Boni dissolved in 1918, Liveright became the firm's major owner. Bon vivant and publishing man-about-town, given to the long shot and the grand gesture, Liveright loved the spotlight. He used the presidency of Boni & Liveright to oppose John Sumner's New York Society for the Suppression of Vice and to fight the Clean Books Bill Sumner sponsored; he vigorously supported his own authors, and writers generally, against obscenity prosecutions in both Boston and New York; and he campaigned publicly for passage of the Vestal Bill, which would have given authors stronger copyright protection.[20]

Liveright also had an uncanny eye for talent. He published O'Neill, Dreiser, Sherwood Anderson, Robinson Jeffers, Hart Crane, Ezra Pound, and E. E. Cummings, for instance; of the writers whose careers I examined in detail, Dorothy Parker, S. J. Perelman, Samuel Hoffenstein, William Faulkner, Nathanael West, and Ben Hecht all issued books through Boni & Liveright in the twenties. Louis Kronenberger, who began his professional career as a junior editor at B & L in 1926 called it "an anchorless, undaunted, undisciplined, messy, magnificent publishing house."[21]

Boni & Liveright was esteemed not only for the quality of its authors, but also for the brilliance and enthusiasm of its editorial staff. Bennet Cerf, Donald Friede, Beatrice Kaufman, Manuel Komroff as well as Kronenberger all worked as editors at B & L at some point in its brief history. Lillian Hellman's first job in New York, for instance, was on Liveright's staff. "A job with any publishing house was a plum," Hellman later recalled,

> a job with Horace Liveright was a bag of plums. Never before, and possibly never since, has an American publishing house had so great a record. Liveright, Julian Messner, T. R. Smith, Manuel Komroff, and a few even younger men had made a new and brilliant world for books. It didn't hurt that Horace was handsome and daring, Julian serious and kind, Tom Smith almost erudite with his famous collection of erotica and odd pieces of knowledge that meant nothing but seemed to; that the advances they gave were even larger; that the sympathy and attention given to writers, young or old, was more generous than had been known before, possibly more real than has been known since. They were not truly serious men, I guess, nor men of the caliber of Max Perkins, but they had respect for serious writing.[22]

What writers admired about Liveright, then, was not only the quality of his list, but also his courtly and deferential manner toward them. "Once an author joined the house," Liveright's biographer, Walker Gilmer explains, "he discovered what it was that Liveright offered that was more important than advertising and royalties: attention, the individual attention the publisher paid to each writer, whether he was a first-time author or was already known."[23] B & L's offices were housed in a swank Forty-eighth Street brownstone, where Liveright presided over the turbulent operations of his talented and temperamental staff of editors, readers, production assistants, and layout artists. T. R. Smith handled the day-to-day editorial affairs of the firm; Liveright devoted most of his time to scouting new talent, cultivating the house's established authors, and publicly championing the freedom of the press and other causes close to writers' hearts. Liveright succeeded so well in great part because writers liked B & L's informal, and sometimes riotous, atmosphere. There was something "persistently convivial" about the place, Louis Kronenberger later said:

> I wonder whether any other publishing house of consequence has ever had so many faithful habitual visitors. Liveright authors and would-be authors, and for that matter former authors, came, certainly, many times on business, but many times as well to their club or their bank or their favorite bar. Friends of various kinds, and sometimes the friends' friends would come and go; and girlfriends of various kinds came too. I was not privy to much of this, but a good deal of it was the meat and marrow of the firm's publishing success. It was in many ways a kind of word-of-mouth success. One author led to another: Sherwood Anderson introduced Faulkner; Harold Loeb, Hemingway; Waldo Frank, Hart Crane.[24]

"Liveright gave a great many parties," Lillian Hellman remembers, and in doing so elevated the literary cocktail party into a fine art. "Any writer on a New York visit, any new book, any birthday was an excuse for what he called an A party or a B party." The A parties were respectable and sedate; the B parties, Hellman recalls "were drunk, cutup sex stuff and often lasted into another day and night with replacements."[25] "The few parties I went to at first," Louis Kronenberger reflected in 1965, "were almost certainly A ones; later, when I was invited oftener, I'm not sure which they were, because I'm not sure that by then any distinction was possible."[26] Such parties, though, served a vital function for both author and publisher: at them writers were the center of attention, they garnered praise and prestige regardless of the modesty of their financial reward. When asked in 1924 why he had entered the publishing business, Liveright replied, speaking to just this point: "to make our home on Forty-eight Street a place where all young and unknown authors may bring their books and their ideas."[27]

In late 1929 and early 1930, Liveright's fortunes plunged with the stockmarket. The victim of his own gambling instincts, innumerable ill-advised investments, and too many failures as a theatrical producer, Liveright was forced to sell his share in the firm to Arthur Pell, its business manager, in 1930. Ironically, Liveright accepted an offer to produce movies for Paramount Pictures. "What do you think of my going to Hollywood?" he asked Eugene O'Neill. "No, I haven't sold myself down the river or anything like that."[28] In Hollywood Liveright often crossed paths with former employees and authors also at work in the movie industry. Lillian Hellman, for one, ran into the publisher five or six times in Los Angeles:

> Some of the old glamor was there, where his name was still famous and his recent history not yet fully understood. But every time I saw him ... I knew, for a simple reason, that the pride was breaking: he would, immediately, cross the room to sit beside me because I alone in the room was the respectful young girl who had known him in the great days, and that the more he drank the more we talked of those days, not so many years before.[29]

In 1932, his option dropped by Paramount, Liveright returned to New York. Alone, penniless and drinking heavily, Liveright caught pneumonia within the year and died. That so profligate a man could survive in publishing attests of to the vitality of the literary marketplace in the 1920s.

Manuscripts in hand, would-be writers knocked on the doors of publishers like Liveright throughout the twenties. The publishing house was at the center of writers' professional lives, the door through which they reached their audience. No matter how much money they made on newspapers or magazines, no matter how many free-lance pieces the editors of the same accepted, aspiring writers longed for the day one of the city's publishers accepted their work. It was not so much a question of money, for most fiction—and especially first novels—rarely sold well; rather, young writers yearned for the literary cache only a book provided. Roger Burlingame, an editor at Scribner's in the twenties and a long-time observer of the publishing industry, believed that, for most authors, satisfaction came only indirectly:

> It is true, for instance, that the immeasurable profit of "prestige" comes only from a book. A "great name" in literature comes wholly from a writer's books. No amount of magazine production, lecturing, radio broadcasting or movie production has a comparable effect. Yet all these highly profitable things are often made possible to an author because of the reputation he gains from one book which may be unlucrative or even costly in itself. For it is a curious fact that a book need not sell in great numbers to build a wide reputation. Libraries, reviews, quotations, prizes, and honors are all concerned in this result.[30]

Moreover, writers and their work formed the center of attention in every respectable publishing house. New York's publishers and editors in the 1920s, if lacking Liveright's magnetism, shared his esteem for writers. "Enthusiasm among a publisher's staff," Burlingame firmly believed, "is something an author is justified in expecting."[31] Publishers and editors invariably tried to

Horace Liveright
(Courtesy of the Academy of Motion Picture Arts and Sciences)

treat writers cordially, although no firm was immune to fights and fallings-out with even highly valued authors. Publishers, editors, and writers shared many of the same personal as well as professional interests, thus they often became friends as well as colleagues. Many had been college or prep class mates. John Farrar, who left the firm of Doubleday, Doran with S.M. Rinehart to start his own house in 1929, observed that all good editors "had a deep appreciation of writers, liked them as friends."[32] Cass Canfield, who joined Harper Brothers in 1924 and assumed its presidency seven years later, believed that the test of any publisher or editor was his ability to find writers before they had displayed their full talents.[33]

Any promising young writer might be the next Sinclair Lewis or Sherwood Anderson, and thus all publishing houses searched for new writing talent. "I had lunch a few days ago with Scudder Middleton," H. S. Latham, a young editor at MacMillan wrote to William Rose Benét in 1920, "and he tells me that your brother is a 'comer' in the fiction world and that it would be a pretty good stunt for me to look him up. I understand that he has a novel under way. If he is not already tied up, may I not have the pleasure of talking with him about it or of reading the novel or such portion of it as is now completed?" "If Holt doesn't kick through," Stephen Benét casually noted on the bottom of this letter, "I guess I'll ship it to this guy."[34]

Though publishers were *usually* solicitous of authors during the twenties due to this enormous interest in new writers and writing, publishers' deference toward authors was also very much tied to the tradition of the gentleman-amateur in literature. William Charvat has described the gentleman-amateur's legacy to the twentieth century author:

> Historically, the creative writer was not a worker or producer, but a gentleman-amateur who exhibited his talent to his social equals but did not depend on it for a living; or he accepted the patronage of a social superior, and was still independent of buyers and readers.... In a pecuniary society under democratic patronage, this proud and independent attitude was an anachronism, but vestiges of it survived until 1850 and later.... Long after Byron and Scott had proved that a gentleman could write for money, we see the mark of the patrician in the American writer's demand for privacy, in dignity in his commercial relations and in his resistance to commercial exploitation.[35]

However anachronistically, much of this "proud and independent attitude" persisted well past the turn of the century among publishers as well as writers. Men entered the publishing industry not only to make money (and that was hardly assured), but also to further the ideals of literature, as they conceived them. "A publisher is a businessman, but he is not merely a businessman," wrote Walter Hines Page in 1904. Without literary judgment and sympathy, Page contended, "he can add little to the best literary impulses or tendencies of his time, nor is he likely to attract the best writers. Every great publishing house has been built on the strong friendships between writers and publishers. There is, in fact, no other sound basis to build on; for the publisher cannot do his highest duty to any author whose work he does not appreciate, and with whom he is not in sympathy."[36] In 1905, Henry Holt, then dean of American publishers, wrote to the *Atlantic Monthly* that, in short, good publishers must "exercise an appreciation of literature in large superiority to financial considerations."[37] Both the syntax and the sentiment shared by Page and Holt are tediously Victorian, but then so was, in its courtly rituals, the author-publisher relationship well into the twentieth century.

Through the years writers for the most part returned their publishers' respect and appreciation. Most writers looked to their publishing houses for both support and counsel. "I speak to my publisher," Richard Harding Davis wrote to Charles Scribner in 1892, "as I speak to my family physician."[38] Writers in the twenties were similarly, if less pompously, appreciative of publishers' attention. Stephen Vincent Benét, for instance, acknowledged John Farrar's letter praising *John Brown's Body* (1927) with the greatest sincerity: "Thank you again for your letter—it has made me very conceited and pleased. It is worth while working in the dark for so long to feel that you might possibly have made a better plumber after all. As for genius, I don't know—but it did take persistence."[39]

Writers expressed their trust and confidence in their houses by continuing to publish with them. Publishers coveted author loyalty most of all. After Scott Fitzgerald published *The Great Gatsby* (1925), his third novel with Scribner's, for instance, Maxwell Perkins heard a rumor in New York that the author might be thinking of moving to Boni & Liveright. Perkins wrote to Fitzgerald, then in Paris, asking for an explanation. "LIVERIGHT RUMOR ABSURD," Fitzgerald wired back.[40] Fitzgerald then composed a long letter to Perkins, expressing his commitment to Scribner's and his personal friendship for his editor. "I have told you many times," Fitzgerald wrote, "that you are my publisher, and permanently as far as one can fling about that word in this too mutable world. If you like I will sign a contract with you immediately for my next three books. The idea of leaving you has never for *one single moment* entered my head." Although initially wary of Scribner's reputation for stodginess, Fitzgerald reassured Perkins, "the personality of you and Mr. Scribner, the tremendous squareness, courtesy, generosity, and open-mindedness I have always met there and, if I may say it, the special consideration you have all had for me and my work, much more than make up the difference."[41] Perkins, for his part, reminded Fitzgerald that he had never asked him to sign a multi-book contract "for the simple reason that it might be right for you sometime to change publishers, and while this would be a tragedy to me, I should not be so small as to stand in the way for personal grounds."[42]

Perkins and Fitzgerald were closer professionally and personally than most editors and authors, but all publishing houses tried to make authors feel that special consideration was being given to them and their work. They were not always successful in this, though, and publisher-writer hostilities flared periodically over both real and supposed wrongs. From at least the time Byron publicly called his publisher a Barabbas, profiting from the sufferings and labors of his writers, there has been tension between author and publisher. If there was a remarkable amount of mutual trust in the publishing industry, there was also a fair share of suspicion, usually about financial matters. Orion Cheney, whose *Economic Survey of the Publishing Industry* (1931) contains a masterful analysis of author-publisher relationships, concluded that the writer's contact with his publisher "touches him at his two most sensitive nerves—the pocket-book nerve and the creation nerve which leads directly to the ego." Consequently these nerves occasionally rubbed raw. "Being touched at only one of them is enough for any human being," Cheney commented wryly. "To the author, his book is the very essense of his being—very often his only throw of the dice for current prosperity." But for the publisher, Cheney pointed out, "the book is just one of a number of troubles and one chance out of many to gain profit—or lose it."[43] This economic tension built into the publisher-author relationship strained the tradition of cordial relations in the late nineteenth century. As writers discovered more and more of their colleagues actually making a living from their writing, many came to believe that their own publishers might be holding out on them. According to John Tebbel's authorative four-volume history of the publishing industry in America, by the 1880s there was a "growing conviction" among writers "that they should no longer endure the prevalent notion that they should be grateful for what was given to them."[44] Publishers, for their part, complained that writers had no understanding of literary economics. In 1870, for instance, Charles Scribner estimated that of every five books published three would fail to make back the cost of printing them, one would break even, and only one would actually make money for the firm and the author. That one success, Scribner and other publishers argued, had to underwrite the failure of the other four books.[45] Publishers continue to make this argument to this day.

At the turn of the century authors condemned the still-extant publishing practice of having writers pay for the publication of their books; they complained that they were unfairly treated in the division of profits; they claimed that publishers took too large a share of subsidiary rights payments; and they chided publishers for resisting stronger copyright legislation. As early as 1890 writers tried putting collective pressure on publishers to correct the worst abuses in the industry, but it was not until 1912, with the formation of the Authors' League, that American writers had any collective means with which to lobby and bargain for better terms.[46]

Many of the touchiest areas of the author-publisher relationship were addressed by their legal contract. Such contracts specified copyright ownership arrangements, the distribution of subsidiary rights, and how profits and costs were to be shared. All these issues had once been settled with a handshake, but after 1880 both sides preferred to sign legal contracts. By 1920 almost every author and publisher insisted on some form of written agreement. The Authors' League and other writers' organizations repeatedly urged the adoption of a minimum basic contract agreement for the industry. Although no such official contract was negotiated in the twenties (nor has it been since), most book contracts were drawn along much the same lines. All dealt, for instance, with the key matters of ownership, compensation, and control.

By 1920 it was well accepted in the industry, for example, that in theory the economic rights to a literary property naturally resided with the author. Copyright protection had been codified first by the Connecticut Assembly in 1783; seven years later Congress passed the first Federal Copyright Act. It provided the author with a fourteen-year exclusive copyright privilege, and two refining laws in the nineteenth century guaranteed the author further protection. Such legislation established the fundamental principle of an author's equity in the product of his intelligent industry. Most contracts after 1900 reflected this fact; thus authors in the twentieth century rarely sold their manuscripts outright to publishers. Publishers, however, sometimes required that first-time authors assign the copyright to a firm as a condition of publication. Such "wholesale assignment" of copyright "transfers the ownership of the work to the publisher," the *Authors' League Bulletin* claimed in its February 1919 edition:

> Now there should be little question that the author is and should remain the natural proprietor, both technical and actually, of his creation ... A complete grant of rights reverses the natural order of things and makes the publisher the technical and actual owner of the author's work and puts the latter in the position of holding a claim to royalties in the place of proprietorship of his book.[48]

The League did not prevail in its effort to halt all copyright transfers: perhaps 25 percent of the novels published in the 1920s were copyrighted in the publisher's name. Often this was merely a precaution against disastrous sales, so that the publisher had a chance to recoup his losses. Orion Cheney, though, echoed the prevailing sentiment in the publishing industry in the twenties when he wrote that "copyright protection of the author's economic rights in his work is an established principle of the civilized world's law," a principle publishers tried their best to uphold.[49] "The book," Maxwell Perkins simply said, "belongs to the author."[50]

The contract also specified how the writer would profit from the possession or assignment of copyright. The writer's financial return came in two forms: royalty payments for books actually sold and sales of subsidiary rights. An average 10 percent for author's royalty prevailed in the industry, increasing on a sliding scale as more copies of a book were sold; 10 percent represented roughly half of the publisher's profit after expenses. Popular authors commanded larger percentages, but very few writers received more than a 15 percent royalty, even on the occasional best seller. Publishers and authors quarreled less over royalty rates, though, than over the reported number of copies sold. A familiar complaint among nineteenth-century authors, for example, was that publishers accounted for fewer copies sold than were actually purchased, thus cheating writers out of deserved royalties. Finally in 1896 the Federal Court decided in Savage v. McNeely that authors had the right to check their publisher's accounts in order to verify the accuracy of royalty payments. Much of this controversy resembled a tempest in a financial teapot, as royalty payments rarely amounted to much: most novels did not make back their publication costs, and even so publicized and popular a novel as *This Side of Paradise* returned Scott Fitzgerald less than ten thousand dollars in royalties for more than three years of work.[51]

Of much greater economic importance in most publishing transactions was the sale of the subsidiary rights attendant to a book's publication: magazine serialization, syndication, motion picture, dramatic, radio and translation rights among them. In the twenties, serialization rights alone often brought more than ten thouand dollars for popular books. The movie rights to even moderate successes often brought several thousand dollars, and payments increased in size and importance throughout the twenties. Publishers and authors agreed that subsidiary rights, like copyright, resided naturally with the author, not the publisher. "A book publisher should be a book publisher and not a dealer in serial, dramatic, motion picture, and other rights," the *Authors' League Bulletin* stated flatly.[52] Orion Cheney, reporting to the National Association of Book Publishers in 1931, concurred: "The subsidiary and by-product rights incident to the writing and publication of a book inhere naturally and completely with the author. From that basic principle, modifications may be developed, but any attempt to overlook, void or obviate that principle can only result in unfairness and antagonism."[53] When a publisher contributed to the success of an author's work and hence the saleability of the secondary rights, though, he was entitled to a share of the income from these rights. Hence during the twenties most rights sales were divided equally between publisher and author. Popular authors at any time, of course, negotiated better terms if they wished and unknown writers often settled for a much less favorable split.

In general, these basic financial arrangements satisfied both sides. "That the relations between authors and publishers are a continous war stirred by mutual disrespect is not true," Orion Cheney concluded. "Very few cases of conflict require arbitration and contracts are adhered to as well as in other fields."[54] The *Authors' League Bulletin,* on behalf of the writers, determined that "when dealing with reliable firms the probability of difficulty in any specific case is slight."[55] In a nutshell, both sides agreed that in terms of proprietorship and compensation the author owned his work; that the publisher should have the opportunity to recoup his losses through secondary rights sales, if a book failed in the stores; and that if a book was profitable, both author and publisher should share equally in that success.

They also agreed on the second basic contractual issue, that of creative control. The book belonged to the author in this respect as well. Publishing contracts stipulated that the manuscript would be published without any changes or eliminations unless they were approved by the author; publishers could refuse to print obscene, libelous, or plagiarized material, but once the book was accepted, publishers were required to print it as the author directed. "In the early days things were quite simple," Alfred Knopf remarked in 1974.

> The books came in; we published them as written. I would never have dreamed of suggesting, say, to Willa Cather or Carl Van Vechten or even Joseph Hergesheimer, with whom I was closest, what they should do . . . The writer's job was to write a book and give it to you.[56]

The best publishers and editors were similarly loathe to interfere with the creative processes of their writers. Most would offer suggestions and advice when asked, but few went further. To an audience of aspiring editors, Maxwell Perkins once said, "The first thing you must remember—an editor does not add to a book. At best he serves as a handmaiden to an author. Don't ever get to feeling important about yourself, because an editor at most releases energy. He creates nothing. A writer's best work comes from himself."[57] Although Perkins developed the reputation of an editor who actively worked with authors to solve their writing problems, his usual advice to them was to follow their own judgment. After offering just such counsel to Marjorie Rawlings, Perkins explained:

> When I write in that do-it-as-it-seems-right-to-you way, it is because it has always been my conviction—and I do not see how anyone could dispute the rightness of it—that a book must be done according to the writer's conception of it as nearly perfectly as possible, and that the publishing problems begin then. *That is, the publisher must not try to get the writer to fit the book to the conditions of the trade, etc. It must be the other way around.*[58]

How strenuously writers exercised this right of control varied from individual to individual. Most worked with the publisher on the choice of title, jacket design, advertising copy, and typography. While some writers scrupulously revised and corrected galleys, others left these chores to the editor and his staff. In short, if he so wanted, the writer could participate actively in the production process to insure that his work reached the public according to his conception.

This is not to say that publishers and authors did not feud at times, particularly when negotiating contracts. The decade of the twenties was not always an era of good feeling in American letters. Publishers balked at paying out large advances, for instance, while writers perpetually charged that advances were far too measly. Publishers complained that the increasing number of literary agents, making impossible demands for their clients, destroyed the traditional author-publisher closeness, much as sports team owners today grouch about high-priced athletes, their lawyers and agents. Writers countered that they needed advisors to handle the financial and legal affairs they themselves found increasingly baffling. Publishers accused writers of switching houses to gain short-term financial advantage; authors in turn accused publishers of taking advantage of their loyalty. The simple handshake, by 1920, was pretty much a thing of the past in contract negotiations.

Given these factors, trust and good will prevailed to a surprising extent among publishers and authors in the twenties. Economic prosperity made negotiating easier for both sides; the entreprenurial flavor of the age insured the continuance of the small independent publisher willing and able to service the writer personally. Alfred Knopf began in publishing with five thousand dollars, and dozens of other men entered the field with even less capital. A book could be published for a few thousand dollars; losses were never catastrophic, and Ivy Leaguers always surfaced eager to buy into a firm. Publishers could afford to take chances. In short, the tradition of the gentleman-amateur lingered on well into the twenties in the form of cordial author-publisher relations. Through their legal contracts, we can pinpoint other essential features of the writer's professional life: his ownership of his literary property, his status as an independent economic agent; and his possession of creative control in the publication process. Each gained the book author much prestige in the literary marketplace.

Playwrights enjoyed roughly the same status in the commercial theater. There was, however, no longstanding tradition of gentlemanly relations between playwright and producer. As late as the 1880s, producers relied for material on pirated English plays, their own writing efforts, and infrequently held competitions. Playwrights rarely received more than a token amount, if even that, for their work, and neither producer nor playwright enjoyed much standing in the literary world. The American theater also had a history of more activist labor organizing among stagehands, actors, and writers than did the more genteel Publishers Row. Traditionally, playwrights and theatrical producers viewed each other with more suspicion than did authors and publishers. In the twenties the Dramatists' Guild succeeded where the Authors'

League had failed in negotiating a standard contract. The Minimum Basic Agreement, signed by the Guild and 152 theatrical producers in 1927, provided for copyright in the playwright's name. It specified that authors would be paid on a royalty basis, and set the minimum royalty of five percent of box office receipts. The Agreement also settled a long-simmering conflict between producer and playwright by insuring the author of at least a 50-percent share of all secondary rights sales, and assigned to the author the right to approve all such sales.

The Minimum Basic Agreement vested creative control exclusively in the playwright by stipulating that the producer could make "no additions, omissions, or any alterations whatsoever without the consent of the Author."[59] The M.B.A. guaranteed an author's right-of-approval over basic casting, direction and set design decisions. In short, the Guild agreement granted playwrights roughly the same basic legal rights and privileges as prevailed for authors in the publishing industry. Thus, playwrights shared with book authors the common professional identity of the *writer:* both were economic free-agents and therefore personally independent; as the creators of their literary property, both were acknowledged by law and custom to be its owners; both retained creative control through the entire production process. If the book belonged to the author, the play belonged to the playwright. As such, both were in a position to insist on cordiality, attention, and respect in their business affairs, even though they could not compete with their publishers or producers in terms of economic clout.

The Minimum Basic Agreement, in fact, merely codified what had been standard practice for more than a decade. The American theater of the twenties, for the first time, celebrated and rewarded its playwrights as much as its stars. As Robert E. Sherwood noted some time later, the entrance of Eugene O'Neill onto the theatrical scene had effectively shattered "the ancient and frequently vulnerable theory that a play that was 'arty' could never get by in the box office." The theater had finally come of age, and playwright and producer both enjoyed their new-found prestige. Broadway in the twenties, Sherwood avowed, had been "a wonderfully exciting place in which to work and progress, as wide open as a virgin continent and as teeming with chances of adventure and fortune."[60]

Consequently both playwright and book author stood closer to center stage in the literary marketplace during the heady days of the twenties than they ever had before. Furthermore, the writer's business affairs offered a foothold into the greater world of the New York literary community, which in the twenties was nothing if not relentlessly social. A great deal of the writer's business itself was conducted out of the office and after hours. George Oppenheimer, who founded the Viking Press with Harold Ginzburg in 1925, believed that "social life and publishing are inextricably interwoven.

Sometimes more business is accomplished at a party, be it cocktail, tea, or rout, than in the office."[61] Thus Horace Liveright was not the only publisher to understand the value of a good bootlegger to a firm, or to realize, in Lillian Hellman's words, "that writers care less for dollars than for attention."[62]

Of that attention, there was no short supply. A publishing contract, a play on Broadway, even a staff position on a respected newspaper or magazine, provided entry into New York's celebrated literary community. "By the mid-twenties," Linda Cirino and Susan Edminston point out in their informative *Literary New York,*

> Midtown—the business district of the city extending from 34th Street to West 59th Street—was bustling with literary activity, most of the harvest but sometimes of the farming variety. Like the Park Row area in the mid-nineteenth century, Midtown was the center of both the theater and commercial publishing. Authors came to do business with their publishers and stayed in the great hotels. Journalists, playwrights, critics, and celebrities socialized in Midtown restaurants, speakeasies, and living rooms. And some even came to write.[63]

Midtown was not only a literary marketplace, then, but also a social environment where writers lived or visited in order to be in each other's company. It was a place where writers knew they were welcome, and welcome even if not well known. The Gotham Boom Mart, the Rose Room of the Algonquin Hotel, Jack and Charlie's Puncheon Club (later the "21" Club), Liveright's townhouse, and illustrator Neysa McMein's studio on 57th Street were all frequent writers' haunts during the twenties. Many other spontaneous gatherings took place daily in restaurants, clubs, and apartments. A row of speakeasies along 52nd Street, for example, catered almost exclusively to the literary trade. At the time, the Algonquin Round Table was the most renowned of writers' meeting places. John Mason Brown, later one of the country's foremost drama critics, joined hundreds of other "stage-struck, print-bedazzled newcomers to New York in the mid-twenties" who dined at the Algonquin hoping for a glimpse of George S. Kaufman, Dorothy Parker, Robert Benchley, Marc Connelly, Alexander Woollcott, or one of the other luminaries who frequented Frank Case's hotel:

> On those occasions, and for us they *were* occasions, when we went to the Rose Room, we could not at our side tables hear what was being said by those men and women whose plays and performances we were seeing, whose books, columns, and reviews we devoured, and who seemed to us the embodiment of Times Square sophistication, gaiety and success. We could only gape at them, and hear their distant laughter, and be hopefully certain that what they laughed at was the ultimate in wit and drollery. We, the younger ones, were not alone in feeling this. Countless older New Yorkers, also avid readers of "the page opposite" in the *World* on which the columns of Broun, Woollcott, Deems Taylor, and Stallings appeared, felt as we did, and so did out-of-towners beyond numbering who flocked to the Algonquin as part of their Broadway pilgrimage.[64]

For writers like Brown, then, the Algonquin Round Table symbolized New York's literary community in the twenties. Budd Schulberg, a long-time student and observer of the writers' public life, believes that although much less true today, writers traditionally moved in much the same social world:

> Before the First World War it was still common for literary folk to fraternize. There was Mabel Dodge's salon for movers and shakers in Greenwich Village, where John Reed, Edna St. Vincent Millay, Big Bill Heywood, and other artists and actionaries passing through would assemble for poetry reading, wine drinking, love-making, and revolutionary dreaming. . . . Even in the Jazz Age it was still literary etiquette for a young man of promise to send politely autographed copies of his new book to Edith Wharton, T. S. Eliot, or other established literary figures of his day. There was every sort of exchange, from Scott Fitzgerald's genteel tea-time encouragement from Edith Wharton and Eliot, to his Long Island drinking bouts with Ring Lardner.[65]

Friendships, marriages, writing collaborations, grudges, and feuds abounded among and between writers. There are many such associations and encounters simply among the forty writers studied here. Marc Connelly and George S. Kaufman collaborated on a number of plays; so did Ben Hecht and Charles MacArthur. Robert E. Sherwood, Dorothy Parker, and Robert Benchley first met on the staff of *Vanity Fair* after the war, and later were charter members of the Round Table. Parker and Lillian Hellman were close friends; Hellman and Dashiell Hammett had a twenty-year-long affair; S. J. Perelman and Nathanael West were brothers-in-law. Sherwood, Maxwell Anderson, Sidney Howard and S. N. Behrman later formed a highly successful production company to stage their own plays. "The world in which we moved was small," Marc Connelly remembered, "but it was churning with a dynamnic group of young people. It seemed like we were together constantly."[66] How small that world actually was later haunted Connelly when his wife left him to marry his best friend—Robert Sherwood.

Thus there is merit in talking about Midtown in the twenties as a literary community in more than the metaphorical sense, inhabited by authors, playwrights, publishers, producers, critics, agents, editors, and any number of other "Broadway and print-bedazzled" hopefuls. This community, and those with an interest in writers and writing everywhere, showered the writer with the intangible but precious rewards of celebrity and prestige. "Artists were looked up to as heroes," Van Wyck Brooks said of New York in the twenties,

> there had never been a time and place so favorable to literary growth. . . . For in the nihilistic air the reverence that religion had once absorbed was redirected toward artists, who were regarded as saints, the craftsmen who had maintained their integrity, who had remained inviolate in a world that seemed generally to be tumbling to pieces.[67]

Marc Connelly
(*Courtesy of the Library of Congress*)

W. R. Burnett discovered the more worldly pleasures of New York awaiting a writer in 1928 when his tough-guy novel about racketeering in Chicago, *Little Caesar,* was accepted by the Dial Press. Burnett's career is, more than anything else, a study in perseverance. After graduating from Ohio State University in 1921, Burnett devoted six years to writing at night without ever selling a line. "I wrote five novels before *Little Caesar,* all rejected," Burnett recalled in 1977.[68] To support himself he worked by day as a statistician for the State of Ohio. Fed up with office routine, he moved to Chicago and found a job as a night clerk in a North Side flophouse. There he met many of the models for the underworld characters who peopled the grim backrooms of *Little Caesar.* A kind note from Maxwell Perkins was the only encouragement he received until a reader at Dial chanced upon *Little Caesar* in a pile of unsolicited manuscripts and convinced his superiors to publish it. *Little Caesar* became a smashing success and launched Burnett on a long and fruitful career. He quit Chicago for New York in 1929, where, to his amazement, writers seemed very much at the center of attention:

> I went to New York on *Little Caesar,* before it was published and during the publication, and stayed there about four months. I couldn't believe it, the way writers were treated. Here I was staying in a beautiful place, right across from the Plaza, a small hotel, a very elegant hotel, with a dining room reserved for the guests [for which] I paid nothing. Nothing. They did it for the publicity. The status, you know, of having a writer in the house. Later on, I stayed at the St. Regis often on the same kind of deal. It was wonderful, after all that rejection and all that work, to be somewhere finally where it made a difference that I was a writer. I was respected for it.[69]

The deference showered on writers extended far beyond free hotel rooms and seven-course meals, however. Countless appreciative letters, for example, poured in from total strangers. Imagine receiving any one of these letters:

> It may be a satisfaction for you to know that your plays have spoken to me personally and spiritually, and enriched my life. I can only hope that by taking strict care of yourself you may be spared for many more years of service for the arts and the country that you have already endowed with your genius.

> I ask nothing more than this honor. That you, who have been my master, scan his pupil's work. Letters are not my *metier.* This one is badly done, I have no doubt. But sir, my heart and my being goes with it.

> I loved it so that if there had been a matinee today I would still be sitting in my seat—waiting to be warmed again—I was deeply moved and deeply grateful and you are wonderful.[70]

Maxwell Anderson received all three, and more like them every week. The first was written by Professor Sculley Bradley; the second by an aspiring playwright, Samuel Burger; the third by Arlene Francis. Almost every writer received such letters. This literary fan mail, the reward of the writer's professional life, was nothing if not flattering to the ego. In the twenties, the writer basked in the warm glow of public celebrity as never before.

In sum, the literary marketplace and the community it supported were firmly rooted in midtown Manhattan during the 1920s. Authors, both would-be and established, from all over the country travelled to New York to be near that marketplace and community. Once in New York, authors discovered a world where, in and out of the business office, a writer was a person of consequence, regardless of how popular or successful. It was a world which valued the writer's creativity; a world where the writer owned and controlled his work by reason of his creative investment; and a world which usually afforded him at least a modest living and invariably the less tangible but no less cherished rewards of prestige, respect, and celebrity.

This brief chapter could not hope to explore, or even suggest, all the varied dimensions of the profession of authorship and the literary marketplace in the twenties. The picture of the writer in the marketplace and literary community presented here, though, should be kept in mind when judging writers' reactions to working in the film industry. For, as we shall see, the studios defined what a "writer" was and did far differently—so differently in Hollywood, in fact, that it presented a serious challenge to writers' conceptions of themselves as "writers" in the Eastern sense. Screenwriting radically differed from playwrighting or book writing, and had its own traditions and its own haphazard and curious history.

2

The Writer and the Silent Screen

However prosperous the literary marketplace in the 1920s, it could not equal the riches of the American film industry, then in its golden age. In 1860 the motion picture was a theoretical probability; in 1885, a technical possibility but still commercially impractical. In 1893 Edison introduced the kinetoscope at Chicago's Columbian Exposition; thirty years later motion pictures were a multi-billion dollar industry servicing a mass audience. By the twenties the prospects for expansion in the movie industry seemed limitless. "The post-war period was one of unrestraint in business as in life generally," film historian Lewis Jacobs wrote in 1939. "To be important a thing had to be big—and the movies became one of the biggest things in American Civilization."[1] In the process, the status and role of the screenwriter inevitably changed.

A number of American novelists, including Theodore Dreiser, William Dean Howells, and Stephen Crane, had been early enthusiasts of the motion picture's artistic possibilities, but a now-forgotten reporter on the *New York World,* Roy McCardell, enjoys the distinction of having been the first professional screenwriter. Prior to 1900, there had been little need for writers in commercial movie making. The first movies shown to the general public were rarely more than short scenes of city street life, galloping horses, auto races, onrushing locomotives and the like. Movie makers were at once camera operators, directors, and lab technicians. There was little money or inclination to hire extra people simply to decide what scene to shoot next. Even when production companies began making simple dramas, the first being Vitagraph's *Tearing Down the Spanish Flag* (1898), there was no need for professional writers. Companies depended on the momentary inspiration of directors, actors, and even office workers for story material. The "script" rarely consisted of more than a hastily scrawled list of shots for the director to follow as best he could.

In 1900 Biograph's Henry Marvin, then the industry's leading advocate of improving the quality of movies, approached McCardell with an offer to pay fifteen dollars each for as many as ten story ideas. Playing times had increased to more than five minutes a reel, Marvin calculated, sufficient time for a modicum of plot development. McCardell quickly submitted ten simple scenarios. Marvin was so pleased with the newspaperman's work that he ordered six of the stories into production and placed McCardell on the Biograph payroll at $150 a week.[2]

McCardell's good fortune caught the eye of many of his colleagues in the city rooms of New York's newspapers. A veteran reporter received no more than forty dollars a week at the turn of the century, and only top-drawer editors earned as much as McCardell was making at Biograph. Soon reporters and re-write men, their minds churning with story ideas, flooded the offices of film manufacturers. Marvin further endeared himself to writers by organizing the first separate story department in a movie production company. As early as 1900, then, the movies were a highly profitable alternative to newspaper work for a select few writers.

Yet Marvin's admirable attempt to improve the quality of his product ran counter to the restricted budgets of early movie pioneers. By 1910 movie making took place on a scale large enough to require craft specialization, and movie makers enjoyed a certain amount of creative latitude. More often than not, though, lack of time and money severely circumscribed such freedom. "There was no opposition to quality," Benjamin Hampton reports, "there was merely no conscious effort to find superior stories, sets, acting, and directing. Writers, scene printers, players, and directors were entirely free to do their work as effectively as they knew how, so long as their ambitions did not require any more film or cost any more money."[3]

In this first decade of the new century the film industry was self-destructively competitive. Companies spent more time in litigation over patent infringements than they did in making movies; cheating and corruption plagued all parts of the industry; violence against competitors was only one of the tactics used to gain a competitive edge. Chaos threatened until, in January 1909, the nine leading manufacturing companies, under the leadership of Edison, finally formed the Motion Picture Patents Company, a trust arrangement wherein each company relinquished its patents to the MPPC, which in turn issued licenses for the equipment's use. The MPPC was a powerful economic organization, and at first enjoyed success in its attempt to monopolize all the major segments of the industry—manufacture, distribution, and exhibition.

The trust did not live long, however, without stiff competition. So potentially enormous were the profits in movie making that dozens of small independent manufacturers and exhibitors openly defied the trust and its lawyers. By 1912, the trust faced increasing public resentment of monopoly in general in addition to the specific opposition of the independents. The battle with the "outlaws," as the trust branded independent producers, lasted until

1914 when the MPPC finally broke under pressure. Two years later, the courts officially broke up the monopoly. The trust war is a fascinating study of corporate maneuver and warfare, and was of crucial significance in the development of the film industry.[4] Three consequences of the trust war were of particular importance to the status and function of writers—and other craftspeople—within the industry: the war increased the incentive to produce attractive, high caliber movies; it speeded the introduction of the star system; and it hastened, if not prompted, the transfer of production facilities from the New York area to Southern California.

A great deal of lore surrounds the move of the movie makers to Los Angeles. Carey McWilliams, for one, believed in 1946 that the independents moved to Los Angeles to elude the patent trust: "Always looking over their shoulders for process servers, the first motion picture 'people' did not live in Los Angeles; they merely camped in the community, prepared, like Arabs, to fold their tents and steal away in the night."[5] Benjamin Hampton also believed that Los Angeles became the home of the movie industry because of its proximity to the Mexican border and its shelter from the trust's lawyers. This tents-in-the-night theory is appropriately melodramatic, but a more plausible explanation for the move is to be found in the region's irresistible combination of good weather, varied landscape, cheap land, and cheap labor. The fact that the Selig Company—a MPPC member—moved to Los Angles two years before the first independent, and that the only producer to make the five-hour drive to the border was avoiding a morals charge, only confirm the speciousness of the tents-in-the-night explanation.[6] By the 1920s, in any case, virtually all film production took place in the Los Angeles area. Although a few studios continued to operate in the East, by 1920 Hollywood and the movies were synonymous. Writers who worked in the film industry now had to move to Los Angeles, a continent away from New York. In Europe, as J. B. Priestley suggested, writers walked to work in films; in America they boarded the Super Chief, isolating themselves from the rest of the literary community.

The trust war also fostered the adoption of the star system, first by the independents and then by the trust itself. The MPPC originally clung to the practice of neither crediting on screen nor publicizing in any way their creative personnel. By doing this, the trust companies hoped to keep salary demands and labor costs under control. Carl Laemmle, the most important independent producer, first challenged the wisdom of this policy and took advantage of movie-goers' increasing interest in the personalities they saw on the screen. Laemmle lured Florence Lawrence, "The Biograph Girl," to his own IMP Productions with the promise of a larger salary, screen credit, and a full-scale publicity campaign. Laemmle's gambit succeeded immediately, and virtually every studio, trust and independent alike, quickly rushed to sign and promote stars of its own. "Acting, historically one of the most precarious of all professions, suddenly found itself among the highest paid on earth," wrote Benjamin Hampton, who himself entered the movie business just before the First World War. "When millions of American movie fans learned to identify their favorites on the screen they changed the status of an entire craft, transferring the balance of power from the employer to the employee group."[7] Mary Pickford, Douglas Fairbanks, Tom Mix, and a handful of other stars became the most powerful figures in the industry. The practice of giving screen credit to a movie's creative personnel quickly spread, and the huge salaries paid the stars helped raise the wages of other craftspeople. The star system, then, contributed to the steady rise in writers' compensation.

Finally, the intensely competitive atmosphere during the trust war and the public's insatiable appetite for new and better movies further increased the demand for professional writers. The independents in particular publicized their movies as costly and innovative productions. One of those innovations, the feature-length movie, quickly became the standard of the industry. By 1915 the trust's usual two or three reel program had been superseded by features of five reels or longer. As movies increased in length, so too did their potential for plot and character development. The demand for writers grew in turn.

Traditionally movie makers had rummaged through the classics for material. The rights to novels, plays and stories in the public domain were free for the asking, and the public had already demonstrated their interest in such material. Within a few short years, though, most of the classics had been adapted to the movies at least once, and the studios were forced to scout out other sources of material. Contemporary best-selling action and adventure fiction provided one likely source: Gene Stratton-Porter, Rex Beach, Richard Harding Davis, and Jack London were among the first novelists to see their work reach the screen. Conflict arose between author and movie producer almost immediately, however, as many companies used current novels and plays without bothering to purchase the right to do so. When Lew Wallace sued Kalem for filming *Ben Hur* without his authorization, and won a fifty thousand dollar award, movie companies more carefully observed the copyright laws. Consequently, motion picture rights steadily increased in value. In 1914, Vitagraph announced that it had paid fifty thousand dollars for the rights to a popular stage play, *Within the Law,* and the average price for any best-selling novel, reached five thousand dollars.[8]

Yet even the vast supply of such popular fiction did not provide enough grist for the movie mill. Following Biograph's lead, film manufacturers actively sought out original story material wherever they could find it. Many even advertised in the growing number of fan magazines; other announced their willingness to train writers in "scenario technique." Correspondence schools promised to "teach the art of scenario writing in a few simple lessons."[9] Although the studios let it be known that less than two percent of the scripts received through the mail actually went before the camera, thousands of submissions poured in.

McCardell had thought his fifteen dollars per story a fortune in 1900; ten years later producers paid fifty dollars for each scenario. Ingenious plots brought twice that amount. This rate compared favorably with that offered by the high-priced magazines of the day, and was far greater than that paid by most newspapers and magazines for similar free-lance work. In 1912, the American Film Manufacturing Company caused a stir when it paid McCardell thirty thousand dollars to write and supervise the production of a serial, "The Diamond from the Sky."[10] Story departments sprung up in every studio, following Biograph's lead. Staffed by ex-newspapermen, publicity agents, advertising copywriters, and many studio office workers with a knack for screenwriting, these departments churned out scenarios as fast as possible. C. Gardiner Sullivan, Edmund Jones, Jeanie MacPherson and Frances Marion were among the first to carve out professional careers as "scenarists." With little training in or allegiance to other forms of creative writing, they thought themselves, at best, technical writers conversant with the new terminology of the screen: cuts, dissolves, fades, wipes, irises, leaders, and the like. They scoffed at the notion that they were artists.

The studios in their pursuit of quality also began to hire *established* writers. In 1914, Carl Laemmle's Universal advertised that such popular authors as Booth Tarkington, Eugene Rhodes, William McCloud and Arthur Stringer were in the company's employ, working on scenarios and occasionally participating in their production.[11] Two years later, Famous Players Film Company made an unprecedented proposal: one thousand dollars each for one hundred scenarios. Famous Players professed their desire, in advertising the offer, "to establish direct contact with the best imaginative brains in the country in permanent association."[12] This permanent association remained a few years in the future in 1916, and few of the manuscripts received by Famous Players were the work of the best minds of the country. This proposal, though, indicates the explosive demand for writers in the industry. Motion picture companies had to find quality vehicles for the newborn stars, and no expense was to be spared.

The trust war, then, was advantageous to the screenwriter in several ways. The battle between the MPPC and the independents fostered the movement toward better, more sophisticated pictures. Also, for the first time writers received screen credit for their contributions. The trust war brought about the first involvement, however tentative, of popular authors with the movies, and contributed to the steady rise in prices paid for story material.

Yet the trust war also meant the transfer of production facilities to California, and the isolation of the screenwriter from the rest of the literary marketplace. Moreover, the star system had, in at least one way, actually *diminished* the status of the scenarist: with a great many temperamental stars making arbitrary decisions, writers were "regarded as hacks," according to Hampton, "whose business it was to shape and distort feeble stories to fit the limitations of the stars."[13] Directors and even production executives, who had always enjoyed the upper hand, now accommodated the most trival demands of their stars. Long-term contracts and morals clauses later tipped the balance of power back to the front office, but during the heyday of the star system just before, during and immediately after World War I, actors enjoyed creative as well as financial control of movie making. In short, three crucial dimensions of the screenwriting profession surfaced during the trust war: its large financial reward compared to other kinds of writing; its relative lack of status; and its lack of creative autonomy.

After the end of World War I, one producer in particular, Samuel Goldwyn, was responsible for the first concerted effort to lure authors to the film industry. Goldwyn's background was typical of many movie producers of his generation. Born in Warsaw to Jewish parents in 1882, Goldwyn ran away to England as a boy, taking the name Samuel Goldfish. At the age of fifteen he sailed to America and apprenticed himself to a Manhattan glove manufacturer. Goldfish's fortunes rose steadily; by 1910 he owned a leather factory and had made his modest mark as an entrepreneur.[14]

The proposed end of the tariff on foreign leather goods threatened to destroy Goldfish's capital in 1913; he sagely sold out of the garment industry and bought into the fledgling movie business. Goldfish joined with his brother-in-law, Jesse Lasky, and a struggling theatrical director named Cecil B. DeMille to form the Lasky Feature Plays Company, and set about learning a new trade. Three years later he dissolved this first partnership and formed a second, the Goldwyn Pictures Company, with the Selwyn brothers, two successful Broadway producers. In 1919 Goldfish changed his name to Goldwyn, and moved the company's operations to a new plant in Culver City, California. He broke from the Selwyns in 1920, reformed the partnership eighteen months later, and ended it for good in 1922. Goldwyn remained Hollywood's major independent producer well into the 1950s: he owned a studio complex in downtown Hollywood had actors, writers, and directors under personal contract and financed and supervised the production of his films himself, distributing them through one of the major studios.[15]

Irascible, unschooled, unsurpassingly energetic, and seemingly with a cigar—and at least part of his foot—always in his mouth, Goldwyn was by some accounts a vulgar philistine and by others one of the best producers in Hollywood. Writers who worked with him through the years usually held to the latter view. Nunnally Johnson, for one, thought Goldwyn an "instinctive man about pictures," and ranked him with Darryl Zanuck and David Selznick as the best movie makers in the industry.[16] George Oppenheimer, for another, who worked as a production assistant and writer for Goldwyn in the thirties, later praised his former boss fulsomely:

> He made good pictures and had high ideals and standards of taste, divorced from the usual Hollywood one-track, narrow-gauged commercialism. Like most producers, he was a maze of insecurities and indecision. He had also been one of the first to realize the worth of the writer.[17]

In 1919 Goldwyn ran the largest production facility in the industry, but he was the only significant producer without a major star under contract. He had suffered a humiliating string of failures in promoting young actresses; only Mabel Normand was a Goldwyn star of any consequence. To counteract this chronic inability to develop stars, Goldwyn struck upon the idea of hiring and publicizing famous writers in their stead. Goldwyn's professed motivation in this endeavor was to improve the caliber of films: "In the poverty of the screen drama lay, so I felt, the weakness of our industry, and the one correction which suggested itself was a closer cooperation between author and picture producer."[18] But Goldwyn must have fancied also the thought of marquees emblazoned with the names of the world's most famous authors, books, and plays. For whatever reason, he decided to employ "star" writers, or failing that, to make writers into stars.

To this end he created the Eminent Authors Inc., in 1919, as a subsidiary of the Goldwyn Corporation. Among the writers Goldwyn wooed to Hollywood in the next two years were Gertrude Atherton, Mary Roberts Rinehart, Rupert Hughes, Elmer Rice, Edward Justice Mayer, Gouvenor Morris, and Basil King. Rex Beach, who had worked well with the producer in the past, also joined the Eminent Authors organization and soon advised Goldwyn on the hiring of other writers. In theory each writer was to receive a percentage of the box-office receipts for the movies he worked on as well as a weekly salary. Each was to work with the scenario department in the development of story material, and then take part in actual production

Howard Dietz, the wunderkind of Goldwyn's publicity department, devoted his full talents to promoting both Goldwyn and the Eminent Authors. A series of full-page advertisements in the *Saturday Evening Post* announced that the Eminent Authors project would guarantee the public that "all Goldwyn pictures are built upon a strong foundation of intelligence and refinement."[19] Another advertisement in *The Movie Mirror* proclaimed that because of the Eminent Authors "the motion picture will now rank with the drama and the novel in importance."[20] Dietz's promotional blitz insured that both the industry and public knew of Goldwyn's attempts to improve the caliber of motion pictures. Goldwyn's competitors, in particular Famous Players-Lasky and Paramount, took enough notice to institute more modest literary hiring campaigns of their own. Adolph Zukor of Paramount

Publicity Photo of Sam Goldwyn and His Eminent Authors (Rupert Hughes, Mary Roberts Rinehart, Basil King, Rex Beach, and Sam Goldwyn)
(Courtesy of the Academy of Motion Picture Arts and Sciences)

concentrated on luring European authors to America. By 1921 he counted Sir James Barrie, Joseph Conrad, Arnold Bennett, Elinor Glyn, and W. Somerset Maugham among the "famous authors actually in the studios writing new plays for Paramount Pictures, advising with directors, using the motion picture as they formerly used the pen."[21]

These initial experiments with established authors produced some successes. The work of Rex Beach, Rupert Hughes, and Elinor Glyn pleased their bosses and all three remained in Hollywood for many years. Beach and Hughes eventually became writer-producers, supervising the making of their own movies. In 1921, while admitting Hollywood's failings in the past, Beach concluded that the Eminent Authors program improved both the writer's lot in the industry and the quality of films:

> There is something to be said for the author who disdained the photoplay heretofore, who was forced to witness the mutilation of his story into unrecognizable caricature. Each side has now made concessions. Each realizes the indispensability of the other. Each has noted with approval the growing demand for the good story, the well-thought-out-plot, characters drawn from life rather than from the stilted lay-figures of the studio. The author is now contesting with the star for supremacy. His own laurels, the many photoplays created from well-known novels in recent months, are proof of his value to the newest and most popular art.[22]

There were also some spectacular disasters. Goldwyn's experience with the Belgian poet and mystic, Maurice Maeterlinck, painfully demonstrated the hazards of hiring writers solely for their name. Maeterlinck's star was on the rise in America after his *Blue Bird,* an operatic fantasy, had met with acclaim in New York. Dietz convinced Goldwyn that signing Maeterlinck would be of enormous publicity value to the studio. Goldwyn cornered Maeterlinck while the poet was on a lecture tour in the United States and offered him $100,000 to join the Eminent Authors. When he upped this offer to include a private villa high in the Hollywood Hills, Maeterlinck accepted. For three months Maeterlinck worked diligently writing his first script. A translator then spent another two months with the script. The Goldwyn production department was alerted to await the commencement of the studio's most spectacular picture to date. Finally, the translated script arrived at Goldwyn's door. Reportedly, Goldwyn burst hysterically into the corridor minutes later, screaming in frustration: "But the hero is a bee! The hero is a bee!"[23]

When Goldwyn looked back on the Eminent Authors experiment a few years after he dismantled it, he was forced to admit defeat: "When the tradition of the pen ran athwart the tradition of the screen, I am bound to say that I suffered considerably from the impact."[24] Like most other producers in Hollywood, Goldwyn attributed the program's failure to the inability of novelists and playwrights to readjust their sights and adapt to screenwriting; in short, they could not write visually. "The great trouble with the usual author," Goldwyn wrote, "is that he approaches the camera with some fixed literary ideal and he cannot compromise with the motion-picture viewpoint. He does not realize that a page of Henry James prose, leading through the finest shades of human consciousness, is absolutely lost on the screen."[25] Most of the writers who hired on in Hollywood during these years, not surprisingly, told a different tale about the Eminent Authors and other special writing projects of the day. Mary Roberts Rinehart, for one, signed a three-year contract with the Eminent Authors in 1919. Of Goldwyn's motives in this endeavor, she later wrote:

> I believe now that Mr. Goldwyn's plan for utilizing the author in the picturization of his story was a perfectly genuine one. I have always given him credit for more vision than falls to the lot of most picture producers. If he saw, in a list of well-known names, a certain publicity value, he also believed that people whose business it was to tell stories could be helpful in transposing them to the screen.[26]

Rinehart knew little of Hollywood's methods, but within a few months she came to understand that her duties at the studio were not to include much writing:

> As early as that summer I found that I had one function in the studio, and only one. That was publicity. Whatever its origin, the Eminent Authors idea ended as a publicity stunt.... I had no place to work. I had a chair in the cafeteria, but that was all, save that the gate-keeper passed my car without question.... According to the press I was making motion pictures; and to support this idea I was being photographed for publicity purposes, on the stage, in the studio garden, on my favorite mount! Nobody believed that compared with me the office boy on the lot was an oriental potentate and the gate-keeper a king. Or that my place on the lot was considerably less definite than that of the waiters in the restaurant.[27]

When Rinehart complained to Goldwyn's story editor that she was no more useful to the studio than "a fifth leg to a calf," he replied that she had not yet learned the knack of screenwriting. "That was largely the story of my three-years' connection with the movies," Rinehart recalled. "When I protested, and I did protest, I was told of the vast gulf between the picture audience and the reading public; I was assured, politely, that I knew nothing of the screen art; and when I threatened to become violent I received a box of flowers."[28] But, to Rinehart, the charge that writers could not learn the technical aspects of screenwriting sounded like sour grapes. If the writer not only had no control over his material but also no real function *at all* in the scripting process, she suggested, neither Goldwyn nor the writers he hired were at fault. Rather, the scenario department at Goldwyn's studio sabotaged the Eminent Authors, and with good reason, for they stood to lose the most if Eastern authors proved to be successful scenarists:

> The stubborn resistance which he [Goldwyn] met was not in the authors, most of them humble in their ignorance of the new art; but in his own organization. If authors could arrange in what sequences their stories were to be developed, leaving to mere technicians the details of that development, the high-salaried scenario department would be superfluous. It required only three days for me to discover this attitude and less than a week to take it to Mr. Goldwyn. A story of mine was being prepared for production, and a skilled scenario writer was assigned to me for my ideas.

> It was immediately clear to me, however, that he did not want my ideas. Nobody about the lot but the management wanted my ideas, or even my story. All they asked of me was to go home and draw my guarantee of fifteen thousand dollars a year and a small percentage of profits which never developed. . . . At the end of that first trip to the coast, in early July of 1919, I departed with the full knowledge that every scenario department regarded authors as nuisances, and not even necessary ones; that no cooperation would be possible, and that they regarded their continued existence as depending on their insistence that the author of a tale neither knew the incidents which should lead to its conclusion, nor the conclusion which should arise from those incidents.[29]

Rinehart left the Eminent Authors program convinced that, whatever Goldwyn's good intentions, the organization was a fraud and a personal embarrassment.

The Eminent Authors were not the only imported writers to complain about their status in Hollywood. Famous Players-Lasky, for example, lured Elinor Glyn, a popular English romantic novelist, to their payroll in 1920 with many of the same promises Goldwyn made to Rinehart. "The plan was that we should proceed at once to Hollywood," Glyn recalled, "spend as long as seemed necessary in studying the technical problems of film production, and then each write a scenario and supervise its translation into a film."[30] Each writer in the program was to receive ten thousand dollars per picture, travelling expenses, and the promise of a better contract if this first movie proved a hit. Although initially enthused with the idea, Glyn soon realized, like Rinehart, that these promises were largely a smokescreen, and that she would have no part in the actual making of movies:

> No one wanted our advice or assistance, nor did they intend to take it. All they required was the use of our names to act as shields against the critics. Every person connected with the production studios, although few had travelled as far as New York, and many were all but illiterates, was absolutely convinced that he or she knew much better how to depict the manners and morals of whatever society or country they were attempting to show on the screen than any denizen of that country or society, and they were not prepared to amend any detail to meet our criticisms.[31]

Glyn also realized that creative control was not to be one of the author's prerogatives in the film industry. The scenario department at Famous Players-Lasky, evidently much like Goldwyn's, was Glyn's principal nemesis: "All authors, living or dead, famous or obscure, shared the same fate. Their stories were re-written and completely altered either by the stenographers and continuity girls of the scenario department, or by the Assistant Director and his lady-love."[32]

Other foreign authors hired by Paramount and Famous Players concurred with Glyn's diagnosis of the writer's plight, and most left as soon as their contracts expired. Somerset Maugham, for one, left Hollywood long before production even began on his first and only movie script. He merely handed in the story and immediately sailed for China, where, Glyn remarked, she had "no doubt he felt much more at home."[33] Glyn, however, remained in Hollywood for more than seven years. Cecil B. DeMille, by then a famous movie director, took the flamboyant divorcée under his wing, and made several popular pictures based on her stories. In fact, the very few Eastern authors who arrived in Hollywood around 1920 who succeeded in the studio did so for one of only two reasons: either, like Glyn, they found a producer or director sympathetic to their work; or, like Rex Beach and Rupert Hughes, they became producers as well as writers. Hence Rinehart attributed Hughes's success to his "sheer ability and patience, and willingness to make himself not only the author, but a technician and even a director."[34] Rinehart, Maugham, and those other authors who could not manage one or the other of these strategies quickly moved on.

Elmer Rice's experience with Sam Goldwyn early in the twenties confirms Rinehart's and Glyn's opinions about the writer's status and role in the studios. Later Rice joined with four other distinguished playwrights—Maxwell Anderson, S. N. Behrman, Sidney Howard, and Robert Sherwood—to form the enormously successful Playwright's Company. At the time of his arrival at the Goldwyn studios, however, Rice was a one-hit playwright with several box-office disappointments in his recent past, and may have doubted his ability ever to repeat his initial success. Born Elmer Riezenstein in Manhattan's Upper West Side in 1892, Rice had studied and then practiced law in New York, all the while harboring the wish to become a playwright. In 1915, Rice's first play, *On Trial,* was purchased and produced by Arthur Hopkins. This courtroom mystery proved a considerable hit. Rice found himself, at age twenty-three, a celebrated and wealthy playwright. In the next five years Rice married and began a family; he informally attended lectures by Dewey, Beard, and Shotwell at Columbia while working on a succession of plays which attracted neither audiences nor much critical favor. Rice had just begun his annual vacation in New Hamphire when Sam Goldwyn called him to New York to discuss a possible screenwriting contract. Goldwyn was frank with Rice about his need to counteract the power of screen stars; he also told the young playwright that he had acquired the screen rights to a number of well-known novels, and wanted "writers skilled in dramatic construction and not conditioned by Hollywood routines" to adapt these books for the screen.[35]

Rice listened with considerable skepticism, but later believed in Goldwyn's sincerity: "He meant what he said; throughout his long, highly successful career he has given greater recognition to the writer's contribution than has any other Hollywood producer."[36] A few weeks after this meeting Rice was offered a five-year contract, beginning at one hundred fifty dollars a week. He accepted at once, and in the summer of 1920 moved to California, rented a house in a modest neighborhood bordering Crenshaw Boulevard, and reported to work at the Goldwyn lot below the Baldwin Hills in Culver City.

Initially Rice found the atmosphere of the studios stimulating. The scenario department held less than a dozen writers, "former newspapermen, or youngsters who had 'grown up' in pictures and had no other writing experience." He liked Jack Hawks, Goldwyn's story editor at the time, "an energetic, unlettered, likeable alcoholic extrovert, well-versed in the routines and clichés of film construction." Rice's first few writing assignments proved not too taxing, and they dovetailed nicely with his particular talent for dramatic construction. Scenario writing was merely "an exercise in dramatic craftsmanship," he decided, "rather than literary art."[37] Although his weekly salary rose by more than a hundred dollars within two months, Rice's enthusiasm for his new venture rapidly faded. "My interest in my new surroundings, acquaintances, and occupation soon diminished," despite the money, Rice later recalled. "Familiarity bred boredom, if not contempt."[38] Although his work apparently pleased Goldwyn, Rice's experience as an Eminent Author abruptly soured:

> The proposed revolution in writing came to nothing. All story material was channelled through Hawks, who vetoed any innovation with the comment that it was "not pictures." Everything went into the old sausage machine and it all came out looking and tasting alike. . . . I had accepted Goldwyn's offer largely on the strength of his promise of creative scope. But he had reckoned without the scenario department's entrenched bureaucracy. The practitioners of the established patterns of picture-making saw in the invasion from the East a threat to their security. . . . In silent-picture days the writer was decidedly subordinate. Goldwyn's Eastern recruits, received with something less than enthusiasm, did not enhance their popularity by frequent affectionate references to the world of the theater. There was general unfriendliness, sometimes amounting to open hostility.[39]

Rice eventually wrangled his release from Goldwyn only after agreeing to invest money in a highly speculative oil deal cooked up by Thompson Buchanan, his immediate superior. The venture produced only dry holes, as feared, but Rice was happily unemployed. Unwilling to commit himself to another long stint under contract, Rice obtained a number of free-lance assignments through the offices of an old friend, Frank Woods, then the story editor at Famous Players-Lasky. But Rice found life at Famous Players no more amenable. "As on the Goldwyn lot," he lamented, "any suggestion that partook of novelty was met with the standard inquiry 'Yes, but will Lizzie like it?'"[40] Although he was now making four hundred dollars a week and further raises were in the offing, Rice quit the movie business. "I had seen enough to convince me that the writer could never have complete freedom of expression in Hollywood."[41] By the winter of 1922, Rice was back in New York at work on another play.

By 1923 Hollywood had dismantled the Eminent Authors project and its variants on the other lots. Most of the established writers who had entered the studios under their aegis had done so with little knowledge of the business or art of movie making. Most naively assumed that they would be welcomed; they also assumed that the same prerogatives existed for scenario writers as did for novelists and playwrights. Judging from their response to screen writing, artistic control was the most important of these rights. After the briefest immersion in studio routines, however, they learned that such was not to be the case. Blocked by the veteran scenario writers in the studios, frustrated in their attempts to see their scripts faithfully rendered on the screen, exploited by the studios for their publicity value yet given no real work, this first wave of Eastern writers—despite their magnificent salaries—left little doubt about their basic unhappiness with the way producers ran studios and made movies. Most echoed Elmer Rice's evaluation of his brief sojoun to Hollywood:

> In a sense those two years were wasted. Creatively I had accomplished nothing. Yet in other ways it had been a valuable experience: a new environment, new acquaintances, new perspectives, ample leisure for reflection and self-examination, which fortified *my belief that nothing is more important than independence of thought and freedom of action.*[42]

The producers, for their part, were scarcely happier with the results of their experiments. Their scenario departments were resentful of the incursion from the East. Although the animosity stirred up during the years of the Eminent Authors diminished in time, it never completely disappeared. Too many established authors, producers complained, wrote scenarios with bees as heroes and then wondered why such scripts could not be produced. A handful of writers did make the adjustment to the ways of the film industry, and publicly the producers refused to deem the experiment a failure, but producers remained wary of hiring famous authors from the East for several years to come. Although writers generally could protest their ignorance of the writer's status and role in Hollywood *before* the Eminent Authors, the experiences of this first contingent of established writers were so well publicized and discussed both in Hollywood and in New York that after 1922 such was not the case. Writers had learned that their mere presence in the film studios was not going to change the basic structure of movie production, nor occasion a flowering of the cinematic art.

The failure of the Eminent Authors project was the least of Hollywood's worries in 1922. As the rest of the economy emerged from the post-war slump, business at the box office wavered. In 1922 movie patronage actually declined for the first time in the industry's history. Further financial woes beset the industry when independent movie-house operators bitterly contested the take-over of major theaters in most American cities by the larger production and distribution companies. In 1921 the independent Motion Picture Theater Owners Association convened in Minneapolis in order to plot tactics to prevent such vertical integration; when the Federal Trade Commission brought suit against Paramount for violation of the anti-trust statutes, movie executives began to panic.

At the same time these financial problems came to a head, a series of scandals rocked the film community. In September 1921 Roscoe "Fatty" Arbuckle, a popular screen comedian, was accused of the murder of a young starlet during a riotous party in San Francisco. Although Arbuckle's guilt was never established, newspapers condemned the excesses, real and supposed, of Arbuckle and his ilk in Hollywood. While Arbuckle's trial was taking place, the director William Desmond Taylor was found murdered in his Los Angeles home. Such sex scandals filled the pages of the country's newspapers and tabloids. Moral leaders in every state cried that vice in Hollywood ran rampant, both on and off the screen. When legislators in thirty-two states considered censorship bills directly aimed at the movies in 1922, industry executives looked desperately for a way to stem the tide of bad publicity, internal strife, and government intervention. On March 14, 1922 the major companies announced the formation of the Motion Picture Producers and Distributors Association, and the hiring of Will Hays as its President. Hays, a Republican politician from Indiana who had served as Warren G. Harding's Postmaster General, was instructed to move on a number of fronts: to improve the public image of the film community; to formulate a system and standards for internal censorship; to arbitrate any labor disputes within the industry; and to prevent federal or state legislation which would regulate the product and practices of the movie companies. In short, Hays later said, he "was to act as a buffer between the industry and the public."[43]

Hays was remarkably successful. He orchestrated a very effective publicity campaign to convince the public of Hollywood's basic rectitude. He helped producers insert morals clauses into the contracts of important stars and craftspeople in order to control their off-screen behavior and protect Hollywood's image. Hays also solved a chronic problem within the industry— the over-supply and exploitation of extras—by creating the Central Casting Bureau to serve as a protective intermediary between the studios and the hordes of hopeful young actors arriving daily at Union Station. Hays also promoted the idea of a screening committee to monitor the content of the films made by

MPPDA members. A code of screen conduct was tentatively approved, but it did not legally bind the member-producers in any way and contained no stringent enforcement procedures. It would be ten years before a strict code of self-censorship was enforced through the Hays Office, but it appeared at least that the industry was moving to assure the "decency" of its product. Hays did not silence criticism of the industry, but he did remove Hollywood's scandals from the front pages, and effectively prevented governmental intrusion into the industry's affairs.

Just when Hollywood's reputation reached its nadir, however, Theodore Dreiser, then one of America's preeminent authors, wrote a curious series of articles about it which reinforced many of the worst fears concerning the film community. Dreiser had moved to Hollywood in 1919 with his mistress, an aspiring actress named Helen Richardson. He planned to observe the film community and possibly sell a few stories to the movies; she hoped for an acting contract with one of the major studios. Dreiser couldn't interest the studios in his work, but he did find Los Angeles a congenial place to write and was content to enjoy the sunshine while Richardson dogged studio-casting directors. Occasionally going to the movies to see what the film community was producing, Dreiser liked what he saw. Indeed, Dreiser told a reporter in 1922 that some film directors were more intelligent and tasteful than the authors whose works they adapted.[44] A year later, however, he told a newspaper interviewer that "whoever imagines that Los Angeles is the Athens of the West must have a good bootlegger. . . . there is no art in Los Angeles and Hollywood and there never will be." The reason for this, Dreiser explained, was that no writer wanted to see his work butchered on the screen. "I myself," he concluded protectively, "would not want my *Jennie Gerhardt* botched up on the screen. I would have my ideas as to how it should be done. But when an author mixes in, he gets laughed at and is only ridiculous."[45]

Dreiser, then, although not himself a principal, apparently knew of the complaints of the Eminent Authors, particularly their frustrating lack of creative control. But Dreiser was only peripherally concerned with the plight of serious writers in Hollywood, perhaps because he had never experienced their difficulties within the studios. When he left Los Angeles in 1922 he had yet to work as a screenwriter. Eight years later he returned to write an adaptation of *An American Tragedy* and then had much more to say, most of it abusive, about the treatment of serious writers and their works by the studios. Dreiser wrote five articles for *Shadowland* and *Redbook* shortly before his departure from the west coast in 1922, but none mentioned screenwriting.[46] Rather, they focused on the ruthlessness, corruption, and sexual exploitation then making Hollywood a national *cause célèbre*. In these articles—incidentally not among his better journalistic efforts—Dreiser described at length the insatiable sexual appetites of the industry's upper echelon and their drug-ridden, off-the-screen orgies; he luridly portrayed the economic and social exploitation of thousands of extras hoping for stardom; and he counted off numerous instances of Hollywood's rampant and craven materialism. Hollywood's depravity merely fueled Dreiser's long-held belief in the world's brutal and impersonal determinism. It is doubtful that many other writers read Dreiser's carping descriptions of Hollywood, or that his opinion was very influential with those who did. *Shadowland* was an obscure monthly entertainment magazine, and only one of the five pieces appeared in the more widely read *Redbook*. Everyone who read a newspaper in America, though, knew of Hollywood's reputation for scandal and corruption. Dreiser's articles would have only confirmed that impression.

Not every writer who ventured to Southern California in the early and mid-twenties, however, corroborated Dreiser's findings about the movie community. For one, Robert Sherwood's impressions of the film industry, published in *Life* at about the same time as Dreiser's, differ greatly. Sherwood had been regularly reviewing movies for *Life,* and had been hearing daily of Hollywood's scandals. He convinced his editor to underwrite a trip to Hollywood "to learn the truth," he wrote at the time, "about this sink of iniquity, this twentieth-century Babylon, this celluloid Sodom."[47] Sherwood was given the grand tour of the studios by Adela Rogers St. John, then a reporter for *Photoplay,* and nightly attended parties at the mansions and hilltop hideaways of Hollywood's *arrivistes.* Sherwood reported that he could not find Dreiser's Gomorrah anywhere. Hollywood was a "normal community inhabited by regular people who go about their business in much the same manner as do people in Emporia, Pawtucket, Little Rock, and Medicine Hat."[48] Hollywood, Sherwood concluded, was simply the dullest place he had ever visited.

In 1927 Carl Van Vechten made a similar trip to Los Angeles for *Vanity Fair,* then at the height of its popularity and influence. Van Vechten was one of the most prominent members of New York's literary society: he was the first dance critic in the American press; Gertrude Stein was his life-long friend (and made him her literary executor); and he was an ardent champion of the Harlem Renaissance and raised a great deal of money for the infant NAACP. Van Vechten wrote a number of fashionable novels in the twenties: *Peter Whiffle* (1922), *The Tattooed Countess* (1924), his best-remembered *Nigger Heaven* (1925), and a Hollywood novel, *Spider Boy* (1927), based on his *Vanity Fair* trip. He was also known in the twenties as much for hosting parties as for writing. Van Vechten abandoned fiction for photography early in the 1930s and became a successful portaitist of writers and theater people.

Because of his reputation as a bon vivant, the editors of *Vanity Fair* commissioned Van Vechten to report on the social life of "America's Famous Film Paradise."[49] Like Sherwood, Van Vechten could find little trace of

Dreiser's Hollywood in the community nestled beneath the Santa Monica Mountains. "The film capital," he concluded, "is not as fantastic as its history."[50] Hollywood parties were on the whole respectable and sedate, largely because most everyone in Hollywood worked long hours—beginning early in the morning—and had little energy for carousing. The women were beautiful and high-spirited, the weather gorgeous, and, Van Vechten found, most of Hollywood's spare energy was spent in sophisticated pursuits and innocent fun rather than debauchery. Van Vechten attended many parties and sampled the fare at Hollywood's better nightclubs and cabarets. He toured the studios with Eileen Pringle, King Vidor, and Jesse Lasky. He heard a few stories in Hollywood of illicit love and delirium tremens, but found scarce evidence to convict the film community of moral turpitude. "In fact," he wrote, "considering the inflated and fantastic atmosphere of the place, I was pleasantly astonished, on the whole, to find so much good common sense, so many really delightful people."[51]

Thus the few reports from authors about the film industry which circulated in Eastern magazines during the mid-twenties suggested that there were far worse places in the world. The climate, the congenial hospitality, and the exotic landscape combined to make most of the visits of Eastern journalists comfortable if slightly dull. Except for Dreiser's censure, these magazine pieces rarely refer to Hollywood's in-fights and scandals. Hays, and the film producers who sponsored him, had succeeded in rehabilitating Hollywood's public reputation. The image which writers and any other readers formed of Hollywood from these popular sources, though, contained little detail of the inner workings of the studios.

During these years, other reports filtered back to writers in the East from the handful of newspapermen, playwrights, and novelists actually working in the studios. By 1925, Hollywood's producers had weathered their Eminent Authors trauma and tentatively resumed their search in New York for experienced writers. By far the most important writer to go to the studios between 1925 and the end of 1927 was Herman J. Mankiewicz. First hired in early 1925, for the next five years Mankiewicz would provide a crucial liaison between Hollywood and the New York writing community.

Mankiewicz was born in New York in 1897, the son of a reporter and editorial writer for a German language newspaper in Manhattan. In 1904 Franz Mankiewicz moved his family to Wilkes-Barre after accepting a teaching post at the Harry Hillman Academy, an aristocratic prep school. The elder Mankiewicz would later became an eminent education professor at the City College of New York, but in Wilkes-Barre he was an intensely frustrated man, a scholar resentfully teaching richer men's doltish sons. Herman was also enrolled in the Hillman Academy, where his father supervised his studies with Prussian severity. Mankiewicz passed Columbia University's entrance examination when he was thirteen, but waited to matriculate for two years until he met the school's minimum age requirement. He majored in philosophy at Columbia, studied desultorily, cultivated the pose of the playwright and litterateur, and eventually received his undergraduate degree in 1916. Under pressure from his father he enrolled in the Graduate School, but dropped out after a semester when offered a job as a cub reporter on the *New York Tribune.* [52]

During the war Mankiewicz enlisted in the Air Corps, and after failing his flying test, joined the Marines early in 1918. He shipped out to France four months later, remained overseas until after the Armistice, and was demobilized with tens of thousands of other recruits in June 1919. Mankiewicz then returned to New York and the *Tribune,* living in a cheap boarding house on East 116th Street. In December of the same year he accepted a job in the Red Cross Office in Paris. He worked in France for six months, then returned to America to be married; he sailed again for Europe in the summer of 1920. Mankiewicz's destination this time was Berlin, where he spent the better part of 1920 looking for a newspaper job. His first break came when *Women's Wear Daily* hired him as a fifteen-dollar-a-week stringer. Early in 1921 he also began sending the *New York Times* occasional news items about the Berlin theater. By 1922, Mankiewicz was eager to return to America, and agreed to act as Isadora Duncan's publicist on an upcoming American tour. Mankiewicz and Duncan came to blows even before they boarded ship, he was summarily fired, and friends then lent the now-desperate young writer enough to pay for his passage home. [53]

Once back in New York, Mankiewicz was hired as a general reporter for Herbert Bayard Swope's *New York World.* When the *New York Times* expanded its Sunday theater coverage, George S. Kaufman—then the paper's entertainment editor—hired the young reporter as his assistant. Mankiewicz became the *Times'* third-string reviewer and wrote occasional features and odd notes for the Sunday editon. He remained in New York until Hollywood called early in 1925, working at the *Times,* unsuccessfully trying his hand at theatrical production, and hoping to write plays himself.

By the mid-twenties, then, Mankiewicz had become a bona-fide member of New York's community of writers, playwrights and journalists. George S. Kaufman and Marc Connelly—two of Broadway's hottest playwrights—were writing plays with him. He dined with the regulars at the Algonquin Hotel, and his name often appeared in the columns of Franklin P. Adams and Heywood Broun. In 1925 Harold Ross asked him to join the original staff of *The New Yorker,* for which Mankiewicz then wrote theater reviews and occasional pieces. [54] He had formed friendships with Dorothy Parker, Robert Benchley, Scott Fitzgerald, Ben Hecht, Charles MacArthur, Robert Sherwood, Ring Lardner, and countless other writers active in New York at the time.

Portrait of Herman J. Mankiewicz, ca. 1930
(Courtesy of the Academy of Motion Picture Arts and Sciences)

Then MGM offered to bring Mankiewicz to Hollywood to complete a story on World War I which he had begun in New York. They offered him a salary of five hundred dollars a week, more than four times what Mankiewicz was making through his *Times* and other writing assignments. With two children, a wife, and any number of gambling debts to consider, he agreed at once. "We nearly lost our minds with joy," Mankiewicz's wife later recalled.[55] Their first sojourn west was to end disappointingly when MGM rejected Mankiewicz's Marine story and could not find him another project. He did, however, earn his first screen credit for a story written with Tod Browning, *The Road to Mandalay,* starring Lon Chaney. The studio billed it as a "Thrilling, Throbbing Romance of Singapore."

Mankiewicz had no sooner returned to New York and the *Times* when Walter Wanger, a film producer and friend, arranged a one-year contract for him with Paramount. Made wary by his previous disappointment, Mankiewicz accepted this offer only after the *Times* assured him he could have his job back if his Hollywood career collapsed. In July 1925, then, Mankiewicz returned to California. He rented a large house in the Hollywood Hills, bought a second-hand Cadillac convertible from Ernst Lubitsch, ordered an expensive new wardrobe of sports clothes, and joined the La Cresta Country Club. His wife remembers him gleefully singing, "We're in the money; We're in the money," as they moved into their villa directly below the HOLLYWOODLAND sign.[56] And Mankiewicz now could almost afford such extravagance: his contract called for four hundred dollars a week *and* Paramount had agreed to purchase four Mankiewicz originals in the next year for five thousand dollars each.

Mankiewicz was treated royally by the front office upon his arrival in Hollywood. B. P. Schulberg, then Chief of Production at Paramount, took the writer under his wing. Richard Meryman, Mankiewicz's recent biographer, writes of their friendship:

> Herman had a son-and-father relationship with Ben Schulberg, another literate, rebellious ex-newspaperman. At night they played pinochle together in Schulberg's den, thick cigar smoke, drinks, outrageous sarcastic anecdotes, guffaws of laughter, and, at dawn, Herman invariably writing a check.[57]

While most writers toiled in small cubicles in the barn-like Writers' Building, Schulberg gave Mankiewicz a lavish office close to his own in the Administration Building. Schulberg's investment in Mankiewicz quickly paid off. An adept title writer, Mankiewicz's original scenarios also proved to be perfect movie material: brisk, action-oriented, and cheap to film.

When the talkies arrived late in 1927, Mankiewicz was one of the few members of Paramount's scenario department with experience in writing dialog. Moreover, for some time Mankiewicz had been promoting the virtues of Hollywood life to his writing friends in the East. For these reasons Schulberg decided to make Mankiewicz the head of Paramount's crash program to create a staff of competent dialog writers. "The Herman J. Mankiewicz Fresh Air Fund," as Paramount's informal recruitment effort came to be known, attracted more than a dozen writers to the studio. Most often Mankiewicz approached newspapermen much in his own image: Lawrence Stallings, Charles MacArthur, Ben Hecht, Gene Fowler, and Nunnally Johnson all came to Hollywood, for instance, on Mankiewicz's invitation. As early as December 1926, Mankiewicz had urged Schulberg to hire Ben Hecht, for one, who was then writing plays in New York. If Hecht didn't write an acceptable script, Mankiewicz promised, then Schulberg could fire them both. The producer agreed and Mankiewicz wired Hecht:

> WILL YOU ACCEPT THREE HUNDRED PER WEEK TO WORK FOR PARAMOUNT PICTURES? STOP ALL EXPENSES PAID STOP THE THREE HUNDRED IS PEANUTS STOP MILLIONS ARE TO BE GRABBED OUT HERE AND YOUR ONLY COMPETITON IS IDIOTS STOP DON'T LET THIS GET AROUND.[58]

By the time the Fresh Air Fund was conceived a year later, though, word *had* gotten around. "Mank told us all," Gene Fowler said, "that it was a gold mine and nobody there was staking a claim."[59] Mankiewicz seemed delighted in Hollywood, his recruits thought, and they willingly took the plunge themselves. If Mankiewicz was pleased with his progress in Hollywood in the late twenties, he still did not consider it a permanent arrangement: "Things are going quite nicely for me," Mankiewicz wrote to George Kaufman in 1928, "and I think I will probably be here for another year or more."[60] He died twenty-five years later, having never left Hollywood.

After the Fresh Air Fund effort, Mankiewicz's work for Schulberg continued to go well. By 1931 he was one of the five or six highest paid writers in the film industry. Schulberg even promoted him to associate producer for Paramount's two early Marx Brothers' classics, *Monkey Business* (1931) and *Horsefeathers* (1932). Years later, Nunnally Johnson theorized of Mankiewicz's early success:

> Mank was a man who liked to manipulate people and the job. And when he came out here, I think Mank figured "These are my kind of people and I can handle them." He was so damned smart he charmed everybody from stuffed shirts like Walter Wanger all the way down to almost idiots and hustlers. Bringing Mank to Hollywood then was like throwing a rabbit into a briar patch.[61]

When Zukor fired Schulberg in 1933, Mankiewicz left Paramount, signed a lucrative contract with MGM, and continued to write successful scripts. In the late thirties, though, as his drinking and erratic behavior increased, his screenwriting star began to wane. It was then that Orson Welles hired him to write the screenplay for *Citizen Kane* (1941), which earned Mankiewicz an Academy Award. His reputation revived, Mankiewicz could pick from among a number of choice projects in the next few years. His drinking and bitterness towards the industry intensified when Hearst's papers smeared him with a hit-and-run driving charge in retribution for the Kane portrayal, and many doors previously open were now shut in his face. For most of his life Mankiewicz had tried to write a hit play, but he died of liver disease in 1953 without the Broadway success he so wanted, and with little remaining stature in the film industry.

Those who argue on both sides of the Hollywood-as-destroyer controversy often cite Mankiewicz's checkered career. Mankiewicz was a better screenwriter than playwright or journalist, most film historians and critics contend, whatever his aspirations as a serious writer. In *Citizen Kane* he wrote perhaps the greatest movie ever made in America, while his efforts for the stage are best left forgotten. Pauline Kael, who did much to document the importance of Mankiewicz's contribution to *Kane*, asserts that he was drinking heavily in New York in the twenties and, given the abject failure of his first plays, faced an uncertain future as a playwright in the East. In Hollywood, Kael maintains, Mankiewicz's talents dovetailed nicely with the requirements of the movies. Mankiewicz and his Fresh Air recruits may have felt that their serious writing aspirations evaporated in the dry Hollywood air, Kael suggests, but their contribution to Hollywood, and the huge salaries they raked in, more than compensated them. For all the charges of writers "ruined" by Hollywood, Kael believes that the Fresh Air writers and Mankiewicz himself

> as a group were responsible for that sustained feat of careless magic we call "thirties comedy."... The recurrence of the names of that group of writers, not just on rather obscurely remembered films but on almost *all* the films that are generally cited as proof of the vision and style of the most highly acclaimed directors of that period, suggests that the writers—and a particular group of them at that—may for a brief period, a little more then a decade, have given American talkies their character.[62]

This has been the basis of the standard cineaste interpretation of Mankiewicz's career for twenty-five years. Many of Mankiewicz's friends, however, were of a different mind. If he was drinking in New York, they charged, he was drinking even more desperately in Hollywood. His was a first-rate mind, they remembered, learned and witty, but in all the years in Hollywood he worked on only one project worthy of his talent. For this he had abandoned a promising career as a playwright, regardless of the commercial failure of his first two plays and his already established reputation as a journalist. Mankiewicz's acquaintances did not totally absolve him of responsiblity for his own plight. Scott Fitzgerald, for one, who had been a friend of Mankiewicz's for a time in New York, talked to Budd Schulberg about Mankiewicz's problems with the studios in the late thirties:

> Scott said he knew Mank (as Herman was always called) very well and considered him a kind of spoiled priest who might have been a genius if he had not become so preoccupied with the private life of Hollywood—some of his best work seemed to go into malicious jokes at the expense of his producers and fellow writers during long liquid lunches at Romanoff's.[63]

Nunnally Johnson, a Fresh Air recruit who eventually became one of Hollywood's most successful producers, considered Mankiewicz's irresponsibility the prime cause of his downfall in Hollywood:

> Mank was a good film writer, but let's say he wasn't dedicated to his art. His whole idea was to see how long he could make a job last. He had very little pride, even ordinary pride. I hired him on pictures a couple of times, but he just wasn't dependable. He was just unreliable. Nothing came of it.[64]

W. R. Burnett, who met Mankiewicz in Hollywood in the thirties, remembers him as a "wild one." "He was a good writer," Burnett continued, "but for all his jokes and pranks and good humor there was something wrong with him in Hollywood, and I never thought he was happy here. All his old friends in New York were big-hit playwrights and he wasn't and it bothered him."[65] Finally, Ben Hecht, one of his closest friends, best articulated these writers' analysis of Hollywood's effect on Mankiewicz:

> Mank died in his fifties, still writing movie scenarios. That he lasted as long as he did surprised me. To own a mind like Manky's and hamstring and throttle it for twenty-five years in the writing only of movie scenarios is to submit your soul to a nasty strain. Manky wrote good movies. One of them, *Citizen Kane*, won him an Oscar. But all of them together won him an early grave.[66]

Mankiewicz's major troubles were in the future, however, on the eve of the introduction of sound. In 1926 and 1927 he was happily a part of the small clique of ex-newspapermen and ex-New Yorkers under contract to the Hollywood studios, which included Lawrence Stallings, Hecht, Robert Benchley (who was hired by MGM in 1925 as an actor), and Edward Justice Mayer. They were joined periodically by literary friends from the East: Fitzgerald wintered in Southern California in 1927; Sherwood spent six weeks in Hollywood in 1926; and Kaufman, Connelly, Van Vechten, and MacArthur all made brief visits either to work or simply to vacation.

This coterie of Eastern writers in Hollywood during the mid-twenties found their life at heart carefree and pleasant. Unlike the Eminent Authors, they had been hired with little fanfare, and had been integrated into the established scenario departments. Hollywood, if lacking the excitement and stimulation of the Great White Way, had its other attractions. The climate was wonderful; the social life gay; the company was attractive and often familiar; and the salaries so enormous that many writers were simply incredulous. "Hollywood money," Charles MacArthur decided, "is something you throw off the ends of trains."[67]

These recruits had fewer illusions about the nature of their work and the studio's expectations than had the Eminent Authors. "I discovered early in my movie work," Ben Hecht later recalled, "that a movie is never any better than the stupidest man connected with it. In the Owner's mind, art was a synonym for bankruptcy."[68] From Hollywood, Lawrence Stallings urged Charles MacArthur, "You should sign the [MGM] contract; the Studio Bosses still hold writers in great contempt, but you'll make a FORTUNE and the work is NOTHING!"[69] Hecht best summed up the attitude of this small coterie of Hollywood recruits when he recalled that he initially "looked upon movie writing as an amiable chore. It was a source of easy money and pleasant friendships. There was small responsiblity."[70]

Yet only a small handful of writers enjoyed the comforts Hecht experienced in Hollywood before the introduction of sound. The Fresh Air Fund, for instance, began only after the studios committed themselves to sound production. Of the forty writers whose careers I examined, only Hecht, Fitzgerald, Nunnally Johnson, and Marc Connelly actually worked as scenario writers in Hollywood during the latter days of the silent era; thus only four of the forty had any first-hand knowledge of the inside of the Hollywood studio. Moreover, the experience of these four men was slight—only Ben Hecht worked as a screenwriter for longer than two months before the introduction of sound. Because of the abject failure of the Eminent Authors program, and because silent films required less actual writing manpower, there simply was not a great demand in Hollywood for novelists and playwrights.

There were, however, other less direct contacts between writers and the Hollywood studios. A handful of writers wrote original stories or screenplays for the major production companies while remaining in New York. Marc Connelly, George S. Kaufman, and Robert E. Sherwood, for instance, worked briefly on scripts while pursuing other projects in the East. These assignments were short-lived, however, and rarely required the authors' presence in the studios. In addition, Paramount operated a moderate-sized production studio in the Astoria section of Queens, and occasionally hired writers from Manhattan to work on movies to be filmed there. Such assignments, judging from the experience of the study group, were rare: only Donald Ogden Stewart and George Abbott actually worked in the Astoria studio before the thirties. In the thirties, Astoria would serve as home for a experimental production unit, headed by Ben Hecht and Charles MacArthur, which attempted to convince the front-office that writers could effectively supervise their own work. Thus only ten of the forty writers I studied had any direct contact with the movie industry in or out of Hollywood before the introduction of sound. And for most of them, this contact was short-lived.

A somewhat larger number of authors did sell the screenrights to their novels or plays to the studios, but this only rarely involved the writer directly with the movie-making process. Publishers, theatrical producers, and agents negotiated the sales of these rights. While large sums were paid for the most popular works, the vast majority of sales were for much smaller amounts. By 1925, motion picture rights averaged about five thousand dollars, still a considerable sum for most authors, and as we have seen, usually more than authors received in royalties. The issue of the sale of screen rights, however, was distinct from that of employment in the film industry. It has also been the subject of its own controversies. One catalyst in the formation of the Dramatists Guild, for example, was the threat posed to playwrights by the influx of Hollywood money into theatrical production in the mid-twenties. When Adolph Zukor and other film producers began to underwrite Broadway plays, authors charged it a conflict of interest, for it was the writer who suffered most, in the form of smaller rights sales, from this practice. The Minimum Basic Agreement reached between producers and playwrights in 1926 ameliorated many of the writers' strongest objections. Nevertheless, a good deal of ill-will was fostered between playwrights and Hollywood during this brief episode, which did nothing to enhance the image of the film industry in the eyes of New York's writers.

Both playwrights and novelists were extremely critical of the film treatment their material received once it was purchased by the studio. Writers persistently complained that film adaptations were at best bowdlerized versions of the original and at worst criminal misrepresentations. An article in *The American Mercury* in 1928, one of the magazines most popular with the writing community, conveyed the essence of writers' objections to the process by which Hollywood obtained and adapted story material. Leda Bauer, a veteran journalist and member in good standing of the New York writing community, pointedly observed that if each studio's story editor had only to deal with producers, selecting story material might be a much simpler task. There existed any number of possible stories which "fitted into a season's schedule, a star's individuality, and a producer's uncomplicated notions, with a bow to the censors." But producers, "these captains of art," as Bauer ironically dubbed them, trust neither their own nor anyone else's story sense. Prospective story ideas have to "run the gauntlet" of story conferees: the director, "who almost invariably has an idea of his own he would like to sell"; the production manager, who refuses to allow "anything to go through that he did not personally engineer"; and a horde of other gentlemen on the payroll of the company—relatives of the producer, relatives and admirers of his wife, men who have been given jobs for business, social or political reasons—all of whom, being obviously unfit for anything really important, are allowed their say in the matter of story-buying.[71]

Eventually the studio purchases a story which "by a miracle, satisfies all the cooks." Still, at least five hazards still threaten the original story idea:

First, it is completely rewritten. This is called translating it to the screen, "because word and picture symbols are so different." When there is no longer any connection with the story on which the screen play was based, it is pronounced perfect, the title is changed to something short, spicy, and completely inapplicable, and the original story is resold to another picture company to go through the same process.[72]

In 1931 Theodore Dreiser became so incensed over this very issue that he took Paramount Picture Corporation to court. Paramount's proposed script for *An American Tragedy* thoroughly emasculated his original story, Dreiser charged, and the studio had not purchased the right to alter its basic plot and meaning. He brought suit against the studio, Dreiser explained, in the name of the "thousands of authors who haven't had a square deal in having their works belittled for screen exploitation."[73] Dreiser eventually lost his suit; the court ruled that Paramount's contract with Dreiser expressly stated that the studio had the right to change Dreiser's story as it wished. Although Dreiser's challenge to the studios did rally authors briefly to demand more say in the adaptation of their material, the weight of the law rested squarely with the studios. Most sales of screen rights to this day do not provide the author any control over the filmed version of his work. Even before Dreiser's suit, though, the sale of screen rights held this double meaning for writers: the lure of lucrative, and often essential income; and also the loss of control over the use of their work and name. Regarded by many writers as a necessary evil, sales of screen rights of their works and the subsequent film versions often times left a bad taste in authors' mouths when Hollywood was mentioned.

Combined with the industry's abiding reputation for corruption, decadence, and scandal, and the public outrage periodically stirred up by censorship advocates and the tabloid press, both the direct and the indirect contacts of a select few Eastern writers with the movie industry had left the Eastern writing community, poised on the brink of the sound era, with some basic trepidations about screen writing. The Eminent Authors experiment and the controversies over screen rights and adaptation created animosity between writers and Hollywood. The Eminent Authors charged that they were merely used for publicity and were given no real function within the studios. They also charged that the professional screenwriters in the industry were undermining them at every turn. Such charges lingered in the pre-sound era.

Yet many reports back from Hollywood, by writers and non-writers alike, suggested that Hollywood was a pleasant place to work. Enormous amounts of money were to be made there. By 1927 there was, on a certain level, an easy familiarity between Hollywood and the Eastern literary community. Broadway actors, designers, directors, and writers had been lured to Hollywood in sufficient numbers to effect social cross-breeding of a sort. For those writers (and they were a small minority of the total writing community) who enjoyed New York's Cafe society, there were frequent contacts, and presumed discourse, with Hollywood's new elite. "It was Cafe society," Leo Rosten perceived, "that bridged the gap between Hollywood and Park Avenue. In the night clubs and restaurants of New York, the scions of the East met the gay, bright people of Broadway and Hollywood."[74] Mary Pickford, Douglas Fairbanks, the Barrymores, Helen Hayes, and countless others shuttled across the continent with increasing frequency. A formal picture taken at Robert E. Sherwood's wedding to Mary Brandon vividly illustrates Rosten's point: among those posing stiffly in formal attire are Sherwood, Robert Benchley, Sidney Howard, Alexander Woollcott, Frank Case, John Emerson (a film director married to Anita Loos), Douglas Fairbanks, Grant Mitchell, and Marc Connelly.[75] Under such circumstances, the thought of Hollywood could not have generated too much hostility among writers.

On the whole, however, most writers in the East remained surprisingly ignorant of the goings-on within the Hollywood studios. Harold Clurman, a theatrical director and one of the founders of the Group Theater in New York wrote of the Group's attitude toward Hollywood:

> In the Group in those days Hollywood was the symbol in the show world of money-making unrelated to any other ideal. It was so remote to us then that we hardly took pains to scorn it. We saw movies occasionally, and liked them perhaps, but we rarely thought of how or where they were made or that we or any of our kind might be connected with their making.[76]

Not only Clurman, but also Clifford Odets, Lee J. Cobb, Franchot Tone, and later Irwin Shaw, William Saroyan, and Elia Kazan of the Group's company would find themselves in Hollywood. But in 1927 they had little need of Hollywood while conditions on Broadway remained so prosperous. And Hollywood had little call for famous Eastern writers so long as studio scenario departments were capable of handling the requirements of the silent screen. The Great Depression, following on the heels of the coming of sound, changed all of that.

3

The Coming of Sound and
the Studio System

The idea of the talking motion picture had intrigued imaginative movie executives and independent inventors since the turn of the century. But while business boomed and profits in the industry remained high, there was little incentive for the major movie companies to undertake the enormous, and enormously risky, capital investment needed to harness sound reproduction to the motion picture. By 1925 most of the majors had considered, and rejected, at least one talking picture scheme, usually because the development costs seemed prohibitive and the sound quality irritating and scratchy. It fell to Warner Brothers, then a small and financially troubled company, to take the major gamble on sound.

The first public preview of Warner's Vitaphone system occurred on August 5, 1926 in their flagship theater in New York. Well attended by the industry's leading executives and financiers, and well covered by the national press, Warner's presentation that night succeeded far beyond it expectations. The program featured a filmed greeting from Will Hays, performances by leading stage and operatic stars, and the premier of Warner's latest John Barrymore movie, *Don Juan,* complete with full-length musical score. The next morning an editorial writer for *Film Daily* captured the enthusiasm generated by the Vitaphone preview: "It seems beyond human conception that the smallest theater in the smallest hamlet of this country can exhibit *Don Juan* with an orchestral accompaniment of 107 men of the New York Philharmonic Orchestra," he rhapsodized. "Can there be any doubt that a momentous event has come to pass in the industry?"[1]

Nonetheless it took the box-office success of Warner Brothers' first feature talking movie, *The Jazz Singer,* released more than a year after the Vitaphone premier, to convince many conservative industry executives of the inevitability of talking pictures. Once convinced that sound was indeed the wave of the future, the major studios rushed pell-mell to convert to sound production. MGM's first sound drama was produced early in 1929, for instance; its last silent movie was made in September of the same year. By the end of 1929, the talkies had taken over. "At Last!," a Warner Brothers advertisement trumpeted, "Pictures that Talk like Living People!"[2]

In Hollywood, construction crews worked double shifts building sound-proofed stages while the front office searched for anyone remotely resembling an audio engineer. The industry's creative personnel also struggled to adapt to the medium's many new demands. High-pitched voices or, more frequently, thick accents doomed some actors to a quick exit from the sound stage. Directors groaned at the restrictions audio recording placed on camera movements and on-screen action: cameras had to be enclosed in huge, sound-proofed closets, and the dull, bulky microphones severely restricted stage movement and blocking. Scenario departments, staffed with experts in plot construction, many of whom had tin ears for dialog, panicked at the thought of full-length talking pictures. And after initially relying on music and sound effects, the movies were soon filled with dialog—often of the most stilted and artificial variety. "The consensus," Lewis Jacobs concluded, "was that the moving picture had, with the addition of sound, forgotten everything it had recently learned" during the golden age of the silent film.[3]

In New York, many writers familiar with the movie industry pondered what sound would do to the screenwriter's status. Robert E. Sherwood, for one, writing in the *American Mercury,* optimistically predicted that the introduction of sound would bring about a virtual renaissance in Hollywood. Sherwood conceded that the first few talkies to reach the public had been embarrassingly primitive, but he argued that once the technicians mastered sound reproduction many of the worst habits and practices of the silent film industry would disappear. With the advent of talkies, for instance, screen actors would have to be skilled and intelligent enough to learn lines and deliver them articulately. Also, the flock of silent movie directors whose only contribution to their pictures had been to bellow through a megaphone for the ingenue to show more thigh would no longer be of use to the studios. "It should be apparent that this type of director is soon to pass on to other fields," Sherwood predicted. "With him will go his by-products, the scenario and subtitle writers, or yes-men." Like many of the other Eastern writers who knew something about the inside of a movie studio, Sherwood did little to hide his contempt for the professional screenwriter of the silent era:

> Of all the classes of laborers in the Southern California vineyards, those [scenario writers] have been the lowliest and most ignoble. While the movies have developed several great directors, many fine actors, and two or three first-rate financiers. . . . they have, in their thirty-years existence, developed only one writer who is worthy of mention; that lone exception is the gifted Miss Anita Loos, and she quit this chambermaid's employment as soon as she could afford to do so.[4]

However the author, Sherwood reasoned, would inevitably enjoy the same status in Hollywood that he did in New York:

> The writer [in Hollywood] will now be boosted into a position of importance that is equal, at least, to that of the director. He will assume the same privilege of responsibility that is enjoyed or regretted as the case may be by the playwright. He will have a great deal to say about the preparation and production of a picture, and his remarks will not all be variations of the affirmative yes.[5]

Sherwood sounded a final cheerful note in predicting that production executives in Hollywood, whom he claimed had only impeded the progress of film art, would be gradually eased from power. The giant corporations headquartered in New York would now run the show, and presumably, keep out of their artists' way.

Although correct in predicting that writers would soon flock to the studios from New York, Sherwood was no clairvoyant and most of his more hopeful predictions never came to pass. Moreover, those authors who had arrived in Hollywood during its frantic conversion to sound production rarely shared Sherwood's optimism about the screenwriter's future status. S. N. Behrman, one of the first playwrights wooed from Broadway, was far less excited by the prospect of the talking picture. After one hit play followed closely by two commercial failures, in 1927 Behrman—like Elmer Rice seven years earlier—questioned his ability to live by playwrighting alone. Behrman had just begun entertaining the notion of working in Hollywood when the Fox studio offered him a $1250-a-week contract. Behrman consulted Arhur Richman, a writer-friend who had already been to the studios, who advised him to hold out for more money. "Producers are happier paying more money." Richman told Behrman. "They feel that a $1250 a week writer can't really be very good."[6] One measure of Hollywood's need for writers at the time is that Fox agreed to raise Behrman's salary, and the young playwright arrived in Hollywood just as the transition to sound was taking place:

> From the moment *The Second Man* was produced I began getting urgent offers to come to Hollywood. The Industry, as it was called, had been through the chrysalis of revolutionary change—from silence to sound. There were great billboards all over Hollywood blazoning an eccentricity of Greta Garbo's: "GARBO TALKS!" It was as if an animal trainer had taught a poodle to converse. One wondered how Miss Garbo had managed before she discovered in herself this special skill. How had she done the marketing or given orders to her servants?
>
> On the bosses, like Winfield Sheehan, the revolution had the traditional effect: it panicked them. The Los Angeles suburb, hitherto wrapped in silence, was forced to join the articulate world. The actors were panicked too. They had, up to then, put all their confidence in "titles," flashed on the screen, to tell their audiences what they were feeling. Now they would utter these titles themselves, and many of them felt only too often justifiably insecure about their

ability to project them. For a long time after I began to work in the Hollywood studios, I found that directors and producers, rocking in the warm cradle of atavism, kept referring to whatever dialogue I wrote as "titles."[7]

The compression of time has made the premier of *The Jazz Singer*, the Wall Street Crash, and the departure of writers *en masse* for Southern California seem almost simultaneous events. Yet while Hollywood geared up for full-scale sound production and writers like Sherwood pondered the talkies' significance for their profession, very few writers actually joined Behrman in the studios before 1930. Producers and writers, not surprisingly given their past history, did not, rush into each other's arms.

Producers, for their part, initially hoped that their veteran screenwriters would prove as competent at dialog as they had at continuity or construction. Resentment between Eastern writers and Hollywood producers still lingered from the disasters of the early twenties, and were only exacerbated by the continual wrangling over the sales of screen rights. It was only after veteran scenarists proved unequal to the task of creating interesting and believable dialog that the "Fresh Air Fund" and other wholesale recruitment campaigns began in earnest. When film producers reluctantly reapproached popular writers in the late twenties, it was often only to offer work in *New York* as "dialoguers"—Hollywood's term for those writers, usually playwrights, hired to fabricate dialog for scenarios whose continuity was written by professional screenwriters. Preston Sturges, for one, worked at Paramount's Astoria studio as a dialoguer on two films, *The Big Pond* and *Fast and Loose*, before he was offered a Hollywood contract.[8] George S. Kaufman, Moss Hart, Marc Connelly, Donald Ogden Stewart, and George Abbott began their screenwriting careers in much the same way. Donald Ogden Stewart remembers: "Walter Wanger of Paramount, which then [in 1929] had studios out on Long Island, asked me to do a picture and I went out there and worked with Harry D'Arrast on *Laughter*."[9] It was only after that film proved popular that Stewart went to Hollywood. "To break me in," Abbott recalls of a similar arrangement with Paramount, "they asked me to do a short subject in their Eastern studio. It was called *The Bishop's Candlestick*, starring Walter Huston, and since they liked it I was soon off to the coast to try my hand at a larger picture."[10]

In 1928 and 1929, many of New York's writers were no more anxious to rush to Hollywood than Hollywood was eager to have them. Prosperity remained the watchword of the literary marketplace in the late twenties. The Crash in October of 1929 had little immediate impact on the publishing world, but in 1931, with all sectors of the economy sputtering if not collapsing, Hollywood's attraction for writers was strong enough for Orion Cheney to describe a new occupational disease, "novelist's nystagmus," caused by "keeping one eye on the typewriter and the other on Hollywood."[11] The Depression hit the publishing world head on in 1933: the number of new titles issued plunged lower than in nearly a decade, booksellers across the country went out of business, and the number of publishing firms filing for bankruptcy mushroomed. For example, Harper Brothers' sales dropped 60 percent, the staff twice agreed to 10 percent pay cuts, and the firm declared no dividends for the year. Scribner's suffered similarly: in 1929 the firm's net profits had been an unprecedented $289,309; in 1932 Scribner's profit had been reduced to $40,661.[12] Even established houses hung on by the skin of their teeth.

Magazine publishers were similarly affected. In 1932 *The Saturday Evening Post,* America's most popular and profitable magazine, reduced each issue from 210 to 102 pages. The *Post* cut in half the number of stories published each week. The prices writers received for stories also plummeted: editors who had once paid $1,000 or more for each story now offered less than $400.[13] The Depression affected the theater even more immediately and profoundly. Although Burns Mantle, reflecting on the 1930 theater season, reassured himself that "the sun shines, the government at Washington still lives, and the living theater has not been crushed, either by economic depression or the threat of cheap entertainment," financial realities belied his optimism.[14] Fifty fewer plays opened on Broadway in 1930 than the year before, and by the start of the 1932 season, only half of the legitimate theaters in New York were open. Half of Broadway's actors were unemployed. Even with ticket prices slashed to one dollar, producers struggled to fill their houses. "The percentage of failures was much higher than usual," the normally blithe-spirited Mantle lamented in that year's annual survey, "as it properly should have been. There were more bad plays than usual. Short bankrolls, inexperienced producers, playwrights sold down the river to Hollywood—a lot of things contributed to these results."[15]

Despite the misery all around them, theater loyalists cited Hollywood as the main culprit in Broadway's decline. Patrons with ever-shrinking entertainment budgets preferred the cheaper talking picture shows to the legitimate stage. According to Mantle, Hollywood's recruitment campaigns, duly noted and bemoaned by all in the theater world, were beginning to have their effect on the quality of Broadway's offerings. By 1933 the number of openings shrank further to 130—exactly half that of the 1926 season—demoralizing producers and playwrights, alike. Of this period in New York Harold Clurman observed:

> About this time I began to notice with sharp clarity the transformation that had come over New York during the past two years. It seemed as if the very color of the city had changed. From an elegant bright grey by day and a sparkling gold by night, the afternoons had grown haggard, the nights mournful. The neon glow that had come to replace the brilliance of the twenties was like a whistling in the dark. The town was visibly down at the heels; it seemed to shuffle feebly as if on chilblained feet.[16]

By 1933, then, the bull market for the writer's work had ended. Hollywood appeared more and more inviting in comparison. The careers of the forty writers I examined in detail confirm that Hollywood did not enthusiastically import Eastern writers—and that writers were not particularly interested in Hollywood employment—until *after* the literary marketplace began to fail. Four writers—Fitzgerald, Nunnally Johnson, Ben Hecht, and Marc Connelly—worked in Hollywood during the silent era. Four more arrived in 1928—George Abbott, Zoe Akins, Sidney Howard, and S.N. Behrman. Another four arrived the next year—Maxwell Anderson, Stephen Vincent Benét, Dudley Nichols, and Samson Raphaelson. In all, only twelve of the forty writers, or 30 percent, worked in Hollywood before 1930. During the first three years of the thirties, as the lights darkened in New York, nineteen of the forty, or nearly half, made the trip to Hollywood. [17]

Chapter 4 explores the experiences of writers in the studios in detail, but a few examples will indicate the range of circumstances which could bring writers to Hollywood. Stephen Vincent Benét, for one, arrived in Hollywood in late 1929. Benét had graduated from Yale ten years earlier, and had spent most of the twenties writing short stories and novels of no great distinction, and without much popular success. A Guggenheim Fellowship in 1926 allowed him to spend a year in Paris, however, where he began a long narrative poem about the Civil War, *John Brown's Body.* Published in 1928, it spent months on the best-seller list and won him a Pulitzer Prize the next year. Benét confidently assumed that the proceeds from *John Brown's Body* would subsidize at least a few years' uninterrupted writing, and he spent the autumn of 1929 writing occasional magazine pieces while planning another long poem. [18] The collapse of the stock market in October, however, wiped out the bulk of his capital. A month after the crash Benét received the following telegram, offering an immediate solution to his plight:

DEAR MR. BENET: ARTHUR HOPKINS SUGGESTED THAT WE COMMUNI-CATE WITH YOU REGARDING THE POSSIBILITY OF GETTING YOU TO PREPARE THE SCREEN ADAPTATION AND DIALOGUE FOR TALKING MOTION PICTURE BASED ON THE LIFE OF ABRAHAM LINCOLN TO BE PRODUCED AND DIRECTED BY D.W. GRIFFITH FOR UNITED ARTISTS CORPORATION STOP MR. GRIFFITH HAS SPENT SEVERAL MONTHS IN GATHERING HIS MATERIAL AND IS NOW READY TO BEGIN ACTIVE WORK ON THE FINAL SCREEN STORY STOP WE WOULD LIKE TO KNOW IF THIS MATTER INTERESTS YOU AND WHETHER OR NOT YOU COULD COME TO LOS ANGELES TO WORK WITH MR. GRIFFITH STOP YOUR PROMPT REPLY BY COLLECT TELEGRAPH WILL BE GENUINELY APPRECIATED.
JOHN W. CONSIDINE JR.
GENERAL MANAGER [19]

Fresh from the success of *John Brown's Body*, and aware that his critical and popular visibility gave him some bargaining leverage, Benét replied to Considine, indicating his interest in the project and also proposing terms:

INTERESTED IN YOUR SUGGESTION ALTHOUGH HAVE STARTED PIECE OF ORIGINAL WORK STOP COULD COME TO HOLLYWOOD FOR A PERIOD NOT LONGER THAN TEN WEEKS PREFERABLY BEGINNING EARLY JANUARY BUT WOULD START IMMEDIATELY IF NECESSARY STOP DO NOT WANT TO BARGAIN SO WILL SET MINIMUM FIGURE ECONOMICALLY POSSIBLE FOR ME WHICH IS TWENTY-FIVE THOUSAND PLUS DRAWING ROOM TRANS-PORTATION BOTH WAYS STOP WOULD EITHER HAVE TO SEE SCRIPT OR BE ASSURED IT DID NOT CONFLICT WITH POSSIBLE PRODUCTION OF *JOHN BROWN'S BODY* ALSO THAT ALL PUBLICITY WOULD PROTECT THAT PROPERTY STOP DELIGHTED POSSIBLE OPPORTUNITY WORK WITH MR. GRIFFITH STOP PLEASE ADVISE ME EARLIEST POSSIBLE AS MUST HALT ALL PERSONAL PLANS UNTIL I HEAR FROM YOU
STEPHEN VINCENT BENET[20]

Benét's money demands were steep even by Hollywood's generous standards; he had not earned twenty-five thousand dollars from his serious writing during the previous ten years. Considine quickly balked at this figure, and also insisted that Benét commit himself for a longer period of time. Benét eventually settled for a twelve- week contract at $1000 per week.[21] He met Griffith in New York and, impressed with the famous director and enthusiastic about the project, set out for Hollywood shortly before Christmas. As we shall see later, the next three months would not be the happiest of his life.

W. R. Burnett is another author who, fresh from a popular success, found himself working in Hollywood, if under slightly different circumstances. In 1930, after his phenomenal success in New York with *Little Caesar,* Burnett decided to vacation in California for a few months. Screenwriting was the last thing on his mind while he visited friends from Ohio then living in the Los Angeles area. As Burnett tells it:

I didn't want to work in Hollywood at all. I came out here and I didn't know anything. I was a greenhorn from Ohio. I didn't know what it meant to have a success like *Little Caesar* in this town. At the time it was terrific, but it doesn't last. How they knew where I was I don't know. I'm out here just on vacation. And I said, "No," and they thought I was crazy. They said, "My God, the money you can make!"

So I finally got a call from Warner Brothers—would I mind coming over and talking to them—and I said, "What about?" And they said, "About a movie." And I said, "I'm not going to write for pictures." and they said, "Just come over and talk to us."

So I went over and talked to them. And I met two very slick guys: Johnny Monk Saunders, the writer, and Graham Baker, the story editor, who was also a writer. They said "Look, Burnett, Johnny Monk Saunders will write the script—all you have to do is just sit in, you don't have to write at all, just sit in and he'll ask you questions about Chicago." They were doing... *The Finger Points,* one of the earliest talkies and a lousy picture by the way.

So I said, "Oh well, what the hell, I don't care." So I asked—I didn't know about money—I said if they'd pay me what I asked, I'd do it. So they said, "What do you want?" I said, "I want a thousand dollars a week," and they said "Fine." They were laughing—you know, they'd have given me $2500. But I didn't know that. So I wrote my father and he said, "You are lying—nobody gets a thousand dollars a week for writing." But I took the job. [22]

Burnett was to fare much better than Benét in the studios. He remained in Hollywood, working as a screenwriter, for more than forty years, during which time he wrote more than a dozen adventure novels.

Benét and Burnett are examples of writers who had some bargaining power in their negotiations with the studios. Nunnally Johnson, in contrast, possessing neither critical reputation nor demonstrated popular appeal, was in a more precarious bargaining position. Johnson worked in Hollywood in 1926 as one of Herman Mankiewicz's recruits, but he quickly returned to his job as a reporter on the *New York Post.* Johnson was well-paid by the *Post,* making about $140 each week, throughout much of the late twenties. He left the paper's payroll, however, in 1930 to try his luck as a free-lance short story writer. He became a popular contributor to the *Saturday Evening Post,* but when the magazine cut back its fiction purchases in 1932, Johnson found more and more rejection notices in his mailbox. Johnson then began thinking again about Hollywood:

You know, I'd write a short story and I had enough experience to know, well, this is o.k., this will sell. And it came back. I felt like a pitcher who was cutting the corner of the plate, and they were calling them balls. I didn't know what to do. That was when I talked to my agent about getting me a job. . . . anywhere. Hollywood sounded the poshest kind of job I could get. But I'd known a fellow named Merritt Hulbert, who was an editor of the *Saturday Evening Post,* and I'd worked with him a great deal, and he'd become story editor at Paramount. That seemed like a good chance. [23]

Even with Hulbert's support, Johnson received only a half-hearted offer from Paramount: three hundred dollars a week and no travelling expenses. Desperate for work, Johnson borrowed the money from friends to make the trip, and signed the contract.

Of these three authors, Benét's hiring was most representative of the group of writers I studied. Hollywood was most interested in writers whose names had some current publicity value. A hit on Broadway or in the bookstalls was the likeliest way to attract the attention of a Hollywood producer. As the Depression deepened, however, more writers' hiring experiences resembled Johnson's. They found that, as their bargaining power diminished, Hollywood's terms became less generous. By the mid-thirties writers like Daniel Fuchs, the young novelist whose *Williamsburg Trilogy* was published to critical raves but indifferent sales, gladly accepted any terms Hollywood suggested.

One by one, and then in droves, authors left New York for Los Angeles. There they encountered business organizations and methods of production far different in history, structure, and practice than those of the literary marketplace. In economic terms, the film industry during the thirties was a mature, vertically integrated oligopoly; a handful of multi-million dollar corporations dominated all phases of the movie business. The production studios themselves were not even the most valuable part of the industry; rather, its economic strength lay in the real estate holdings of these studios' parent corporations. When the movie makers moved to California during the trust war, the industry's money men had remained in New York, buying out smaller competitors, building or leasing large chains of theaters, and attending to their ever-growing financial empires. By the thirties, ten times more capital was invested in theaters and land than in production facilities.[24] The studios, in effect, existed only to supply their parent corporations with a steady supply of product. Ultimate financial control in the industry, then, rested in the hands of executives and financiers in the East.

The industry was so consolidated by 1938 that the staff of the congressionally mandated Temporary National Economic Committee reported that the film industry had developed over the course of thirty years "from an activity in the hands of a large number of small and financially weak individuals to an industry controlled by a few large companies which dominate its policies and control its actions."[25] In the thirties, the number of these large companies had thinned to eight: Columbia Pictures, Corporation; Loew's, Inc., of which Metro-Goldwyn-Mayer was the production subsidiary; Paramount Pictures, Inc.; Radio-Keith-Orpheum Corporation; United Artists Corporation; Universal Corporation; and Warner Brothers Pictures, Inc.[26] These eight organizations owned and operated the only production facilities of any consequence in Hollywood. Between them, they manufactured 95 percent of the pictures exhibited in the country's first-run movie houses.[27] Thus, while there were dozens of publishers and hundreds of theatrical producers in New York, authors taking on screenwriting assignments invariably worked for one of these eight "majors." Of the forty writers I examined in detail, for example, only Nathanael West ever worked for another production company.[28]

The movie studios in Hollywood, then, were tied to commercial organizations whose major purpose was not making movies but rather exhibiting them. These organizations demanded a seemingly ever-increasing supply of pictures. All of the studios in Hollywood faced the essential economic challenge of meeting this demand while keeping down production costs, because by the 1920s movie making had grown into an enormously complicated, time-consuming, and expensive process. Each movie involved dozens of specialized crafts and cost several hundred thousand dollars. The eight major production studios spent tens of millions of dollars annually on their payrolls, to maintain and improve their physical plants, and to service the debts accrued during rapid expansion. "The production of films, essentially fluid and experimental as a process," film historian Tino Balio concludes, "is harnessed to a form of organization which can rarely afford to be either experimental or speculative because of the regularity with which heavy fixed charges must be met."[29]

As the cost of filmmaking skyrocketed during the twenties and thirties, motion picture executives in both New York and Hollywood sought to rationalize and streamline the production process. Companies came to rely heavily on formula pictures—standardized melodramas, Westerns, romantic comedies, adventure and action movies—tailored to the talents of their stars. By doing so, studios could re-use or recycle sets, costumes, casts, and even scripts, at considerable savings. Since many movies had to be made simultaneously in order to meet production quotas, and since the studios needed to keep their full-time workers productive, the manufacturing process was fragmented into its component stages and craft specialties. Like a worker on any industrial assembly-line, movie employees—be they electricians, set designers, or major stars—performed their specific jobs on one movie and then moved on to others. Robert Sklar observed in *Movie-Made America* that by the late twenties

> the once anarchic adventure of putting together a movie had become as specialized, organized, and as routinized as collective creative work could be. The major studios had developed departments, inventories, and experts capable of producing any object, image, or sound from all the world's cultures and epochs: researchers found out the right cut of any jacket or hair style; property men and women secured or made historically correct furnishings; sound men reproduced the sounds of bygone machines, and stunt men the feats of ancient heroes.[30]

It fell to the management hierarchy of the studios to orchestrate the complex process of motion picture production. Traditionally the director had been the kingpin of movie making, approving all casting, scripting, and technical decisions related to production. But beginning in the late twenties, the home offices began to hire supervisor-managers to take control of the studios. By the thirties the managers, supervisors, and executives of the studios, who came to be known collectively as *producers,* or the *front office,* held rarely disputed power in Hollywood, controlling the actual manufacture, as well as the content, of the movies those studios made.[31]

Initially the title "producer" referred only to the presidents and chief executives of production companies—those men with the most power and influence in Hollywood. MGM's Louis B. Mayer, Warner Brothers' Jack Warner, Paramount's Barney Balaban, Universal's Carl Laemmle, and Columbia's Harry Cohn all functioned in this capacity. These men conducted labor negotiations, supervised the maintenance and expansion of the physical plant, dealt with the most crucial financial concerns of the production company, and reported directly to the home office in New York.

As the studios' operations grew in size and complexity during the twenties, these men often delegated responsibility for actual production to a second-in-command, usually an executive vice-president in charge of production. Irving Thalberg at MGM, Darryl Zanuck at Warners, David Selznick at RKO, and Carl Laemmle, Jr. at Universal all worked at one time or another in this capacity. These two types of managers, whose official titles and precise duties varied from studio to studio, formed Hollywood's true elite—socially, economically, and in terms of the power they wielded within the walls of the studios. In concert with a battery of lawyers, accountants, and other administrators, and directed by the officers of the parent corporation in New York, the front offices of each production company determined the number of pictures to be made each year, allocated funds among the various classes of pictures to be made, and drew up budgets and shooting schedules for each picture.

Reporting to the front office were any number of lesser managers initially known as supervisors but by the thirties also called *line producers,* directly responsible for the making of a certain portion of the studio's yearly output. Line producers also advised the front office on the selection of story material, the hiring and assigning of both creative personnel and key technicians, and the setting of specific budgets and schedules for each movie's manufacture. The line producer then supervised each particular movie's progress from story idea to final cut. Thus the line producer was the only person associated with a film's making who worked on a movie from beginning to end. Each line producer usually had subordinates of his own, associate or assistant producers responsible for individual pictures or managing one aspect of a production if the producer was working on a single important movie.

The most important producers in the thirties had been in the business for years. They had acquired their power and status through decades of shrewd bargaining, long-shot gambling, educated guessing, and more than a measure of ruthlessness. All, though, had demonstrated that they could make movies the public wanted to see. Many were from lower-class immigrant families, and a disproportionate number were Jews who had begun their working lives in New York's garment industry, a highly speculative and often treacherous business in its own right. Most thought of movie making as a business rather than as an art. They thought of movies, in the words of Bosley Crowther, "as bulk product, rather than individual gems."[32] Yet line producers and those front office men like Thalberg and Selznick who kept their hand in the actual movie-making process had to be sensitive to more than financial matters. Leo Rosten has ventured to list the qualities of a good producer:

The producer should possess the ability to recognize ability, the knack of assigning the right creative persons to the right creative spots. He should have a knowledge of audience tastes, a story sense, a businessman's approach to the costs and mechanics of picture making. He should be able to manage, placate, and drive a variety of gifted, impulsive, and egocentric people.[33]

Never known for their modesty, most producers would have recognized in themselves the model for Rosten's perfect producer. Jesse Lasky, for one, who for years supervised production at Paramount, wrote of the producer's character in his aptly titled autobiography *I Blow My Own Horn:*

The producer must be a prophet and a general, a diplomat and a peacemaker, a miser, and a spendthrift. He must have vision tempered by hindsight, daring governed by caution, the patience of a saint and the iron will of a Cromwell. His decision must be sure, swift and immediate, as well as subject to change, because conditions change continuously in the motion picture industry. The producer's resources must be such that no contingency can stop him finding a star, soothing a director like a super-Tallyrand, or, in all night conference in shirt-sleeves and heavy cigar smoke, doctoring the scripts by his own creative power.[34]

As we shall see in the next chapter, most writers felt that Hollywood's producers, with rare exceptions, could not measure up to Lasky's sterling description.

Beginning shortly after the introduction of sound, the cadre of supervisory personnel in the studios, including producers and their associates, grew enormously. At the same time, the number of creative workers in the studios remained fairly constant. Many new producers were competent, creative persons; many more were poor relations, inept in-laws, and simple incompetents. In the early thirties, the joke began circulating in Hollywood that the the only *ism* producers believed in was nepotism. A Screen Directors Guild report issued in 1938 confirmed the increasingly top-heavy management structure of the studios: while 34 producers made 743 movies in 1927, ten years later 220 producers were required to make only 484 pictures.[35] Executives in New York lamented the inherent wastes of this bloated managerial class; workers in the studios ridiculed its incompetence. The producers' ability to make movies the public would pay to see muted the objections of the former; the producers' authority silenced the later.

Yet producers could not directly control every aspect of a picture's production. As Robert Sklar points out, they came in the early 1930s to concentrate on those few vital areas where they could be most assertive:

Under the circumstances only the most powerful and obsessive producers and producer-directors could retain personal control over all the complex facets of filmmaking. A significant part of what the producer was selling to the public—the "production values," costumes, sets, music, location shots—was largely determined by preliminary budget decisions. Studio specialists and craftworkers could be counted on for as high quality work as their money allowed. It was in the realm of story, direction and performance that the producer took his chances; and there the manipulation of personality became so subtle a game that it often turned into an end in itself.[36]

Eastern writers arrived in the studios, then, just as the producer was coming to power in Hollywood, and just as producers realized that, as Sklar observes, "to gain control over story and script was to have your hand on the creative pipeline and to dominate the entire filmmaking process... The manipulation of writers, therefore, became as essential a part of the producer's power game as the manipulation of stars."[37] Eastern writers came to Hollywood as the pawns of producers in their battle for power with directors; their arrival, Sklar concludes, "turned out to be the final decisive act in the producers' successful drive for control."[38]

From their vantage point at the top of the studio hierarchy, producers charted, then guided, the course of each picture through the three basic stages of its making. *Pre-production* involved all the work preparatory to the actual photography. The producer in preproduction acquired or commissioned a story "property," then assembled the director, principal actors, and writers. The producer would either assign talent from his own studio's contract rosters, or arrange to borrow another studio's employees, or sign someone not currently under contract to a short-term (or length-of-picture) contract. While the writers and the producer worked on the movie's script, the technical departments designed and built the sets, assembled props, tested make-up, designed and made costumes, scouted locations, and performed the scores of other tasks to be done before filming could begin.

The second, or *production,* stage involved all the work actually done before the camera. This was the most labor-intensive and therefore costly phase of a movie's manufacture, consequently, producers constructed shooting schedules to maximize the use of every actor and set. Delays invariably occurred: bad weather on location, temperamental stars, broken equipment, and mishandled film stock all habitually held up or shut down production. Thus producers coveted directors who ran workmanlike sets and kept the number of delays to a minimum.

In *post-production* the editors cut the movie, the musical score was recorded, the actors overdubbed any poorly reproduced dialog, any scenes the producer disliked were reshot, and the laboratory manufactured the final print and its copies. The publicity department then constructed an advertising campaign around the movie's plot and stars, the picture was previewed at a neighborhood theater in the Los Angeles area, and after revision, then released to the general public.

The screenwriters' work was confined almost exclusively to pre-production. They were given an idea or story to develop into an outline or *treatment*—a short summary of the proposed script's plot and characterizations. If the producer approved the treatment, writers then began work on the actual scenario. During the scripting process, writers and producers met in story conferences called by the producer to review the writer's work, and to provide a platform for the producer's own ideas. The frequency of these conferences and the matter of which staff members participated in them varied from studio to studio. Irving Thalberg and David Selznick constantly conducted such conferences, often on a daily basis. Thalberg, for instance, frequently gathered his staff after a film's first preview to evaluate the audience reaction and discuss possible reshooting or re-editing.[39] Jack Warner, on the other hand, usually let his screenwriters finish complete drafts before scheduling meetings. Also present at the story conference could be the director, the story editor, the unit manager, and any number of production assistants. In any case, the story conference was the producer's chief means of input and control of the scripting process. How that control was exercised varied enormously from producer to producer, but, as we shall see in the next chapter, was crucial to Eastern writers' experiences in the studios.

Once the scenario was completed, the studio submitted it to the Production Code Administration for approval. The Code, a further strengthening of the Hays Office's initial self-censorship efforts, was formally adopted by the Motion Picture Production and Distributors Association in 1930.[40] This agreement was a collective response to the added possibilities for offense and profanity inherent in sound production. It was also a response to the wave of new writers entering the studios who, unaccustomed to Hollywood's traditional taboos, were submitting scripts on controversial subjects and containing too-frank dialog. The Code proscribed any immoral or illegal actions on the screen which went without punishment or reform. In part, the Code directed:

1. No picture shall be produced which will lower the moral standards of those who see it. Hence the sympathy of the audience should never be thrown on the side of crime, wrong doing, evil or sin.
2. Correct standards of life shall, as far as possible, be presented. A wide knowledge of life and living is made possible through the film. When right standards are consistently presented, the motion picture exercises the most powerful influences. It builds character, develops right ideals, inculcates correct principles, and all this in the attractive story form.
3. Law, human or natural, shall not be ridiculed, nor shall sympathy be created for its violation.[41]

Dozens of unacceptable actions were spelled out in the Code, including:

The use of liquor in American life, when not required by the plot or for proper characterization, will not be shown.

The techniques of murder must be presented in a way that will not inspire imitation.

The sanctity of the institution of marriage and the home shall be upheld. Pictures shall not infer that low forms of sex relationships are the accepted or common thing.

The treatment of low, disgusting, unpleasant, though not necessarily evil, subjects should always be subject to the dictates of good taste and a regard for the sensibilities of the audience.

Obscenity in word, gesture, reference, song, joke, or by suggestion (even when likely to be understood only by a part of the audience) is forbidden.[42]

In short, the Code cut the movies off from many of the most pressing social and moral issues confronting American society, and it severely restricted the range of character and plot possibilities available to the screenwriter. Although approved as the standard of the industry in 1930, it was not until 1934 that compliance with the Code's provisions became mandatory. Producers after that time were reluctant to begin shooting a movie until Joseph Breen, the head of the PCA, had approved the script, ordered revisions, or declared it totally unsuitable.

The Hays Office was a logical target for writers' hostility, and screenwriters invariably ridiculed the strictures of the Code. But the most experienced screenwriters learned to blunt the full effect of Breen's censorship. "You would learn to put in four or five incidents or bits of dialogue that they could take out so that they would let you leave in other things," Donald Ogden Stewart remembered. "You didn't make a deal with them but they wouldn't want to take out too much so you'd give them five things to take out to satisfy the Hays Office—and you'd get away with murder with what they left in."[43]

Once the Hays Office approved a script, the writers' work was complete, and they moved on to the next assignment. Writers rarely took part in production or post-production. Some studios and producers expressly prohibited writers from even visiting the sound stage during filming. Directors, producers, and actors constantly altered the scripts writers presented them, and none wanted angry authors around protesting these changes.[44]

On rare occasions, though, writers were asked to take part in production. If problems with the script occurred during shooting, they were sometimes called in to rewrite certain passages or scenes. Such *script doctoring* was high-pressured and lucrative work, since each day of lost production cost the studio thousands of dollars. A few producers and directors hired writers to work on the set regularly, suggesting improvements in the script as shooting progressed.

William Faulkner, for example, served just this function for Howard Hawks on a number of pictures.[45] Generally, though, from the producer's point-of-view, the writer was hired to write, and once he finished the script, his further service was unnecessary.

This, then, is a very brief outline of the screenwriter's role in movie production under what came to be called the studio system. Hollywood's large scale, producer-controlled, assembly-line method of production was neither as monolithic nor as systematic as this name implies, and each of the eight major studios had a distinctive history and character.

United Artists was unique among the eight in that it was not a production company *per se,* but rather the distribution organization for a group of independent stars and producers. It had been formed in 1919 by Charles Chaplin, Mary Pickford, Douglas Fairbanks, and D. W. Griffith—all then near the height of their popularity—as a means of reaping larger shares of the profits of their pictures. Each of the four owned his or her own production studio; their joint organization merely arranged distribution in return for a small percentage of the gross. Joseph Schenck acted as president of United Artists through the twenties, before being replaced by Al Lichtman, who, in turn, was succeeded for a brief time by David Selznick. Samuel Goldwyn became a major stockholder in the corporation in the thirties after the founders' popularity had waned, and he distributed his films through United Artists for most of the decade. United Artists was a small company by Hollywood standards, and hired relatively few writers. Only Stephen Vincent Benét, Ben Hecht, Robert E. Sherwood, and Preston Sturges of the writers I studied worked for United Artists during the thirties.[46]

Universal was the oldest of the majors, formed in 1912 by a group of independent manufacturers and exhibitors under the leadership of Carl Laemmle. Laemmle, a Chicago clothing merchant and nickelodeon operator, moved Universal's production facilities to Los Angeles in 1914, and a year later built Universal City, then the largest studio in the industry. Universal's studios have remained at the same San Fernando Valley site ever since. In 1929 Laemmle appointed his son, Carl Jr., head of production, although the elder Laemmle remained the nominal head of the corporation until banking interests forced him out in 1936. Universal's best years were those just after World War I; by 1930 its power and prestige in the industry had dimmed substantially. The Laemmles ran their studio in a benevolent and quixotic manner—their employees knew them as "Uncle Carl" and "Junior"—and this casualness eventually proved to be their downfall.[47]

Three former Laemmle employees, Joseph Brandt and the Cohn brothers, Jack and Harry, founded *Columbia Pictures* in 1924.[48] Originally Columbia was only one of a number of shoestring operations located on Gower Street in downtown Hollywood, an area nicknamed "Gower Gulch," and "Poverty

Row." Frank Capra, who became the studio's most successful director in the thirties, vividly describes Columbia's ramshackle plant:

> To a dozen or more shacks forming a square around an inner courtyard, succeeding fly-by-nighters had added additions to additions with all the playful abandon of children piling odd-shaped cigar boxes on top of each other—two sides were now three stories high; the third, two stories; the fourth, one and a half.... Narrow halls, rising and falling with the uneven levels, tunneled through the maze; partitions honeycombed it into tiny "offices"; afterthoughts of exposed pipes for water, gas and heat pierced the flimsy walls; criss-crossing electric wires—inside and out—tied the jerry built structure together to keep it from blowing away.[49]

Harry Cohn acted as Columbia's production chief and successfully adopted Thomas Ince's shooting on paper method among other efficiencies, in order to stretch the studio's meager resources. Cohn was a vulgar and profane man by all accounts—Capra for one recalls that he "snarled out of the side of his mouth with the best of them"—but he alone among the Gower Gulch producers built his marginal operation into a major Hollywood studio.[50] In 1932 Cohn assumed the presidency of Columbia while keeping his position as chief of production—the only executive in Hollywood to hold both posts. In the movie industry, Harry Cohn *was* Columbia.

Warner Brothers also dated from the early twenties. Harry, Jack, Albert, and Sam Warner began in the industry as exhibitors and distributors in the East. Shortly before 1920 they moved to California with many other small movie companies. By 1925, Warner Brothers Pictures had expanded to include the corporate remains of the Selig, Lubin, Essaney, and Vitagraph companies, all pioneers in the industry. This ambitious acquisition campaign, which also involved the purchase of several theaters, almost bankrupted the Warners. Only the popularity of a series of Rin Tin Tin movies kept the studio afloat. In the mid-twenties Warner Brothers was in such financial hot water that management asked its employees to contribute to the budgets of several productions, and Warner was saved from certain failure only when its gamble on sound production paid off beyond all expectations.[51]

With the profits from *The Jazz Singer,* Warner Brothers acquired the large First National Production Company and thereby vaulted into the front ranks of the industry. *The Jazz Singer* also allowed the Warners to build a new studio complex in Burbank. Of the four brothers, Jack served as chief of production in Hollywood from the twenties until well into the 1960s. During the thirties, Jack Warner's studio specialized in melodramas and action pictures. It counted among its stars James Cagney, Edward G. Robinson, Humphrey Bogart, Bette Davis, Ida Lupino, and John Garfield. Warners also produced a number of movies on serious social themes during the thirties. The quality of the studio's contract roster, its commitment to socially significant pictures, and the basically workmanlike atmosphere which prevailed on the Warner's lot all contributed to its being chosen the most admired studio in a poll of screenwriters taken in 1940.[52] W. R. Burnett, who worked at Warner Brothers off and on for twenty years, said of the studio:

> Warners was so far better managed than the other studios it wasn't funny. Warners had a system. They decided that they were interested in a property. The property was bought or optioned. It was then given to a producer and a writer. It was up to them to get a shootable script. When they were satisfied with it, they took it to Jack Warner, and he said we re-write this part, or we shoot it, or we abandon it. Very few scripts were abandoned, because they knew what they were doing to begin with. That's what made the studio—they didn't waste all that money and time. That's the way it was done. Writers liked it because they knew if they worked on a script the chances were it would be made.[53]

Twentieth Century-Fox was born of the 1935 merger of one of the industry's oldest production companies and one of its youngest. William Fox, one of the industry's pioneers, began as an arcade owner in Brooklyn, expanded his holdings to include fifteen theaters in the New York area, created a film exchange, and then moved into production in 1912. By the late 1910s Fox had developed a number of popular stars, including Theda Bara, William Farnum, and Tom Mix. His profitable integration of production, distribution, and exhibition holdings were envied by the rest of industry. In the early 1920s, however, as popular taste became more sophisticated, Fox's stars lost much of their glitter; his studio lost ground to the trendier Paramount and MGM. Fox then dispatched Winfield Sheehan, an ex-newspaperman and former member of the New York Police Department, to Los Angeles to take control of the studio. By the end of the decade Sheehan had restored much of the company's luster in the Hollywood community. Sheehan had strengthened Fox's hand to such an extent that Fox attempted to take over the business empire of his arch-rival, Marcus Loew. The Wall Street Crash, a threatened Justice Department investigation, and a disabling car accident conspired to foil Fox's bid for industrial supremacy; shortly thereafter he was even ousted from his own company. The Fox Corporation never recovered from these misfortunes, and only the subsequent merger with the Twentieth-Century Pictures Corporation rescued it from insolvency.[54]

Twentieth Century had itself been formed in 1933 by Joseph Schenck (the ex-production chief at United Artists), William Goetz (Louis B. Mayer's son-in-law), and Darryl F. Zanuck. Mayer and Nicholas Schenck provided additional financial help during the first year of the company's existence. Zanuck, who had been Jack Warner's right-hand man in the late twenties, supervised production at Twentieth Century from the time of the merger until 1956.[55]

In an industry known for its convoluted histories of merger and acquisition, *RKO* possessed the most labyrinthine corporate geneology of all. The company was largely the brain child of Joseph P. Kennedy, who in 1928 brought together his own Film Booking Office, the Keith-Albee and Orpheum theater circuits, and the Radio Corporation of America, which had entered the movie industry after the introduction of sound. This hybrid was named the Radio-Keith Orpheum Corporation. RKO suffered hard times during the Depression. In the span of three years it went first into receivership and then into bankruptcy. Its ownership changed hands several times, but a steady stream of films continued to pour from its plant under the direction of several production chiefs, including the tireless David O. Selznick.[56]

Although RKO, Twentieth Century-Fox, and Warner Brothers were all formidable enterprises, Paramount and MGM towered over the rest of the industry in the 1930s. *Paramount* took its name from the distribution company begun in 1915 by an ex-patent company exchange operator named W. W. Hodkinson. Hodkinson distributed the films of two independent production companies, Adolph Zukor's Famous Players Company and the Lasky Feature Plays Company, which merged in 1916 to form the Famous Players-Lasky Company. Famous Players-Lasky eventually grew to take over Hodkinson's firm and several other smaller companies. Zukor, a chilly, calculating schemer known throughout the industry as "Creepy," directly began an aggressive expansion campaign, building new theaters and ruthlessly acquiring older ones. He came very close to capturing control of the entire industry in the early twenties, but concerted pressures from independent theater and exchange operators, the Justice Department, and rival film financiers thwarted his plan. During the twenties, though, Paramount reigned without peer in Hollywood. B. P. Schulberg, Budd Schulberg's father, served as General Manager of Zukor's West Coast studio from 1925 through 1935, when he was replaced by Emmanuel Cohen. Caught unprepared by the public demand for sound pictures, and over-extended financially because of Zukor's appetite for theater expansion, Paramount was buffeted harshly by the Depression. After two years in bankruptcy, it was reorganized in 1935 with Barney Balaban as president and Y. Frank Freeman in charge of production. Through all this financial turmoil, Paramount remained a leading film factory in Hollywood, and in most years was second only to MGM in the number of contract writers, actors, and directors on its payroll.[57]

Metro-Goldwyn-Mayer operated the industry's flagship studio in the 1930s. MGM was the production arm of the theater empire assembled by Marcus Loew with the help of Joseph and Nicholas Schenck. Loew was a classic movie mogul. Born in New York in 1870, Loew was working as a cloth cutter in a garment industry sweatshop before his twelfth birthday. He patiently advanced in the garment trade until, in 1907, he had acquired enough capital to purchase his first theater—a vaudeville house in downtown Brooklyn. He netted $60,000 during his first year as a showman, programming vaudeville acts and short films geared to the family trade. In late 1909, with help from the Schubert brothers, he opened two more theaters in Manhattan, the Yorkville and the Lincoln Square. In the ensuing years he carefully bought properties throughout the city and eventually dominated the New York theater market.[58]

Loew's chain continued to grow and prosper in the late 1910s, but it was not until 1920 that Loew moved directly into production when he acquired the Metro Picture Corporation, begun in 1915 by Louis B. Mayer, a Boston theater magnate.[59] Loew's first picture after taking over Metro proved to be an enormous success, *The Four Horsemen of the Apocalypse*, which introduced Rudolph Valentino. Although Loew was known as a conservative, frugal businessman, he could not resist building on the initial success at Metro by acquiring two other production companies, the Goldwyn Picture Corporation and a smaller firm started by Louis B. Mayer after his separation from Metro. This merger of the Metro, Goldwyn, and Mayer companies occurred on April 17, 1924. Mayer served as Vice President and General Manager of the newly named Metro-Goldwyn-Mayer Company, and Irving Thalberg, Mayer's young assistant, was named Second Vice President and Supervisor of Production.[60] Mayer and Thalberg took up their duties at the old Goldwyn studio in Culver City, a fifty-three acre plant whose nucleus was Thomas Ince's original California facility, Inceville. "This plant," a writer for *Fortune* magazine related, "presents the appearance less of a factory than of a demented university with a campus made out of beaverboard and canvas."[61]

While Mayer concerned himself with administering the studio and diverting as much money to himself as he could, Thalberg quickly built MGM's reputation as the studio with the most exciting stars and most lavish movies. In an industry built on glamor, MGM became the most glamorous studio of them all. By the thirties, it possessed a reputation for sophistication and spare-no-cost productions unmatched in Hollywood. Clark Gable, Greta Garbo, Spencer Tracey, Norma Shearer, William Powell, Judy Garland, Mickey Rooney, James Stewart, Joan Crawford, and Myrna Loy were but a few of MGM's contract players. Thalberg also gathered a staff of producers which before long became the largest and most capable in the industry. At one point, Thalberg had ten associate producers reporting to him, including Paul Bern, Eddie Mannix, Harry Rapf, Bernard Hyman, Hunt Stromberg, Albert Lewin, and David O. Selznick. By the 1930s Thalberg had also acquired the largest and most expensive staff of writers in the industry. In 1932 the studio counted sixty-eight writers under contract, with weekly salaries totalling $40,000.[62] Accordingly, MGM became the largest importer and employer of writers from the East.

Thus these eight major studios differed greatly, due to their various corporate histories and the play of personality among top management. However within the Hollywood-as-destroyer legend they tend to be lumped together. In the studio system, the legend relates, writers were bound like indentured servants to their employers through long-term, standardized contracts. Regardless of how extravagant their salaries, once signed to these contracts writers were then required to put in long hours within the studio walls. The writers themselves often fostered this impression, as we shall see in the next chapter, but contracts were not as uniform nor of as long a duration, salaries were not as large, nor were working conditions as rigid, as the legend suggests.

As long as the management of talent was the key to any studio's success, the legal contract remained the practical instrument of its control. "The option contract," Hortense Powdermaker reported in 1950, "which binds the employee to the studio for seven years and permits the studio to dismiss him at the end of six months or one year, without having to show cause, smacks more of medieval power relations between lord and serf, than of employer and employee in the modern world of industry."[63] Robert Sklar, speaking of the studio system in the thirties, concurred: "All important screen players, and many writers and directors as well, were obliged, as a condition of obtaining work, to sign contacts binding them to a studio for seven years. The studio's commitment, however, was for no more than six months; the contract gave it an option to renew at the end of every half-year period or to let the agreement lapse, setting the employee at liberty."[64] The experiences of the writers I studied, however, indicate that the studios in reality did not rely as heavily on the seven-year contract as most film historians suggest, nor did they often hold their writers to the full seven-year term when such contracts were employed. I examined thirty contracts signed by one or another of the forty writers under consideration and discovered that the writer's contractual time commmitment varied greatly. Six week and three month contracts, in fact, were just as common as longer-term agreements. One-week and even one-day contracts were not unheard of, and some studios often preferred to use length-of-picture contracts, under which a writer was hired to work on a single script, or even part of a script. Furthermore, the actual time writers spent in a studio under any specific contract averaged a little under six months.[65] Thus the image of the writer laboring away for endless years under the terms of an onerous contract is a misconception. In fact, writers complained more often about short contracts than about long ones. The variety of contractual arrangements between writers and studios suggests again as well that the studio system was less systematic than supposed.

There is also a tendency to inflate the amount of money writers received while working in the studios. Hollywood salaries *were* large in comparison to what writers, on the average, made in New York. H. N. Swanson, who perhaps negotiated more movie contracts than any other literary agent, estimated that in the thirties the average salary received by writers was $1000 a week.[66] The contracts I examined support Swanson's estimate: $950 a week was the average per-week salary. Budd Schulberg's $50 a week junior writer's contract was the smallest; Ben Hecht's $3500 *a day* salary while working for David O. Selznick on *Gone With the Wind* was the largest. Yet such salary figures are deceiving in that writers rarely if ever worked a full fifty-two weeks a year. Leo Rosten's data concerning screenwriters' salaries, drawn from studio payroll records, corroborate this fact: of the 238 writers working under contract at Warner Brothers, MGM, Twentieth Century-Fox and Paramount in 1938, only 165 earned more than $15,000 a year. The median salary of these 165 writers was approximately $25,000, or half what a writer earning $1000 a week would make working a full year.[67]

Although records concerning the yearly earnings of the members of the study group are scarce, William Faulkner's 1937 income at Fox of $21,650 is perhaps representative, given Rosten's data.[68] Such a sum, while considerable in 1930s dollars, scarcely allowed writers to live in opulence. Moreover, as so many writers often complained, writers were paid substantially less as a group than actors, directors, or producers. While eighty actors, fifty-four producers, and forty-five directors earned $75,000 or more in 1938, only seventeen writers did.[69] By Hollywood standards, then, writers' salaries were anything but exorbitant. They rarely allowed, in George Jean Nathan's phrase, for "the potential of mauve motor cars, marble dunking pools, English butlers, and seven-dollar neckties."

Finally, as a general rule, writers under contract were required to be present in the studios during working hours, normally from ten to five, with half a day on Saturday. Some studios, however, were more vigilant in their supervision of their writers' work schedules than others. "When you worked at Warners, you didn't screw around," W. R. Burnett revealed. "Jack Warner checked the sheet—you had to be there at 9:30, or you'd get a notice, and you couldn't leave early." But on the MGM lot, "they didn't know where the writers were most of the time or care—they didn't give a good goddamn whether you ever showed up."[70] H. N. Swanson recalls that many producers allowed their writers to work off the lots so long as deadlines were met and they were available for story conferences.[71] At least fourteen writers in the study group, for example, worked outside the walls of the studios at some point in their Hollywood careers. Samson Raphaelson, for one, while working with Earnst Lubitsch on a series of highly successful movies for Paramount, rarely spent more than a few afternoons a week in the studio. S. N. Behrman, for another, frequently worked at a back table in the Brown Derby. According to his secretary at the time, Dashiell Hammett always worked at home—and usually in his bathrobe—while on the MGM payroll during 1934-35.[72] Thus the image of the long-suffering screenwriter chained to a studio desk does not square completely with the facts.

In sum, the introduction of sound tremendously increased the film industry's need for novelists and playwrights with an ear for dialog, but Eastern writers rarely turned to Hollywood before the Depression had throttled the literary marketplace in New York. Once on the West Coast, writers confronted a business enterprise far different than publishing or the commercial theater, one in which a handful of fairly large corporations mass-produced movies using a version of the assembly-line. Although Hollywood's critics often speak of the studio system as monolithic and mechanical, little was predictable about life in the studios for the writer save that he would be relegated to working at the will of the manager-producers who controlled the production process, and that his contribution to movie making would usually be limited to the preproduction stage. In the next chapter, I will look more closely at the studio system from the writer's perspective. For all the variety of this system, Eastern screenwriters shared a remarkably coherent view of how the studios operated, and the writer's role within them.

4

The Writer's View of the Studio System

When Stephen Vincent Benét accepted United Artists' *Abraham Lincoln* assignment, he decided to spare his family another uprooting after years of wearying travel, and so he reported to Hollywood alone. Benét did not relish the idea of a long separation from his family, and was wary of what Hollywood would hold, but he was determined to give the assignment his best. Thus Benét convinced Griffith to make their trip across the country a working one. Travelling in the plush drawing room style to which the famed director, if not the young author, was accustomed, Benét was a bit awed by Griffith. But he was quickly won over by the director's charm. "I like Griffith," Benét wrote to his wife Rosemary upon arriving in Hollywood, "he certainly has been extremely decent to me. He is kiddable—which I didn't expect—and really laid himself out to be pleasant."[1] Before reaching Los Angeles, they had cut Griffith's lengthy original script by a third. Both were delighted with their working relationship, and the author felt that he was off to a good start in the movies.

Once in Southern California, Benét did not have to wait long for his first glimpse behind the studio's walls. "We got in last night," he informed his wife, "and today I have eaten an orange, walked under palm trees, gone out to the studio, met dozens of people whose names I will never remember, been photographed with Mr. Griffith, seen and heard screen-tests of various Lincolns and Ann Rutledges, etc.,"[2] Benét was excited and somewhat disoriented by Hollywood's exotic landscape and the workings of the studio. He wrote home that he was keeping his eyes open and his mouth shut while finding his bearings in this new environment: "The sun is actually out, the roses and poinsettias in bloom in the lush garden. It is all quite mad. And everthing has gone well so far.... At present I am giving my celebrated imitation of a piece of furniture."[3] Benét's only complaint initially was homesickness for his wife and family. In closing his first letter to Rosemary from Los Angeles, he reminded her, and himself, of the reason he had come: "I am lonelier than I can think about and miss you more than words can say. Gee. Only—at the worst—

83 days more.... We're going to get a nice house out of this—concentrate on the house—I am."[4]

After a week in California, Benét found time to write a more detailed description of Hollywood:

> This is Wednesday. Let me recount a little about this madhouse. In the first place Hollywood—Los Angeles, Glendale, Pasadena, etc etc—is one loud, struggling Main Street, low-roofed, mainly unsky-scrapered town that struggles along for twenty-five miles or so, full of stop and go lights, automobiles, palm-trees, Spanishy—& God knows what all houses—orange drink stands with real orange juice—studios—movie theaters—everything but bookstores. I am the only person in the entire twenty-five miles who walks more than 4 blocks, except along Hollywood Boulevard in the evening. There are some swell hotels—up in the hills or between L.A. and Hollywood—& a few nightclubs. But in general, everything is dead, deserted at 11:30 P.M.[5]

In a letter written to his good friend John Farrar, Benét reiterated his initial mock-exasperation with Hollywood and its pretensions: "You must see this place sometime, John. You would have more fun. It is all quite crazy from the flimsiness of the houses to the gentlemen who talk about Screen Art. But worth a visit."[6]

Benét was assigned an office at Griffith's Feature Productions studio in downtown Hollywood. The studio was like any other business, he reported to his wife, in that people spent most of their time gossiping and watching the clock. "I get to the office about ten—work till about 1—either with Griffith or without him—lunch—work from about 2 to 6—or not but anyhow am around the office—walk back here-eat—if there's nothing else—a movie—letters—read—bed. A chaste and sober life."[7] Benét's first reports to his wife and friends in the East, then, indicate that he was at ease in the film community, if not knowing quite what to make of it. "This is a madhouse," he wrote to his agent shortly before Christmas, "but I don't mind."[8] There were occasional visits from old friends who were also working in the studios. "Sidney [Howard] is around the corner at the Goldwyn Offices," Benét informed John Farrar. "I'm having dinner with him tomorrow night. He is fine and hopes to get out of it soon. So do I. But, as he remarked when I called him the other day, one has to have the jack."[9]

If Benét was glad to be working with Griffith, the director, for his part, was so pleased with Benét's work that he talked of another assignment at a larger salary. Yet Benét wanted no part of the offer, whatever his respect for Griffith. "I've been extremely non-commmittal," Benét wrote his wife. "I've worked on this one and I think they'll get their money's worth. I wouldn't sign a new contract for sums untold. Not without you, dearie. Life simply isn't worth it."[10]

Shortly after the first of the year, Benét and Griffith completed their script and submitted it to United Artists' front office for approval. Then Benét's real difficulties in Hollywood began. What enthusiasm he had mustered for screenwriting waned during a seemingly endless round of story conferences in which their script was rehashed and rewritten. In Hollywood, Benét moaned, "a story isn't a story but a conference."[11] Particularly irritating was the intrusion of the "money boys" of the front office in the scripting process. Compounding Benét's problems was Griffith's decreasing power at United Artists. After years of inactivity, Griffith possessed neither financial nor artistic control over his movies. Joseph Schenck, UA's President, and John Considine, its General Manager, made the ultimate decisions about all production affairs during Benét's stint at Griffith's studio, including scripting matters. The interference of these men and their many lieutenants incensed Benét. By the middle of January they had ordered, and rejected, several script revisions. Benét's mood blackened. On January 23 he complained to Rosemary:

> All *this* week we have been working on what-I-hope-will-be-the-last-but-which-undoubtedly -won't version. With some of the money boys, including my friend Mr. _____. I said he was a Yale man. Add to that the simple words "son of a bitch"—and, I think, you have him. All we need now is Mr. Schenck—old black Joe himself—to make things a real family party.... I'm sorry to bawl all this out to you. But it vexes me to see ignorance and stupidity and arrogance enthroned and time and talent wasted.... I am bending every effort to get away as soon as I can but this damn thing seems endless. There is no system and no sense—just a rat-run of politics.[12]

Later that same day, Benét exploded again in a letter to his agent, Carl Brandt. Brandt had suggested the Hollywood trip in the first place—a fact the author did not let him forget:

> The next time you sign me up on a 12 week contract to come out here for any amount of money, there is going to be a good deal of blood flowing around the Brandt office. Happy Lincoln's Birthday and so's your old man!
>
> Of all the Christ bitten places and businesses on the two hemispheres this one is the last curly kink on the pig's tail. And that's without prejudice to D. W. Griffith. I like him and think he's good. But, Jesus, the movies!
>
> I don't know which makes me vomit worst—the horned toads from the cloak and suit trade, the shanty Irish, or the gentlemen who talk of Screen Art. I have worked in advertising and with W. A. Brady Sr. But no where have I seen such shining waste, stupidity and conceit as in the business and managing end of this industry. Woopee!
>
> Since arriving, I have written 4 versions of *Abraham Lincoln,* including a good one, playable in the required time. That, of course, is out. Seven people, including myself, are now working in conferences on the 5th one which promises hopefully to be the worst yet. If I don't get out of here soon I am going crazy. Perhaps I am crazy now. I wouldn't be surprised.
>
> At any rate, don't be surprised if you get a wire from me that I have broken my contract, bombed the studio, or been arrested for public gibbering. Don't be surprised at all.[13]

Six days later, insult was added to injury when stories appeared in *Variety* and other papers suggesting that Considine was displeased with Benét's work and had ordered his script completely rewritten.[14] Furious, Benét fired off a scorching telegram to Brandt, directing him to advise United Artists that "the story must be retracted at once or I will sue."[15] Considine agreed immediately to the retraction, and ordered the studio's publicist, Harry Brand, to write a press release to that effect. Benét may have been more shocked with the content of the retraction than the original articles, for it stated that "Stephen Vincent Benét, prize poet and winner of many literary honors, is seriously considering an offer to write a series of scenarios for the talking screen."[16] That, of course, was the farthest thing from his mind. This release also reported that the poet planned to return to Hollywood as soon as possible (even though he had not yet departed). His script for *Abraham Lincoln* was hailed as "the most forward step yet made in creative screen writing and the first scenario that combines real literature and box office values."[17] In a separate telegram to one of the columnists who had printed the original story, Considine denied vigorously that he was dissatisfied with Benét's work. He asserted that "Benét has written the finest dialogue scenario it has been my pleasure to read in nine years of motion picture work."[18] "Everyone in our organization shares my enthusiasm for its perfection," Considine continued, "and not one change has been made in the original nor would I permit anyone to change a word in the original manuscript."[19] This was patently untrue. Nonetheless Benét was satisfied with the retraction, if incredulous of its content, and dropped his threat to sue. After one final story conference, attended by Joseph Schenck himself, Benét drew his final week's salary. He left Hollywood on February 8, completely soured of the experience. "Meet me in Chicago next Friday," he wired his wife, "and how glad I will be. Love and rejoicing. Steve."[20] Ten years were to pass before Benét would again consider an assignment in Hollywood.

Benét's screenwriting career, although briefer than most, provides a useful introduction to Eastern writers' views of Hollywood and the studio system. The attitudes revealed in Benét's letters about his work for United Artists illustrate many of the key concerns and complaints of Hollywood's literary recruits, whether they served one hitch in the studios or many. First, the great majority of Eastern authors, like Benét, went to Hollywood for financial reasons. Money *was* their motive, as the Hollywood-as-destroyer legend maintains. "Some lecture & some write for the movies," Benét had written his brother in explanation of his trip west, "and I say it's spinach anyhow, no matter how it's boiled."[21] To his wife, he had promised, "We're going to get a nice house out of this—concentrate on the house—I am."[22]

Some writers sought a Hollywood paycheck desperately, others diffidently. John Dos Passos's attitude, like Benét's, lay between the two extremes. Paramount hired Dos Passos in the summer of 1934. He was to work with the director Joseph von Sternberg on an adaptation of Pierre Louys's *La Femme et le Pantin,* presumably because he was familiar with Spanish history and culture. Dos Passos contracted rheumatic fever shortly after arriving in California, hence he did most of his work for von Sternberg via the bedside telephone at a friend's house. Years later, Dos Passos assessed his general financial situation at the time he accepted Paramount's offer:

> This was the period of the Great Depression. It didn't affect me much personally. Katy [his wife] owned the Provincetown house where we made our headquarters, and I scraped up what money I could for trips. I used to tell people I had been just as broke before the stockmarket crash as after it. My books could hardly have sold less anyway.[23]

Shortly after reaching Hollywood in late July of 1934, Dos Passos justisfied his working in the movies in a letter to his friend Ernest Hemingway. "I was in a sort of gap in my work and I thought I might as well take a stab at it, restoring my finances and taking a look at the world's great bullshit center."[24] Dos Passos quickly grew bored and dissatisfied. *"Je ne suis pas heureux,"* he confided to Edmund Wilson, but he did work the five weeks of his contract.[25] He was relieved when it was not renewed, and after a few months' further recuperation, he left Los Angeles never to return to a studio payroll.

William Faulkner's economic situation was even more precarious than that of Dos Passos. His novels, too, had brought him no substantial income. What royalties had accrued for *Sanctuary,* his most profitable book, were frozen due to his publisher's insolvency. So, in late 1931, Faulkner too considered the Hollywood option. "I have the assurance of a movie agent that I can go to Hollywood and make 500.00 or 750.00 a week in the movies," he wrote to his wife from New York in December, "Hal Smith will not want me to do it, but if all that money is out there, I might as well hack a little on the side and put the novel off."[26] In April MGM offered Faulkner a six-week contract paying five hundred dollars a week. Overdrawn at the bank, and with no other prospects in sight, Faulkner accepted. As Joseph Blotner writes of Faulkner's decision:

> He really did not want to go. But the Cape & Smith royalties appeared blocked and there was no immediate prospect of magazine sales. No one had picked up the serial rights to *Light in August,* which would not go on sale for six months. Where else could he make $500 a week? It would be like selling a short story every week for six weeks. He kissed his family goodbye and boarded the train out of Oxford.[27]

Although Dorothy Parker's financial plight was less severe than Faulkner's, she too went to Hollywood for the money. Stopping in Denver en route to California, she wrote to Alexander Woollcott: "I am afraid it is only too true about Hollywood. The Paramount contract, or Kiss of Death, has come. It is for ten weeks, and it seems the only way to get out from under the suffocating mass of debt my doting husband calls Dottie's dowry."[28] Two years later, Parker told a reporter, "I want nothing from Hollywood but money and anyone who tells you that he came here for anything else or tries to make beautiful words out of it lies in his teeth."[29]

Benét, Dos Passos, Faulkner, and Parker are but a few of the authors who signed Hollywood contacts out of economic necessity. Maxwell Anderson, Scott Fitzgerald (in his later years), James M. Cain, Nunnally Johnson, and Nathanael West also openly admitted that they went to Hollywood to liquidate their debts or solve other dire financial problems. Even writers with healthy bank accounts viewed Hollywood employment in strictly financial terms. For example, while Robert Sherwood waited for rehearsals to begin for *Reunion in Vienna* in 1931, he decided to go to Hollywood and accept any temporary assignment his agent could find there for him. But, he assured his mother, "If I do sell my soul to the cinema, it will be for a tidy sum."[30] His agent arranged such short-term employment and at the requested tidy sum—a $7500 two-week contract with Howard Hughes—thus Sherwood returned once more to Hollywood.[31] Thornton Wilder was another financially secure author who could not resist the large sums Hollywood offered. In a letter to an old friend written in 1934 aboard the Sante Fe Chief, he confided that while he had planned to go to New Mexico for a rest and vacation, he could not afford to refuse a short-term contract at a huge salary which MGM had offered him.[32]

Perhaps no writer, rich or poor, was more obsessed with Hollywood's golden promise than John O'Hara. In the early 1930s O'Hara was one of any number of young writers scratching out a living in New York on the sales of occasional pieces to the magazines and newspapers. He even tried his hand for a time at movie publicity, working in Manhattan first for Warner Brothers and then for RKO. Neither job lasted long, but they did acquaint O'Hara with Hollywood's largesse. In 1932 O'Hara was at the low point in his young career. Recently divorced, drinking heavily, and unable to find the time or money necessary to complete a sustained piece of fiction, O'Hara confessed to his brother: "I am looking around for a good job. I dream of going to Hollywood and making large sums there, but I don't suppose that will ever come true, so I am on the make here."[33] By early 1934, however, O'Hara had managed to convince the publishing firm of Harcourt Brace to advance him enough money to complete his first novel, *Appointment in Samarra*. His agent sent the galleys to Paramount, but the studio rejected the novel as "too strong" for the movies. They did, though, offer O'Hara a job writing dialog at $250 a week, which the author readily accepted early in June.[34] He jubilantly announced the news to his brother, and mused about his new-found wealth:

I leave Thursday for Hollywood on a contract that calls for my services for at least ten weeks. Thirty days before the ten weeks have elapsed they are to let me know whether they want me for another three months, so I'll be out there until November 20. Dear, dear; that means I won't be home in time for Mary's birthday. Anyway, I'm going to work for Paramount. They read galley proofs of my novel, and they said they couldn't buy it, but they want me so they got me. I'm so excited about the trip, and the prospect of being able to buy a Ford phaeton of my very own, and a new suit, and some razor blades. A week from today or tomorrow I'll be in greener pastures made green by exactly the fertilizer I have to offer.[35]

Two months later he reported that Paramount had indeed picked up his option. "So far I haven't done a picture," O'Hara conceded, "but they say they like my work. What they really like is that a novelist is content to work for what I'm getting."[36] O'Hara returned to New York in September, still without a completed script to his credit. A year later, though, and infatuated with a nineteen-year-old Wellesley College coed, he again contemplated a trip to the west coast. He wrote to Scott Fitzgerald: "Barbara and I are most likely to get wed the minute I sign a Hollywood contract. I have no money and her family are against me, so I'll take the Hollywood thing and will work at it until we have a good stake, then we will leave there."[37] Neither the marriage nor the Hollywood assignment materialized, but O'Hara continued to consider Hollywood as the easiest solution to his chronic financial problems. In 1936, while reviewing his career options with Charles Pearce, Harcourt Brace's respected editor, he confided "I may do some movie work for the quick touch."[38] Later that year he accepted a writing assignment from Sam Goldwyn, and reassured his publisher that, once again, he had taken the job strictly for the money.[39] O'Hara went to Hollywood on similar short assignments throughout the late thirties and early forties, always hoping to strike it rich, but never quite catching on with the studios.

There were some writers who did have non-financial reasons for seeking Hollywood employment. Zoe Akins, for example, after many years as a successful playwright in New York, moved to California in 1928 hoping to cure her tuberculosis, and shortly thereafter began the first of many Hollywood contracts.[40] Scott Fitzgerald and S. N. Behrman arrived in Hollywood hoping to revive their careers after repeated failures in the East. William Faulkner's romance with Meta Carpenter in Hollywood may have been an added enticement to leave Oxford. Other writers went out of a mixture of curiosity and wanderlust, or to gather material for their serious work.[41] Yet O'Hara's letters are an accurate reflection of the extent to which, in the early thirties, the trip to Hollywood was primarily a financial expedition. This part of the Hollywood legend, at least, is accurate. But as we shall see, Hollywood money was not to be an ideal or easy solution to these writers' economic woes. It often caused more problems than it solved.

John O'Hara, 1930s
(Courtesy of the Library of Congress)

If writers agreed on the reason for going to Hollywood, the same cannot be said of their reaction to the landscape and culture they discovered in Los Angeles. Their impressions ranged from delight to disgust. Many writers, especially those who had been active in New York's literary society, found Los Angeles to be deadly dull. "This place is just like Asbury Park, New Jersey," Nathanael West informed Josephine Herbst upon arriving in Hollywood in 1933, "the same stucco houses, women in pajamas, delicatessen stores, etc. There is nothing to do, except tennis, golf, or the movies.... In other words, phooey on California."[42] But Dorothy Parker, one of New York's more celebrated bon vivants of the twenties, delighted in her new life and surroundings in Southern California. To Alexander Woollcott, she wrote enthusiastically:

> Aside from the work, which I hate like holy water, I love it here. There are any number of poops about, of course, but so are there in New York—or, as we call it, The Coast—and the weather's better here. I love having a house, I love its being pretty wherever you look, I love a big yard full of dogs.[43]

Finally, George Oppenheimer also savored the amenities of life in Los Angeles. After spending the twenties in New York as a playwright and publisher, Oppenheimer was hired by Samuel Goldwyn in the early thirties as a writer-production assistant. Admittedly star-struck, Oppenheimer was strongly attracted to Hollywood. In his autobiography, he recalled his excitement upon first arriving there:

> I loved it. Disillusion had not yet set in. It was, in fact, a long time coming. I was employed, free of debts, and moving in an ambience of glamor. Small wonder that I too was beglamored. From early youth I had been impressed by celebrities. Now I was living among them, not of them as yet, but with them.....I wanted Hollywood with all its rewards and its forfeits, its comfortable living and its mental comfort. I was hooked.[44]

This diversity of opinion about Southern California's ambience only confirms the study group's diversity of taste and temperament. Some felt confortable only with New York's pavement under their feet; others preferred the dust of a country road. Some were gregarious, others reclusive; some family-oriented, others notorious hedonists. That these individuals were writers didn't exempt them from other social identities and roles, much less the exigencies of personality. Moreover, because writers as a group are valued traditionally for their individuality, they are notorious iconoclasts. Ask a group of writers to describe the color of a turquoise stone and some will say it is blue, others green. Still others undoubtedly will see in it another color entirely. Their varied reactions to Los Angeles' landscape and culture, in short, are not surprising.

Given their wide range of personalities and temperaments, however, the degree to which these writers shared similar responses to the world of the studios *is* truly remarkable. Writers came to understand the workings of the studios and their own status and role in them in very much the same way. Once involved in the actual movie-making process they, like Benét, formed very strong and, on the whole, highly critical opinions of the studio system. Whether successful or not, whether their involvement in Hollywood was brief or prolonged, whether or not they continued to write in other mediums, these writers tended to categorize those with whom they worked, define their own position in the studios, and describe the functions of the studio system in much the same terms. This "writer's view" of the studio system cannot be taken as an accurate or objective description of the system; it is not how the studios *really* worked. Rather, it is evidence of the fundamental beliefs, attitudes, and values *shared by these writers* which determined the way they, *as writers,* viewed their world. Writers' reactions to the studio system, then, only make sense in light of the beliefs, attitudes, and values attendant to the identity of the "writer" that these individuals had learned in New York's literary marketplace, for it is the consistency with which writers judged Hollywood in terms of New York that seems the operant factor in their experiences in the studios. That their reaction, in the main, transcended the vagaries of personality further attests to the importance of their identities *as writers* to each of their complete self-images.

Simply put, the members of the study group arrived in Hollywood believing that they had been hired as writers. And, as we have seen in Chapter 1, being a writer to them meant acting as independent agents, with legal and creative control over their work. As such, writers were valued in New York for their individuality and creativity. They would quickly learn that in Hollywood the "writer" was defined not only differently, but diametrically so. The remainder of this chapter examines this "writer's view" of the studio system, and finds in it an explanation of why these authors, as a group, and despite the wide range of their actual experience in the studios, were disturbed, demoralized, and angered by their time spent on studio payrolls.

Social scientists speak of a given social structure as being the composite of many different social identities and the interaction of those identities.[45] For these Eastern writers, the most significant identity, other than their own, was that of the producer. Comments about producers, as individuals and as a class, fill the pages of authors' letters, articles, and contemporary journals. Directors, technicians, and actors—all important in the making of movies—merit only occasional references. Of the producers' standing within the studio system, writers had little doubt: they were the industry's elite. "Throughout Hollywood the caste system prevails," George Abbott once explained. "At the top, you find the producers, then the directors, then the important actors. Next come the writers and technicians.... The producers are about evenly divided between talented men and parasites."[46] "Very quickly I learned that the front office held all the cards in the studio game," Samuel Hoffenstein told an interviewer in 1940, "and that writers held none."[47] Similarly, George S. Kaufman held that "in spite of all the money they throw at us, we don't have any real standing in the studios. The producer is top dog."[48]

Writers' relationships with Hollywood's top dogs were rarely ones of mutual respect. The management ranks of the studios teemed with the kind of producer, Sidney Howard charged, "who is neither director nor writer and would like to be both."[49] Howard explained that such producers were like Australian Kiwis, who have wings but cannot fly. Other writers were even less charitable. Benét had characterized producers as "horned toads from the cloak and suit trade" and as "shanty Irish."[50] S. J. Perelman concluded that producers were "hoodlums of enormous wealth, the ethical sense of a pack of jackals, and taste so degraded that it befouled everything it touched."[51] Gene Fowler best captured the sense of these writers' attitudes toward producers when, in a letter to Ben Hecht, he reported:

> My brief contact with Mr. Zimbalist was funny. . . . It seems that when he announced to Louis B. Manure [sic] that I was being hired, that still-born version of the Pontifex Maximus sent out word that I was to come hat in hand. I came, but it was not my hat which was being gripped. I was asked if I had any "mental reservations" concerning producers. I replied that I had reservations "not only mental but also physical." This did not help my economic needs.[52]

Many producers, for their part, possessed a healthy animus toward the writers in their employ. Irving Thalberg's remark that writers were a "necessary evil" in the film industry was often cited by authors as evidence of the hostility of even the best producers. Samuel Marx, MGM's story editor, once explained of the producer-writer relationship:

> It was part of my job to see that these writers and their assignments were compatible, but in the eyes of one of the MGM executives I was not exactly suited to the job. In a story meeting one day, he gazed glumly at me and observed, "the trouble with our story editor is that he *likes* writers!"[53]

A story told to Lincoln Barnett of *Life* magazine by Charles Brackett and Billy Wilder illustrates perfectly the antagonism between writers and their producers:

> Several years ago Paramount, their alma mater, lent them to MGM for a special project. They were summoned into conference with Sidney Franklin, MGM's top executive producer, whose customary relationship with screen writers is somewhat less personal than that of a zoo curator with inmates of the small mammal house. Outlining the work at hand, Franklin would recurrently turn to Charlie Brackett and say, "Jack, would you lower that window," or addressing Billy Wilder he would command, "Steve, take your feet off that chair."

After a half hour of this treatment, Brackett rose to his feet. "Mr. Franklin," he said haughtily, "my name is Charles Brackett. I'm too old and too rich to put up with this sort of nonsense. If you call us once again by any other names than our own, we'll walk out that door and never come back." The fact that MGM dispensed with their services three days later did not dim the luster of the moment.[54]

If writers quickly determined that producers enjoyed the most status in Hollywood, it did not take them much longer to decide who possessed the least. Despite the fact that thousands of extras, laborers, and technicians were virtual ciphers on the studio lots, and were paid accordingly, in the eyes of Eastern writers only they themselves occupied the bottom rung of the Hollywood status ladder. Comments to this effect lace their commentaries. John Dos Passos, for example, while recovering from rheumatic fever and his stint at Paramount, informed Scott Fitzgerald that, based on his limited observation of the studio system, "the screen writer is certainly a lamentable specimen."[55] Mildred Cram, a promising young writer hired by MGM in 1930, seconded Dos Passos's judgment. In an article written for *The American Spectator* four years after she reached Hollywood, she sadly concluded:

> There is no prestige attached to being an author in Hollywood. An author (of standing) in London, in Paris, even in New York, enjoys a certain distinction. He is acceptable. He is even desirable. His opinion is worth something. But when he reaches Hollywood, he finds himself curiously, unexpectedly anonymous. The arrival of Joan Crawford at the Metro-Goldwyn-Mayer studio in Culver City is an event. Her lavish car rolls through the gate, onto the lot. Bayard Veiller parks across the street, in Charles Bickford's service station. I may be wrong, but I do not recall ever having seen an author's car within the sacred precincts. I believe the gateman would slam the iron portals in Vicki Baum's face. But Shearer and Garbo are of the elect. So, even, is Jimmie Durante.... The author is the most unimportant cog in the Hollywood wheel.[56]

It did not take Budd Schulberg four years as a screenwriter to come to the same conclusion. "Since I had been brought up in the place," Schulberg has written, "I had no illusions about it. I had learned from intelligent producers like Irving Thalberg, David Selznick, and my father that even the wisest of them looked upon the screenwriter as low man on the totem pole."[57] A celebrated exchange between William Faulkner and Clark Gable illustrates Cram's point concerning writers' anonymity in the movie community. It was the habit of Faulkner and Howard Hawks to go hunting whenever they could break away from the studio. On one such trip they were accompanied by Clark Gable, then at the height of his fame, who shared their passion for the outdoors. Driving to the Imperial Valley for some dove shooting, Hawks and Faulkner talked about contemporary literature. As Joseph Blotner reconstructs:

Rather than freezing, as he usually did when most people advanced literary gambits, Faulkner began to talk freely. Gable was silent for awhile but then manfully began to hold up his end of the conversation. "Mr. Faulkner," Hawks remembers his saying, "what do you think somebody should read if he wants to read the best living writers?" Faulkner answered, "Ernest Hemingway, Willa Cather, Thomas Mann, John Dos Passos, and William Faulkner." There was a moment's silence. "Oh," Gable said, recovering, "do you write?" "Yes, Mr. Gable," Faulkner replied. "What do you do?"[58]

There were constant reminders within the studio of the writer's inferior status. When Scott Fitzgerald arrived at MGM, for example, he noticed immediately that the doors to producers' offices were embellished with gold name plates. The names on writers' doors, on the other hand, were typed on removable slips of paper.[59] At Warner Brothers, Faulkner was installed in a corner room on the first floor of the Writers' Building. Faulkner's was one of six such tiny offices opening onto a secretarial pool, an arrangement derisively known as "The Ward" by Warners' contact writers.[60] While Gene Fowler and Ben Hecht were working at MGM, they were assigned to David Selznick's production unit, which enjoyed its own quarters in a separate building. Selznick "occupied the entire lower floor as befitted a movie producer of note," Hecht noted. "Fowler and I were shoe-horned into one of six upper floor offices as befitted movie writers of note."[61]

Discrimination against writers, Hecht and Fowler soon discovered, even extended to office furnishings. The two writers were surprised to find no couch in their office. "Inquiry of the studio's maintenance department," Hecht remembered, "revealed that MGM had a rule against placing couches in writers' offices." [62] Fowler complained to Major Everest, the man in charge of the studio's efficiency problems, and then reported to Hecht:

> "Major Everest explained the situation to me," said Fowler. "It is studio law that no writer may have a couch in his office. The major feels that at the sight of a couch in his office a writer would become overwrought with lewd thoughts and thus impair his maximum efficiency.... It's the goddamdest example of discrimination against literary men ever recorded. Every producer, director, and actor in the establishment is allowed a couch in his office on which to seduce any females he fancies, including the Seven Muses. But, by God, not writers! It makes one feel that literature was an art practiced only by black men in Alabama.[63]

Writers believed that they received such second-class treatment even on those rare occasions when they accompanied film crews on location. The most famous example of this occurred when Budd Schulberg and Scott Fitzgerald made their trip to Dartmouth College with Walter Wanger's production unit to shoot location footage for *Winter Carnival*. The entire crew checked into the cozy Hanover Inn; the two writers, though, discovered that Wanger had made no reservations for them. Instead, they were led to an unheated attic room with a double-decker cot—"a perfect symbol of the writer's status in Hollywood," Schulberg remembers Fitzgerald muttering.[64]

Similarly, Donald Ogden Stewart rudely learned that all would not be as in New York for the writer when he realized that at formal dinners in Hollywood, one was seated "according to importance at the box office. Writers, if invited at all, sat at the bottom of the table, below the heads of publicity but above the hairdressers."[65]

Nowhere were studio hierarchies more evident than in their commissaries. Daniel Fuchs, who kept a fanciful diary during his stint at RKO in 1938, recorded that the studio's other contract writers introduced him to the ritual of lunch at the commissary:

> They pick me up at twelve for lunch at the commissary, where we all eat at the "round table." That is, the lesser writers($100-$500) eat at a large round table. The intermediates ($500-$750) eat privately or off the lot. The big shots eat at the executives' table along with top-flight stars and producers. They shoot crap with their meals.[66]

W. R. Burnett, who worked at many of the studios in the thirties, confirmed the impressions of Fuchs and Wilder: "The commissaries all worked pretty much the same way. The $500 writers at one table, the $2,000 ones somewhere else. The producers ate off by themselves. No one said a word, but everybody knew where to sit."[67]

George Abbott worked as both a writer and a producer at the Fox studio, and thus experienced commissary lunches from both perspectives. Abbott described in his autobiography a hypothetical lunch at the executives' table, revealing the importance placed on status in the studios. After waiting through the morning for a conference with "Mr. Big," an important producer, Abbott imagined:

> word comes that Mr. Big is going to be tied up with some men from the New York office until three o'clock, but that you are invited to have lunch in the executive dining room—that is, if you are a producer or a director you are so invited. If you happen to be an actor you are not, and if you should be someone as low as a writer, you have no chance at all....
>
> In the executive dining room, the talk in your honor may turn politely to the legitimate theatre of New York City, but it soon veers back to the one topic of interest to them all: pictures, past and present. Sometimes baseball or prizefights creep into the conversation, or motor cars, or stock prices—and, of course, broads. After a while, Mr. Big comes in, flanked by two or three assistants. He takes his place at the head of the table and presides after his own fashion. He may be the type of man who has whispered conferences, but he is more likely to relax and direct the conversation at will. If he tells a story, everyone listens; if he makes a joke, everyone laughs. Just to keep a veneer of democracy, a reckless fellow will argue with him, or even make a joke at his expense. But Mr. Big is clearly the king and everyone at the table automatically becomes a yes-man.[68]

A person's status was so obvious in the commissaries that dining there often was a painful experience for the lesser writers on the lot. Lillian Hellman, for one, travelled to Hollywood in 1930 when her husband, playwright Arthur Kober, was hired by MGM. Kober arranged for his wife to work as a reader on the MGM lot. Later Hellman was to have one of the most envied writing contracts in the film industry, but during this period she was very much aware of her low rank in the studio hierarchy, and nowhere more painfully than in the commissary. To avoid its humiliations, she even resorted to eating on a bench in the studio's back lot:

> It was not a good place to eat lunch, but it was better than going to the studio commissary where I had to pass a large table for famous directors and writers, some of whom knew my husband and thus had to make the kind of half-bow, acknowledged in all worlds where classes are sharply marked to mean you are above the ordinary but not enough above it to include you in the circle.[69]

In the commissaries, then, writers learned what they came to feel was the governing principle of studio life: status and prestige in any occupation were not a function of talent, ability, training, or experience; rather, they were based on the sizes of the weekly paycheck. Only those writers with healthy salaries commanded attention. Almost every writer, large paycheck or small, understood this and resented it. "In this town," a writer told Leo Rosten, "I'm snubbed because I only get a thousand a week. It hurts."[70] Daniel Fuchs's diary reveals how he learned of this principle. Fuchs wrote a screenplay for a fictional RKO producer he called Kolb, who immediately rejected it and assigned him to another producer. Fuchs asked his agent to find out why this had happened. The next day Himmer, the agent, dropped by with an explanation: "See, what it was was this: when Kolb came to put you on his budget he called up to find out what your salary was. That's how he found out you get two hundred." "So?," Fuchs asked. "So. Kolb figures he deserves the best writers on the lot. He told them he wouldn't put up with any two-hundred-dollar trash. It's a natural reaction."[71]

Fuchs, as "two-hundred-dollar trash," was still a leg up on some studio writers. According to the writers themselves, there were three basic strata of writers in Hollywood: Fuchs's salary placed him at the bottom of the highest, or *contract writer,* category. The *reader* was the most menial of the three classes. Only Lillian Hellman and Budd Schulberg of the study group actually worked in this capacity. Hellman, who worked for a year as a reader on the MGM lot courtesy of her husband's influence, recorded in *An Unfinished Woman* what that job entailed:

> In order to get the job you had to read two languages—or pretend that you did—and you had to write the kind of idiot-simple report that Louis Mayer's professional lady story-teller

could make even more simple when she told it to Mr. Mayer.... Twelve men and two women sat in a large room in a rickety building on stilts, and every small tremor—and California had a number of tremors that year—sent the building atilt. When you finished a manuscript (you were expected to read at least two a day) you went into another large room and waited your turn for one of the half-broken typewriters. It was said that if your reports showed signs of promise you would be promoted to what was called a junior writer position, but after that I don't know what became of you because I never was promoted.[72]

Budd Schulberg actually *was* promoted. Schulberg's first job upon returning home after graduating from Dartmouth was as a reader for David Selznick. He was paid $25 a week, standard for the position, "to read on the average of one novel a day and write a twenty-page synopsis of the plot, sketching in characters and main situations."[73] Schulberg advanced to junior writer after he did some work which pleased Selznick on the script of *A Star is Born*. With the promotion went a raise to fifty dollars a week, increasing in steps through the length of a five-year contract. In an article about motion-picture writing published about the same time, Sidney Howard criticized Hollywood's habit of hiring junior, or "younger," writers as he called them: "Every studio has on its payroll a group of so-called 'younger writers,' ranging in age from eighteen to sixty, who draw very small salaries, sit in very small offices and, because they have not acquired a thing known in Hollywood as 'prestige,' waste their lives in the process of being 'broken in'."[74] Schulberg experienced first-hand the treatment Howard described. "The trouble is," he groaned, "that when they hire you as a junior writer they rate you as kind of excess baggage—you are supposed to sit around and mature and nobody fancies the idea of letting you work with them."[75]

Schulberg worked as a junior writer for six months, to his increasing frustration. He submitted a number of scripts, all of which were immediately shelved. Finally he approached Selznick, an old family friend, and asked out of his contract. Their encounter clearly supports the belief of the writers that even in the eyes of Hollywood's most literate producers, writing seemed a second-class occupation:

I sent David a note asking him as a personal favor *not* to pick up my option. At last, after long hours of "standing by," I was ushered into his spacious Colonial office. David was at the height of his fame and power then, a sort of latter-day Thalberg. My note had bruised his feelings and he grumbled that he was pretty disappointed in me. I grumbled back, with the license of having known him since childhood, that I was pretty disappointed in him, too: all those months of writing scripts for the shelf without so much as a kind word from him! "I realize we've carried you on the roster as a writer," Selznick acknowledged, "but frankly I think you've shown damn little initiative. Why, when I was your age and working for your father I flooded B. P. with memos, memos on casting, memos on story purchases, on cutting costs, on judicious cuts after previews—all day long I kept feeding him memos. I must've written over a thousand. But you, I don't think you've sent me two memos since you've been here."

"Sure, David," I said, "but the difference is you were practicing to become a producer. I want to be a writer."

"Yes, I know," David Selznick said, his voice dulled with disappointment. "You told me you wanted to be a writer. But I felt if I kept you with me long enough sooner or later your producer's blood would begin to assert itself."[76]

Selznick grudgingly granted the young writer his release. Other than Schulberg, the only writer of those I studied closely to be hired as a junior writer was William Faulkner, but that was by Warner Brothers in the 1940s. All others were hired as contract writers, although at widely varying salaries. As they learned in the commissary, though, not all contract writers were treated equally. Segregation according to salary was an unwritten code in the studios. In Hollywood, you were what you were paid. According to Lillian Hellman, the effects of this code were felt even outside the studio walls. When in Hollywood with her husband, she reports:

We had pleasant evenings with our best friends, Laura and Sidney Perelman and Laura's brother Nathanael West. The five of us, and a few others, stayed close together not only because we liked each other but because we were in what was called "the same salary bracket." Then, and probably now, if you were a writer who earned five hundred dollars a week you didn't see much of those who earned fifteen hundred dollars a week.[77]

F. Scott Fitzgerald, in the notes for his novel about Hollywood, *The Last Tycoon*, conceived the following pay scale for screenwriters:

Junior Writers	300 [dollars a week]
Minor Poets	500
Broken Novelists	850-1000
One Play Dramatists	1500
Sucks	2000
Wits	2500 [78]

Dudley Nichols, the ex-newspaperman who was one of Hollywood's highest paid writers, complained as bitterly as anyone in the industry about the practice of pegging prestige to salary. He told a reporter in 1937: "You have to be blind not to notice within a week's time that everyone accepts the dollar sign as the only indicator of a writer's worth. It's a pernicious notion. But you can't ignore it or pretend that the system doesn't work that way."[79] "There was a general feeling" among producers, Donald Ogden Stewart, another successful screenwriter, decided, "that the more money they'd spent the better it (a script) must be."[80] Finally, this comment from Nunnally Johnson succinctly summarizes the Eastern writers' belief that the money standard was all-pervasive in the studios: "I hadn't been in Hollywood more than two weeks before I noticed that I wasn't considered a writer, but a $300 a week writer. That was alright, but I quickly learned that nobody thought much of $300 a week writers."[81]

In sum, Eastern writers felt that producers not worthy of their respect governed the studios. A caste system, with these producers at the top and writers at the bottom, dominated the studio system. Even a lower-level producer enjoyed more prestige, these writers decided, than they did. Within each occupational group prestige appeared to be solely a function of salary. Yet whether a writer made $200 or $2000 a week, he remained a writer and therefore a second-class citizen in the studio community. As screenwriter Lester Cole later said, writers believed that they were regarded as "the niggers of the studio system" by studio executives.[82] Office space and the commissary ritual were merely two of the most obvious, and ultimately superficial, manifestations of the low esteem in which writers, even highly paid writers, were held.

Writers' irritation with these manifestations of Hollywood's perverse status-consciousness and their obsession with money as a sole indicator of value, however, were minor compared to their displeasure with its method of movie making. In particular, writers complained bitterly about the role assigned to them in that process. Their observations of Hollywood's system of film production cluster in three basic areas: the story conference; the practice of collaboration and team writing; and the granting of on-screen credit. In each of these areas writers' frustrations and complaints often focused on their relationships with movie producers.

To a man, writers echoed Benét's lament that "a story isn't a story but a conference." The incessant holding of meetings where producers picked apart the writers' work annoyed the latter to no end. As Robert Sklar pointed out, the story conference was the producer's principal instrument of control over the content of the movies he made. Writers were well aware of this fact and resented it. Most writers felt that the great number of conferences served no useful purpose in the scripting process, as a sampling of their remarks suggests. Sidney Howard, for one, decided by the mid-thirties that too many producers operated "without the wisdom to see that another man's way of telling a story may be as good as their own. Their determination to get their picture script written and rewritten until it coincides exactly with their own conception is more likely to choke out the last germs of spontaneity and life."[83] Ben Hecht recalled that "as a writer in Hollywood I spent more time arguing than writing. My chief memory of movieland is one of asking in the producer's office why I must damage the script, eviscerate it, cripple and hamstring it? Why must I strip the hero of his few semi-intelligent remarks and why must I tack on a corny ending that makes the stomach shudder? Half of all the movie writers argue in this fashion."[84] Samuel Hoffenstein, responding to a reporter's question, best summed up Eastern writers' attitudes toward the story conference: "What's wrong with the movies? It's simple— the story conference."[85]

Nothing so demoralized writers as the constant, and to their mind unnecessary, revisions ordered by producers in these meetings. Benét, we recall, had written of United Artists: "Since arriving I have written 4 versions of *Abraham Lincoln,* including a good one, playable in the required time. That, of course, is out. Seven people, including myself, are now working in conferences on a 5th one which promises hopefully to be the worst yet."[86] "Writers had a saying in those days," W. R. Burnett later recalled, "'A script is never written, only rewriten.'"[87] Sidney Buchman, who experienced conferences from both ends of the table as a writer and then producer for Harry Cohn at Columbia, admitted to a reporter in 1938: "Meetings are essential if the producer has the good sense to work with the writers and guide them, not control them. But more often than not they're no more than an excuse for the producer to throw around his weight—and, I might add, show off his stupidity. I know a lot of writers who don't sleep very well the night before a conference. I sympathize—I did my own share of thrashing around."[88]

Writers also constantly complained about producers' vacillations concerning story direction. They would be able to satisfy producers, writers felt, if only the producers could decide what they wanted. Dorothy Parker's comments in a letter to Alexander Woollcott, are only partially facetious:

> We are summoned to labor on a story of which we were told only, "Now we don't know yet whether the male lead will be played by Tullio Carminati or Bing Crosby. So just write it with both of them in mind." Before that, we were assigned the task of taking the sex out of "Sailor, Beware." They read our script, and went back to the original version. The catch for the movies, it seemed, was that hinge of the plot where the sailor bets he will make the girl. They said that was dirty. But would they accept our change, that triumph of ingenuity where the sailor just bets he will make another sailor? Oh, no. Sometimes I think they don't know *what* they want.[89]

Another aspect of these writers' dislike of the story conference strikes at the heart of their contempt for producers. Soon after arriving at the studio gate, many writers were shocked to learn that most producers didn't read; hence their reliance on conferences. Writing well, authors decided, was less important than the ability to talk up a storm. Sidney Howard described the producers' aversion to the written word more diplomatically than most of his colleagues:

> The first story conference is an essential milepost in the screen writer's contribution to the making of a picture. It is then that he tells the producer and the director the story of the picture which the one is to produce and the other to direct. I have often thought that this contribution is the most important function that he has to perform, because directors and producers are notably reluctant readers.[90]

Sidney Howard, 1930s
(*The Billy Rose Theatre Collection, New York Public Library*)

Howard betrayed a tinge more sarcasm, though, in the same article when he suggested that "most picture executives are *busy, busy* men who would not be given to reading under any conditions."[91] Still, George S. Kaufman's characterization of producers as "on the whole, a ruck of illiterate idiots" better represents the collective opinion of those writers.[92]

This attitude was based at least in part on the Hollywood policy of using synopses and short outlines of story material so that producers would not have to read the originals in their entirety—be they books, plays, or scripts. Writing these synopses was the job of the studios' readers, including at one point Lillian Hellman. Budd Schulberg remarked of this practice that his father was "one of the few, if not the only, tycoon who preferred books to synopses."[93] MGM went so far as to hire someone (Hellman's "professional lady storyteller") whose sole function was to read aloud to the studio's producers the essentials of the synopses supplied by the readers—a practice writers looked upon with a mixture of horror and amusement.

When James M. Cain reached Hollywood in 1931, he was shocked to find that even the story editor at Paramount, Percy Heath, had not read any of his work. Cain thought it absurd that a studio would hire someone without the slightest knowledge of his talents.[94] Daniel Fuchs devoted two entire entries in his diary to one example of just this indifference to the written word:

May 24—
Barry, front-office man, sent me to another producer, Marc Wilde, who gave me the full shooting script of "Dark Island," which was made in 1926 as a silent picture. "My thought," said Wilde, "is to shoot the story in a talking version. However, before I put you to work on it, I want to find out what you think of it, whether you care to work on it, et cetera. So read it."

May 25—
I didn't like "Dark Island" at all, but I didn't want to antagonize Wilde by being too outspoken. I asked him what *he* thought of it. "Me?" Wilde asked. "Why ask me? I haven't read the script."[95]

A great deal of vitriol vented by writers toward producers, in fact, centered on just such examples of producers' ignorance. Writers grew fond of trading stories and barbs about their producer's philistinism. Some comments, like Benét's reference to the horned toads from the cloak and suit trade and the shanty Irish, were tinged with malice and often blatantly prejudicial. Others were less offensive but no less pointed. Typical is a story told by S. N. Behrman in a letter to Alexander Woollcott. Behrman had been working on an adaptation of *Liliom* at the Fox studio, where his producer was Sol Wurtzel, a charmingly forthright if unsophisticated man whom Woollcott had known in New York. "I must tell you my new Sol Wurtzel," Behrman wrote Woollcott. While driving back from Palm Springs with the producer after listening to some new Gershwin songs, Behrman remarked that he thought Ira a clever lyricist. He gave as an example the lines: "I'm reading Heine/You somewhere in China." "That's no good," Wurtzel had said. "I inquired why not," Behrman related, "'Because,' he shouted, 'it brings up a picture of a fellow with glasses reading a book and it kills the romance!'"[96]

Finally, W. R. Burnett's experience while working on *The Finger Points* at Warner Brothers illustrates perfectly the conclusion most writers drew from their hours in story conferences. It also suggests the way in which some writers learned to cope with the system:

> Little by little I learned how to work in the picture business. Johnny Monk Saunders and I—I was drawing a thousand a week and he was drawing more than that—we sat there for three weeks and we never talked about the picture once. I began to get nervous, so I finally said to Johnny, "What are we supposed to be doing here?" He said, "Don't worry about it," and we talked for another week about nothing. So the next week—Monday—we get a call from the producers: "Come in you guys and tell us what you've got." And I thought, "Goodbye, there goes the job." But Johnny said, "No. Don't do anything." Meanwhile apparently he'd been thinking while we were just horsing around. And he said, "When we go in you don't say anything, just sit there and nod, or say 'okay, that's good Johnny, yeah, that's right'." We went in and he told them a rough outline of the picture, and they said, "Fine boys, go to work!"
>
> That's how I learned how you manipulate things in Hollywood—it's mostly talk. You have to be a good talker and a good salesman. It doesn't matter how well you write.[97]

An additional irony for writers was some producers' obsession with the speed with which their authors worked. Despite the innumerable story conferences called by producers and the interminable delays they engendered, and despite the long periods during which contract writers waited to be assigned to projects, many writers felt pressured to work quickly. Speed was the cardinal virtue in the studios. One of the main reasons there was any interest in William Faulkner's service after his initial debacle at MGM, for instance, was that he could produce scripts rapidly, often writing an entire draft in less than two weeks.[98] Fitzgerald, on the other hand, suffered because of his reputation as a slow worker. S. N. Behrman happened across a "Writers Available" memorandum one day while on the MGM lot in the late thirties:

> It was a macabre list: playwrights who had written one success twenty years ago and had not been heard from since; novelists whose novels you could not remember. But I saw one name that gave me a turn—Scott Fitzgerald. It made me angry. To be on a list of the available in Hollywood was to be on a deathlist. When Bernie [Bernard Hyman, a producer at MGM] came in I let him have it on Scott. "He's easily one of our greatest writers," I said. "Maybe he is," said Bernie, unruffled, "but he's slow." I expressed myself on Scott to other producers. I got the same reaction from all of them, that he was slow.[99]

Mildred Cram's introduction to screen writing and the necessity of speed was much the same as many other Eastern writers. Hired by MGM to adapt one of her short stories, she reached Hollywood unschooled in the techniques of screen writing. Upon first entering MGM, she recalled:

> I was presented to the general supervisor, or associate producer, who was to be responsible for the production. Across his desk were to pass the myriad details of casting, direction, sets, costumes, sound, photography, publicity. He was a taciturn terrifically busy executive. Very charming. Scrupulously polite, ironic, and fundamentally, suspicious. He had never heard of me, and distrusted my ability. It never occurred to him to apprentice me for a few days to a seasoned and expert screen writer. I was told, simply, to *hurry, hurry.* [100]

Thus the biggest contradiction (and to many writers, hypocrisy) of studio life: delays caused by producers' caprices were tolerated, but writer-caused delays were not. While writers constantly griped about the time wasted while they waited for assignments or for producers to pass judgment on their scripts, writers also complained that they were expected to create with mechanical regularity and speed. "There's no fooling around here," Nathanael West informed Josephine Herbst of his duties at Columbia in 1933. "All the writers sit in cells in a row and the minute a typewriter stops someone pokes his head in the door to see if you are thinking."[101] Writing under such handicaps, Ben Hecht decided, especially writing under the pressure of deadlines and the hot breaths of producers, was normal procedure.[102] Writers who met deadlines found themselves in demand; those who didn't found their names, like Fitzgerald's, quickly placed on "Writers Available" lists.

A second studio practice which writers detested was that of enforced collaboration. As I noted in Chapter 3, not all writers objected to collaboration as such; many worked voluntarily with a sympathetic partner. What raised writers' ire was compulsory collaboration, which in Hollywood took two basic forms: the assigning of partners to work together on the same script; and what came to be known as the Thalberg system, the assigning of the same script to a number of writers for successive revisions. That two writers would sometimes be given the same script to work on simultaneously, but without either knowing it, is confirmed by John Dos Passos. "It turns out," Dos Passos revealed to Edmund Wilson, "that all the while [he was writing] a young man, whose name I believe is Nertz, was writing the real screenplay behind the scenes,"[103] Scripts were not written in Hollywood, as Burnett recalled, but rewritten. Some studios used team writing more than others. Writers considered MGM the worst offender in this regard, followed closely by Paramount and Twentieth Century-Fox; constant rewriting was less the rule at Warner Brothers and Columbia. Still, it was rare for any film at any studio to be the sole work of one author or a regular team. Collaboration was the industry norm, and a norm despised by Hollywood's Eastern writers. "It was like laying linoleum," despaired Budd Schulberg, "different people working on different little squares."[104] While many producers judiciously used writers in teams, others seemed to think that the more writers who worked on a script the better it would be. Nunnally Johnson, for example, remembers one producer at Paramount, Harold Hurley, who habitually assigned different writers to *each* character in a story.[105]

The rationale behind this practice was that it promoted efficiency and used the special talents of each writer to enhance the total effect of a film—the whole being more than the sum of its parts. Writers disagreed with both of these premises. Rather, writers argued, team writing sprang from the producers' compulsive need to dominate the scripting process. As Sidney Howard observed, "This [collaboration] not only wastes untold quantities of money— such producers have more than once spent close to a half a million dollars in screen writers' salaries—but deprives the finished picture of any homogeniety of style."[106]

Producers often paired Eastern writers with more experienced studio hands, as in the case of W. R. Burnett's work with John Monk Saunders on *The Finger Points.* Few collaborations, though, worked as well. Writers more often complained that they were teamed with studio hacks of little talent or sensibility. Samson Raphaelson quickly determined when he arrived in Hollywood in 1930 that "your standing with other writers from back East depended almost entirely on how little interference you suffered at the hands of the hacks."[107]

Writers also came to dread the moment when a producer assigned them partners to help "polish" the scripts they had written alone. More often than not, such a "polish" involved complete rewriting. This, for example, happened to Scott Fitzgerald at MGM, where he had written what he thought was a fine adaptation of Remarque's *Three Comrades* for Joseph Mankiewicz. Mankiewicz read Fitzgerald's script and then assigned a studio veteran, Ted Paramore, to help Fitzgerald revise it. The two men worked together for the better part of a week, with Paramore making suggestion after suggestion for extensive revision much to Fitzgerald's increasing annoyance. Finally, he dashed off an angry letter to his collaborator spelling out his objections in detail. One of the more revealing documents concerning Eastern writers' problems with collaboration, it is worth quoting at length:

> Dear Ted:
>   I'd intended to go into this Friday but time was too short. Also, hating controversy, I've decided after all to write it. At all events, it must be discussed now.
>   . . . I totally disagree with you as to the terms of our collaboration. We got off to a bad start and I think you are under certain misapprehensions founded more on my state of mind and body last Friday than upon the real situation. My script is in a general way approved of. There was not any question of taking it out of my hands—as in the case of Sheriff. The

question was who I wanted to work with me on it and for how long. *That was the entire question* and it is not materially changed because I was temporarily off my balance.

At what point you decided you wanted to take the whole course of things in hand—whether because of that day or because when you read my script you liked it much less than Joe or the people in his office—where that point was I don't know. But it was apparent Saturday that you had and it is with my facilities quite clear and alert that I tell you *I prefer to keep* the responsibility for the script as a whole.... About the whores [one of Paramore's changes] again it is a feeling, but, in spite of your current underestimation of my abilities, I think you would be over-stepping your functions if you make a conference-room point of such a matter.

Point after point has become a matter you are going to "take to Joe," more inessential details than I bothered him with in two months. What I want to take to Joe is simply this—the assurance that we can finish the script in three weeks more—you've had a full week to find your way around it—and the assurance that we are in agreement on the main points....

But, Ted, when you blandly informed me yesterday that you were going to write the whole thing over yourself, kindly including my best scenes, I knew we had to have this out.... If you were called on this job in the capacity of complete rewriter then I'm getting deaf. I want to reconceive and rewrite my share of the weak scenes and I want your help but I am not going to spend hours of time and talent arguing with you.... I didn't write four out of four best sellers or a hundred and fifty top-priced short stories out of the mind of a temperamental child without taste or judgement.

This letter is sharp but a discussion might become more heated and less logical. Your job is to help me, not hinder me. Perhaps you'd let me know before we see Joe whether it is possible for us to get together on this.[108]

Fitzgerald and Paramore continued their uneasy alliance for another month, and then submitted their revisions to Mankiewicz. To Fitzgerald's horror, the producer then rewrote it himself. In the process, Fitzgerald believed, the last vestige of his once-fine script was obliterated. In a famous letter to Mankiewicz, the demoralized author wrote:

Well, I read the last part [of the script] and I feel like a good many writers must have felt in the past. I gave you a drawing and you simply took a box of chalk and touched it up. Pat has now become a sentimental girl from Brooklyn, and I guess all these years I've been kidding myself about being a good writer.... To say I'm disillusioned is putting it mildly. For nineteen years, with two years out for sickness, I've written best selling entertainment, and my dialogue is supposedly right up at the top. But I learn from your script that you've suddenly decided that it isn't good dialogue and you can take a few hours off and do much better.[109]

Fitzgerald then catalogued a number of script changes made by Mankiewicz, and detailed his objections to them. In conclusion, he pleaded:

My only hope is that you will *have a moment of clear thinking*. That you'll ask some intelligent and disinterested person to look at the two scripts. Some honest thinking would be much more valuable to the enterprise right now than the effort to convince people you've improved it. I am utterly miserable at seeing months of work and thought negated in one hasty week. I hope you're big enough to take this letter as it's meant—a desperate plea to restore the dialogue to its former quality—to put back the flower cart, the piano-moving, the balcony, the manicure girl—all those touches which were both natural and new. Oh, Joe, can't producers ever be wrong? I'm a good writer—honest. I thought you were going to play fair. Joan Crawford might as well play the part now, for the thing is as groggy with sentimentality as *The Bride Wore Red,* but the true emotion is gone.[110]

Mankiewicz did not restore the cuts, and the film was shot from the producer's revised script. Ironically, Fitzgerald received his only screen credit for the movie. Fitzgerald scholars and film historians have debated the merits of Mankiewicz's changes for years. These two letters, though, do confirm the truth of Budd Schulberg's statement that "it was because he [Fitzgerald] cared about the scripts he had worked on at MGM...that he suffered when those scripts were wrenched away from him and rewritten by producers and writers he considered his inferiors."[111] Moreover, whether or not such rewriting was in fact justified, these letters do capture vividly the frustrations *felt* by Eastern writers when their work was rewritten. Fitzgerald's troubles with Mankiewicz and Paramore became an oft-told tale among writers in Hollywood. Ben Hecht's version, for instance, clearly reveals his sympathies:

Scotty had toiled on a movie script for four months in the studio. He handed it in proudly to his boss, who had never written anything, had not even sold a he-and-she joke to a newspaper, but fancied himself a writer. He redictated the Fitzgerald script in two days, using four stenographers. He changed all the dialogue.[112]

Fitzgerald's troubles with Mankiewicz were only the most well publicized of many such conflicts. Another incident prompted Nunnally Johnson to express his dissatisfaction with "writing by committee" in a letter to Edgar Watson Howe:

There's little satisfaction to be got out of movie writing. I'm really glad you got some entertainment out of the Chevalier picture, but I got next to none, nor any pride or satisfaction out of what came of my months of work. A collaboration between two people is bad enough in writing, but in the movies the collaboration is infinite. Everybody has an oar in it. Nobody's stuff is respected or considered, or, as it often happens, even read. The loudest-mouthed man is always the victor in any difference of opinion. It's dreadful.

And when the thing is finally produced, any one writer (whatever he may claim for professional reasons) knows in his heart that scarcely 10% was his. It's as if 15 cooks made a pan of biscuits; the best average anyone can claim is that he threw the salt in, or the baking powder. And against this unhappiness is the money needed for the 8 or 9 mouths I have to feed.[113]

Collaborations so enraged some writers that they actually refused to accept on-screen credit for their work. Maxwell Anderson, for instance, quit MGM in 1930 in disgust and returned to New York. He then sent the following instructions to his agent:

In regard to the money still due me from Metro, I won't quarrel with the extra day. If they say I quit on Monday, let them have their way. But as for the releases they want me to sign, I read these releases on the coast and refused to sign them because they were inaccurately stated. I'm willing to sign a general release of all work done at Metro, but I'm not willing to put my signature to a series of papers which state that I am the sole author, among other things, of "Trader Horn," "Cheri-Bibi," and God knows what.

I wish you to transmit these sentiments of mine to Mr. Hendricks and tell him that when he draws up reasonable releases, I'll put my name to them—and not before.[114]

Similarly, Clifford Odets, although he worked on more than a half-dozen scripts in the thirties, accepted credit for only one—*The General Died at Dawn.* "The others were rewritten for me after I left town by four or five hacks to each script," Odets told a reporter for the *New York Times* in the forties, "and rather than share credit for what they churned out between gin rummy games, I decided to pass up fame and keep my self-respect."[115]

Writers' frustrations often came to a head over just this issue of credit. Yet because in Hollywood, as Budd Schulberg observed, "they say that you are only as good as your last picture," writers were more concerned with acquiring credits than refusing them.[116] Before the advent of the Screen Writers Guild, a studio's producers determined who received such credit. It was a power often abused, to writers' way of thinking. Producers, writers charged, often gave themselves undeserved writing credit. Nunnally Johnson remembers that one producer at Paramount, Bernard Glazer, was credited as a writer on almost every movie he produced. "This happened so often," Johnson has said, "it made writers sore, and their first organization was to keep these Goddamned producers from putting their names on anything they chose to sign."[117] After writing a number of successful movies for Warner Brothers, W. R. Burnett's name gained some commercial value in the studio's eyes. Thus he soon found himself credited on movies for which he had not written a word:

They'd take my name and put it on a movie whether I wrote it or not. They could do anything. The producer puts his brother-in-law on the payroll. The next thing you know his brother-in-law's a writer, although he can't write at all. That was a wide-spread practice, putting people's names on who didn't deserve it, as well as credit stealing. Then the Writers Guild went in and they stopped it cold.[118]

As a general rule, more writers worked on any given script than could be credited, which had two unwelcome implications for writers. First, it meant that many writers could work for years without receiving credit, as had Fitzgerald before *Three Comrades.* Writers often worked on scripts which were promptly shelved, so that when they did work on one which finally reached the screen, and they were not credited, they were predictably furious. Second, those writers who worked on the first and intermediate drafts of a script most likely found their efforts uncredited. Charles Brackett formulated a simple rule about this phenomenon: "He who writes last gets credit."[119] This put writers in the unfamiliar, and uncomfortable position of competing against each other. They survived in this Darwinian world only by resorting to deviousness. Donald Ogden Stewart best described the kind of ploys writers were forced to use:

> In those days the first thing you had to learn as a writer if you wanted to get screen credit was to hold off until you knew they were going to start shooting. Then your agent would suggest you might be able to help. The producers had the theory that the more writers they had to work on the scripts the better they would be. It was the third or fourth writer that always got the screen credit. If you could possibly screw-up another writer's script, it wasn't beyond you to do that so your script would come through at the end.... It became a game to be the last one before they started shooting so that you would not be eased out of screen credit.[120]

Writers constantly complained that the system of granting credits was corrupt and counter-productive in that it insidiously pitted writer against writer. It was not until the Screen Writers Guild won recognition from the studios in 1941, however that a method for fairly arbitrating credit decisions came into being. Until that time writers continued to despise "the kind of hypocrisy and infighting," in the words of S. J. Perelman, "one had to practice in order to exist in the industry."[121]

Thus the writers' situation in Hollywood, as writers themselves perceived it, differed radically from that in New York. Writers were completely stripped of what I have termed their autonomy—their basic right of legal ownership and creative control of their work. Without this right, they were not writers in their own estimation, but rather hacks. At the root of the problem was the absolute power of the producer, which made the relationship of the writer and the producer, as Budd Schulberg pointed out, inherently unnatural: "When had writers—not willing hacks but *real writers*— hired out as indentured literary servants? For a writer to work not *with* someone, which is different but possible as we see in the theater, but *for* someone is to enter the slave quarters or the kindergarten."[122] The "real" writer possessed autonomy, hence it is not surprising that Eastern writers felt it impossible to be a "real" writer in Hollywood, where ownership rights were signed away on the dotted line and creative control lay in the producer's hands. Ben Hecht played a slight variation on this theme when he noted that "however cynical, overpaid, or inept you are, it is impossible to create entertainment without feeling the urges that haunt creative work." "The artist's ego," Hecht concluded, "even the ego of the Hollywood hack, must always jerk around a bit under restraint."[123]

Maxwell Anderson, in a letter to John Mason Brown, spoke to just this point. In Hollywood, Anderson complained, "the writer has *no control* whatever."[124] In an article written a few years later, Anderson expanded on the importance of this simple observation:

If you are a playwright and go to Hollywood, you discover that there are no authors in moving pictures. There are no authors because the picture companies own all the copyrights and are registered in Washington as the writers of the scripts turned out by the hired hands on the lot. They can change what you write and they will. After you've written your damnedest, they'll set seven galley slaves to work on it, singly and in groups, and by the time the product is ready for consumption it will taste like all the rest of the soup in all the other cans labeled with the trade-mark of your studio. A playwright on Broadway fails far oftener than he succeeds, but he's nobody's hired man. What he has written is his own and may be changed only with his consent.[125]

Thus writers' hostility to Hollywood hinged in large part on just this issue of autonomy. They also came to believe, though, that the vagaries of the studio system—the producer's arbitrary exercise of his power, the endless story conferences, and the obsession with team writing—prohibited writers from pressing into service just those individual creative gifts and abilities which made them writers in the first place. The studios did not value or appreciate individuality and creativity, writers believed, but rather demanded adherence to formula and convention. James M. Cain, for one, decided that to be successful in Hollywood a writer must park his talent and critical judgment alongside his car, outside the studio walls:

It is this, I think, that makes a writer sick at his stomach when he walks on a movie lot, causes him to feel that in some vague way he is a prostitute of the arts. It is not that he is jealous of the actor. It is not that he has highfalutin notions about the sanctity of writing compared with the other branches of the business. He gets off some nonsense to that effect, of course, and half believes it. But the trouble is not that. It is inherent in the business. Imagination is free or it is not free, and here it is not free. It serves the medium, instead of the medium serving it, and once that is felt, that is the end of pride, of joy in getting things down on paper, of having them appear in front of your eyes.[126]

Charles Brackett defined the writer's basic nature and his plight in Hollywood in much the same terms:

We write. The producer performs the editorial job. It's up to him to say on what sort of writing he will risk the company's investment. If there is a profound difference of opinion between writer and producer as to the direction a story should take, one of two things happens: the writer walks out, or the finished product stinks. For it happens to be a basic fact that a writer can't write decently against his profound convictions.[127]

Many writers came to believe that they were paid large salaries not to use their talent, but rather to suppress it. "The process by which the screen adaptor goes to work," Sidney Howard sadly concluded, "is in itself designed to cancel out inspiration."[128] In like manner, Scott Fitzgerald confessed to Maxwell Perkins after he was dropped by MGM in 1939 that he finally understood the essential paradox plaguing writers in the studios. "We brought you here for your individuality," Fitzgerald realized producers were saying, "but while you're here we insist that you do everything to conceal it."[129] Ben Hecht made the identical point when he reflected:

> I have always considered that half of the large sum paid me for writing a movie script was in payment for listening to the producer and obeying him. I am not being facetious. *The movies pay as much for obedience as for creative work.* An able writer is paid a larger sum than a man of small talent. But he is paid this added money *not* to use his superior talents.[130]

It is clear, then, that the identity of the "writer" Eastern authors had learned in New York ill-prepared them to understand—much less cope with—the studio system. Yet just this identity had become a fundamental aspect of each individual's self-image, and, as such, was not easily shaken. Moreover they judged the studios in terms of this identity. Working in Hollywood posed a severe threat to the traditional notion of what a "writer" was and did, and, in the process, threatened Eastern writers' beliefs that they were, indeed, "writers."

The strain was often acute. Mildred Cram was only half-joking when she observed in 1932, after just two years in Hollywood: "The unlucky ones—those who remain, who expose themselves over a period of years—become, eventually, quite mad. The Hollywod state of mind, at its best, ranks with the more important insanities: *dementia praecox,* dipsomania, *l'idée fixe,* neurasthenia, or any of the homocidal obsessions."[131] Robert Benchley, for one, fell prey to such despair. After spending most of the thirties in Hollywood, Benchley's frustration surfaced one night at a Garden of Allah party attended by Dorothy Parker, Scott Fitzgerald, Robert Sherwood, and a few other friends from New York. Pointing to Sherwood, whom he accused of staring at him pityingly, the normally placid Benchley screamed: "Those eyes! I can't stand those eyes looking at me and thinking of how he knew me when I was going to be a great writer! And he's thinking now look at what I am!"[132]

Benchley was not unique. Although writers often hid their despair behind a smokescreen of sarcasm and humor, as we have seen, their misery was palpable and widespread. For all of Faulkner's public demurrals that his Hollywood trips were merely financial godsends which did not affect him much one way or the other—statements that Hollywood's apologists quickly cite when discussing his career—his private letters reveal a far darker attitude toward the film industry. In 1937, as just one example, he wrote to his wife:

> Nothing has happened yet. As far as I know, I will be through at the studio Aug 15 and will start home sometime during that week, though according to my contract they can give me an assignment and hold me overtime until I finish it. I will let you know of course as soon as I know myself. It's hot here and I don't feel very good, but I think it's mostly being tired of the movies, worn out with them.[133]

Publicity Still of Robert Benchley in Hollywood, 1930s
(The Billy Rose Theatre Collection, New York Public Library)

During a later trip to Hollywood, and in an affecting letter to his agent, Harold Ober, Faulkner clearly expressed his ennui and beseeched Ober to find some way to get him off the Hollywood treadmill:

> I think I have had about all of Hollywood I can stand. I feel bad, depressed, dreadful sense of wasting time, I imagine most of the symptoms of some kind of blow-up or collapse. I may be able to come back later, but I think I will finish this present job and return home. Feeling as I do, I am actually becoming afraid to stay here much longer. For some time I have expected, at a certain age, to reach that period (in the early fifties) which most artists seem to reach where they admit at last that there is no solution to life and that it is not, and perhaps never was, worth the living. Before leaving here, I will try to make what contacts I can in hopes to do work at home, as this seems to be the easiest way I can earn money which I must have or at least think I must have. Meanwhile, have you anything in mind I might do, for some more or less certain revenue? My books have never sold, are out of print; the labor (the creation of my apocryphal county) of my life, even if I have a few things yet to add to it, will never make a living for me. I don't have enough sure judgement about trash to be able to write it with 50% success. Could I do some sort of editorial work, or some sort of hack-writing at home, where living won't cost me so much as now, where I support a divided family, that is myself here in hotels, etc., and a house at home whose expenses don't alter whether I am here or not.[134]

Benchley and Faulkner were not the only writers to suffer from *mal de Hollywood*. "I suppose I know fifty writers," declared James M. Cain in 1932, "and I don't know one who doesn't dislike movie work, and wish he could afford to quit."[135] But very few could afford to turn their backs on Hollywood. Nor was Hollywood money the "quick touch" O'Hara and many others had hoped it would be. For those whose contact with Hollywood was short-lived, the price-tag was not too steep, just a vague feeling that they had in some way cheapened themselves. This, for instance, was John Dos Passos's attitude, as expressed in a letter to Malcolm Cowley:

> I've said good-by to Paramount, so I feel very much better. It's not exactly anything to be unhappy about (except when you find all the money going to pay back debts) but its nothing to feel very good about either—it's like endorsing absorbine junior or Beauty mattresses.[136]

The emotional cost for other writers, like Benchley and Faulkner, was far greater. Writers came to feel that they were betraying their talent in two ways when they accepted Hollywood money. First, Hollywood work took them away from the writing that mattered most to them. As Faulkner, for one, informed his publisher, Hal Smith, who was waiting for the manuscript of *Requiem for a Nun:*

> I shall have to peg away at the novel slowly, since I am broke again, with two families to support now, since my father died, and so I shall have to write a short story every so often or go back to Hollywood which I don't want to do. They are flirting with me again, but if I make a nickle [sic] from time to time, I will give them the go-bye.[137]

Clifford Odets, for another, expressed the same sentiment in a letter to John Mason Brown written in 1935. After quarreling with Brown's review of *Paradise Lost,* Odets confessed:

> I don't think I would write this letter to you, except that it is near dawn and I'm feeling fairly low because I will shortly have to give four months of my life away to earn some money [in Hollywood] instead of working the notes here into a hot shouting play.[138]

Writers also came to feel that, in applying themselves to a medium for which they had little respect, they were denigrating their talent; it was "like playing a piano in a whorehouse," as S. J. Perelman described the feeling. Thus the idea that writers were prostituting their talent in Hollywood was not merely the invention of irate, movie-hating theater partisans in New York, as Hollywood's defenders often claim. "High salaries in the paradise of the west," Maxwell Anderson ruefully admitted, "are the mess of pottage for which independent artists who work in Hollywood must sell their birthright."[139] Eastern writers were fond of repeating Samuel Hoffenstein's pointed irony about their condition: "The movies: They tear you away from your home, draw you into a pigsty of people, make you do stuff that disgusts you, rip out all of your ambition of inventiveness, reduce you to a hack—and what do you get out of it? A fortune!"[140] This jest struck painfully close to home.

When Ben Hecht had been in Hollywood before the introduction of sound, he had often urged writer-friends in the East to join him in collecting Hollywood's large salaries which required so little effort. Hollywood seemed very much the goose laying golden eggs. But his experience in the thirties chastened him dramatically. Although hidden to him earlier, the cost of those fat paychecks in wounded egos, lost self-esteem and coopted values, was now all-too-painfully clear:

> I've written that it was easy money—and that's a misstatement if you examine the deed. Writing cheaply, writing falsely, writing with "less" than you have, is a painful thing. To betray belief is to feel sinful, guilty—and tastes bad. Nor is movie writing easier than good writing. It's just as hard to make a toilet seat as it is a castle window. But the view is different.[141]

In sum, Eastern writers found considerably more than they bargained for when they disembarked from the Super Chief at Los Angeles's Union Station. Those who expected to act as writers in Hollywood as they had in New York quickly discovered their sad mistake. Even those who held few illusions could not easily abandon their self-image as writers, so thoroughly learned in New York. For writers, Hollywood was New York turned topsy-turvy: instead of owning and controlling their work as independent economic agents, they found themselves employees, workers stripped of all proprietary rights; instead of their individuality and creativity being admired and rewarded, it was all too often prohibited or penalized; instead of editors, publishers and theatrical producers who acted as friends as well as business partners, they dealt with movie producers who were their absolute bosses in what was frequently an antagonistic relationship; and, finally, instead of receiving prestige because they were writers, they found themselves *denied* prestige because of their profession. The studio system, then, judged in terms of the world view of the New York literary marketplace, was an unmitigated disaster.

Gene Fowler is the kind of writer that Hollywood's defenders cite to refute the Hollywood-as-destroyer legend. He was an ex-newspaperman, accustomed to deadlines, rewrites, and other commercial demands; he wrote a number of fine movies in the thirties; he made a considerable amount of money as a screenwriter; and his best non-movie writing was done *after* he had begun working in the film industry. In short, he enjoyed great success in Hollywood and would appear to be a likely friendly witness on behalf of the film industry. Yet a letter from Fowler to a New York magazine editor, Burt MacBride, written in the late thirties, scarcely gives the impression of a happy man, contented in his work. MacBride asked Fowler's advice about coming to Hollywood and working for the movies. Fowler's reply, even discounting his usual hyperbolic, slighly profane prose, reveals a man deeply frustrated and angry at the writer's status in Hollywood:

> In your position as editor, you deal at least with a semi-literate public. In short, you and your colleagues are able to read, and it is conceivable that your subscribers pick out a word here and there. The situation is immeasurably different in Hollywood. The mumping hyenas who control this abysmal "industry" cannot read, write, nor converse intelligently. They throw all men's sprigs of laurel into a sort of witches' broth and give their public a Mickey Finn.... I am reminiscently aware that the glitter of Hollywood gold blinds us all at the beginning.... A woman raped by a Senegambian leper is much better off than the man who has yielded to the gilt phallus. Your well-seasoned editorial brain will be set upon by golden black-jacks, split infinitives, ten-cent suggestions and a superlative disregard for anything that resembles a constructive idea. A bogus chastity belt, studded with clichés, stolen ideas, claptrap formulae, will be riveted on you. A censorship that stinks like the seventeen streets of Jerusalem will oppress you until you swim in your own night sweats.... For Christ's sake, Burt, unless you are sentenced by a Federal judge to exile in this artificial paradise, keep on producing magazines. Kick Desire in the balls and stay reasonably content.[142]

In short, Fowler seconded Budd Schulberg's opinion that, all things considered, "the Hollywood system of using writers as assembly-line mechanics was colossally wasteful."[143] By the late thirties such complaints about the film industry were well known to the literary community nationwide. Like Fowler, most authors with Hollywood experience warned their fellow writers to stay away from the movies if at all possible. They admitted that they had not been able to change appreciably the studio system—the screenwriter's status and role remained much the same as a decade earlier. Nonetheless, the flow of writers westward continued unabated through the late thirties and into the forties.

Nor had writers' reactions upon first entering the studios changed much in the intervening years. Neither Southern California in general nor the studios in particular struck writers as hospitable. Most writers continued to feel lonely, out-of-place, frustrated in their work, and depressed generally by their new cultural and working milieu. Helen Deutsch's response is representative of those writers who first arrived in Hollywood in the early forties. Deutsch, a journalist and short story writer, had also served as the Group Theater's publicist for a time. In 1940, though, she found her income falling as she placed fewer and fewer of her stories with magazines. Against the advice of her friends in the Group who had worked in the movies, she signed a contract with MGM and left for the West Coast.

While in California she wrote freqently to Mab Maynard, a former Group Theater actress who had married Maxwell Anderson. Her letters were filled with talk of mutual friends, politics, and gossip. But most often she wrote of her work in the studios and reaction to Hollywood, echoing the complaints and concerns of Hollywood's post-sound literary recruits.

"I have been wined and dined and am having a very gay time," Deutsch apprised Maynard shortly after reaching California, "but I don't like the atmosphere of Hollywood—all the caginess, the competition, the gossip, the conversation all on one subject, and mediocrity spreading itself like the proverbial green bay tree."[144] Three months later she acknowledged the truth of the Andersons' warning: "This is a voice crying from the wilderness. You and Max are so right about Hollywood. However I am making money so I mustn't complain."[145] In the fall of 1940, suffering from the Eastern writer's most common malady—homesickness—she wrote Maynard that "last weekend I was so lonely and depressed I wanted to fly to New York and just quit everything here."[146]

In the spring of 1941 Maynard received a letter from Deutsch revealing that even though she was making steady progress up the Hollywood ladder, she found little satisfaction in her work. "I have done several radio shows," Deutsch informed her friend,

and I just finished a rewrite job on a Dietrich picture. I told them the stinking thing stank but they seemed to like it and I got a bonus in addition to my salary.... Why don't you come out here and spend a few weeks with me? I'm dying to see you. You're lucky to be living outside of New York. I hear the war is making things pretty awful there. Out here of course nothing registers very deeply on anybody; they just go on thinking that nothing is more important than the problems of whether she does or does not in reel five.

I met Sam Lauren, who told me about *his* first weeks in Hollywood. He was working on "The American Tragedy" [sic] and was ordered to find a way of justifying the murder that

Clyde commits—"in 300 feet." He was completely baffled until he met Arthur Kober who said it was easy. All you had to do was open the picture with a shot of Clyde as a baby being dropped on his head by his nurse. My favorite movie assignment to date, however, is an order to find a way for the boy and girl to "meet cute."[147]

That fall Deutsch became a full-time contract writer at MGM, and was also asked to do an original story in her spare time. For all the feverish activity these projects entailed, Deutsch was plagued with the by-then all-too-familiar Eastern writer's ennui: "I don't know why I bother really," she confided in November, "it isn't much fun."[148] Her mood further blackened when the Goldwyn studio hired her and then shunted her from script to script. "I still don't like Hollywood, or working in pictures," she wrote the Andersons:

At the moment I am working for Samuel Goldwyn. I was hired for a story about Washington, but one afternoon, as is his wont, Mr. Goldwyn fired the writers on the Lou Gehrig picture and before I knew it I was writing a baseball picture. Herman Mankiewicz was also on it, Dorothy Parker was writing one sequence and Alan Campbell, who they teamed with me on the Washington picture, was also on the Gehrig picture (but he very wisely got the flu the first day and is still at home). A few days ago I announced that I wanted to go back to the Washington story, as I was completely rattled and didn't know who was writing what.

I want to write for magazines again. I like writing and I hate politics. I have learned that writing in Hollywood is 80% politics.[149]

Deutsch's unhappiness in Hollywood and her dislike of its system of using writers, so manifest in these few letters, parallel uncannily Benét's thoughts written a decade earlier. But unlike Benét, she did not leave quickly. Despite her wish to return to her career as a fiction writer, Deutsch was to remain in Hollywood for several years before eventually finding her way back to New York.

Raymond Chandler, another author who first worked as a screenwriter in the forties, also clearly expressed what I have termed the writers' view of the studio system. By 1943, Chandler had authored four well-known mystery novels, two of which had been sold to the movies. In mid-year Paramount offered him a thirteen week contract at $750 a week, which the financially strapped author accepted. In the next two years Chandler collaborated with Billy Wilder on an adaptation of James M. Cain's *Double Indemnity,* which garnered an Academy Award nomination for Best Screenplay. Chandler also "polished" dialog on a number of half-completed scripts; he wrote an original screenplay, *The Blue Dahlia;* and he worked briefly on an adaptation of his novel, *The Lady in the Lake,* while on loan to MGM. Chandler received four screen credits for his two years' work, including a sole credit for *The Blue Dahlia.* His salary jumped to $1000 a week, with a guaranteed twenty-six weeks, employment each year for the length of a three-year contract.[150] To all outward appearances, he had met the challenge of screenwriting.

Yet Chandler was anything but satisfied with his work or the film industry. Wilder's patronizing attitude had irritated him. He bridled when directors cavalierly discarded the dialog he had laboriously "polished." An admittedly slow worker, he hated the pressure of deadlines, especially when his finished scripts then lay dormant for months. When his script for *The Lady in the Lake* was completed by another writer, Chandler considered it so embarrassingly bad that he refused to have his name associated with it.[151] As early as September 1944 Chandler had considered working up an article about writers in Hollywood. "There are some devastating things to be said on this subject," he informed the *Atlantic Monthly's* Charles Morton. "It is high time someone said them."[152]

"Writers in Hollywood," Chandler's thoughts on this subject, eventually appeared in the November 1945 issue of the *Atlantic*. They form a remarkably concise and cogent portrait of the studio system from the Eastern writers' perspective. While writers' perceptions of the film industry in the 1930s often appeared in bits and pieces, Chandler in the mid-forties crystalized their most salient observations and provided a coherent overview of Hollywood's ills as diagnosed by writers. As such it provides a splendid summary of the writers' view of the studio system, and, by implication, a declaration of the writers' traditional identity and prerogatives.

"The making of a picture," Chandler began, "ought to be a rather fascinating adventure. It is not; it is an endless contention of tawdry egos, some of them powerful, almost all of them vociferous, and almost none of them capable of anything much more creative than credit-stealing and self-promotion."[153] "Hollywood," as Chandler defined it, "is a showman's paradise." But showmen made nothing. They merely exploited the work of others. While publishers and theatrical producers were showmen too, they exploited that which was already made. On the other hand, "the showmen of Hollywood control the making—and thereby degrade it." Like most every writer (and some producers and directors), Chandler believed that "the basic art of motion pictures is the screenplay; it is fundamental, without it there is nothing." And like most writers, Chandler felt that producers' control of the scripting process was Hollywood's Achilles' heel:

> But in Hollywood the screenplay is written by a salaried writer under the supervision of a producer—that is to say, by an employee without power or decision over the uses of his own craft, without ownership of it, and, however extravagantly paid, almost without honor for it . . . In so far as the writing of the screenplay is concerned, however, the producer is the boss; the writer either gets along with him and his ideas (if he has any) or gets out. This means both personal and artistic subordination, and no writer of quality will long accept either without

surrendering that which made him a writer of quality, without dulling the fine edge of his mind, without becoming little by little a conniver rather than a creator, a supple and facile journeyman rather than a craftsman of original thought.[154]

Chandler here identified the crux of writers' dissatisfaction with the film industry: screenwriters could not succeed without surrendering that which made them writers in the first place—their personal and artistic independence. "Writers are employed to write screenplays on the theory that, being writers, they have a particular gift and training for the job," charged Chandler, "and are then prevented from doing it with any independence or finality whatsoever, on the theory that, being merely writers, they know nothing about making pictures; and of course if they don't know how to make pictures, they couldn't possibly know how to write them. It takes a producer to tell them that."[155] And tell them producers did in the seemingly endless rounds of story conferences. For where the creative impulse surrendered to arbitrary authority

that which is born in lonelinesss and from the heart cannot be defended against the judgement of a committee of sycophants. The volatile essences which make literature cannot survive the clichés of a long series of story conferences. There is little magic of word or emotion or situation which can remain alive after the incessant bone-scraping revisions imposed on the Hollywood writer by the process of rule by decree. That these magics do somehow, here and there, by another and even rarer magic, survive and reach the screen more or less intact is the infrequent miracle which keeps Hollywood's handful of fine writers from cutting their throats.[156]

The writer's independence was shackled further when producers teamed authors of authentic ability with veteran screenwriters too long used to compromising. Chandler had only contempt for the run-of-the-mill studio professional:

There are writers in Hollywood making two thousand a week who never had an idea in their lives, who have never written a photographable scene, who could not make two cents a word in the pulp market if their lives depended on it. Hollywood is full of such writers, although there are few at such high salaries. They are, to put it bluntly, a pretty dreary lot of hacks, and most of them know it, and they take their kicks and their salaries and try to be reasonably grateful to an industry which permits them to live much more opulently than they could live anywhere else.[157]

Thus the writer, especially the Eastern writer, was low man on the Hollywood totem pole. "The very nicest thing Hollywood can think of to say to a writer," Chandler noted sarcastically, "is that he is too good to be only a writer."[158] His fundamental contribution to whatever art a movie possessed was systematically belittled and obscured from the public. In Hollywood, Chandler charged, "a deliberate and successful plan" existed "to reduce the professional screenwriter to the status of an assistant picture-maker, superficially deferred to (while he is in the room), essentially ignored, and even in his most brilliant achievements carefully pushed out of the way of any possible accolade which might otherwise fall to the star, the producer, the director."[159] Nor was there much hope for any change in this sorry situation:

> There is no present indication whatever that the Hollywood writer is on the point of acquiring any real control over his work, any right to chose what that work shall be (other than refusing jobs, which he can only do within narrow limits), or even any right to decide how the values in the producer-chosen work shall be brought out. There is no present guarantee that his best lines, best ideas, best scenes will not be changed or omitted on the set by the director or dropped on the floor during the later process of cutting.[160]

In sum, Chandler brilliantly explicated the contrast between the status and role of the "true" writer (he of the New York literary marketplace) and that of the screenwriter. The former was autonomous, the latter subject to the producer's arbitrary power; the former personally independent, the latter merely an employee. One was valued for his creativity, the other instructed to suppress it. The true writer was rewarded with the inestimable gift of admiration and prestige; the screenwriter, no matter how well paid, worked in anonymity. The work of the true writer was imaginative and enriching; the work of the writer in Hollywood, as Chandler said, "has no more possibility of distinction than a Pekinese has of becoming a Great Dane." Such would remain the case until "somehow the flatulent moguls . . . learn that only writers can write screenplays and only proud and independent writers can write good screenplays, and that present methods of dealing with such men are destructive of the very force by which pictures must live."[161] The film industry, needless to say, received Chandler's articles with no great enthusiasm. "Let me report that my blast at Hollywood has been received here in frozen silence," Chandler informed Charles Morton. "My agent was told by the Paramount story editor that it had done me a lot of harm with the producers at Paramount."[162] Within the month, the studio suspended Chandler indefinitely.

Despite this barrage of animus aimed at the studio system, Eastern writers did enjoy pleasant moments in Hollywood. They were not always embroiled in enervating battles with the front office. Once outside the studio gates, their time was their own. Few authors were so cramp-souled or embittered that they did not enjoy the amenities of life in Southern California, amenities made possible by the weekly checks issued at the studios' payroll windows. "It was, in truth, an amiable place," remembered Ben Hecht, "despite its high heartburn and mortality rate. Nowhere else could talent find so many matters for assault and diatribe. And talent did not have to make its protests as did the poet Bodenheim, freezing in a hall bedroom and sustaining himself on stolen liquor and discarded sandwiches. It could do its inveighing from barbecue pits, ornate rumpus rooms, and, of course, those swimming pools."[163]

If to be in Hollywood was in some sense to be in exile, Hollywood's insatiable appetite for actors, directors, musicians, and craft-people of all sorts from New York and Europe insured that authors did not suffer their exile alone. Writers could always locate at least a small group of like-minded emigrés in town at any given moment. "One of the joys of being in Hollywood," commented Marc Connelly, "was the presence of so many friends from New York."[164] Similarly, S. N. Behrman realized that "there were few [other] places in America where you could go out to dinner with Harpo or Groucho Marx, the Franz Werfels, Leopold Stokowski, Aldous Huxley, Somerset Maughan, George and Ira Gershwin."[165] Writers often found themselves at the lavish formal dinners, movie premiers, gala social events, cocktail parties and opulently staged weekend brunches with which Hollywood society teemed.

Yet Eastern authors, for the most part, preferred the company of their fellow-writers and other imported artists. Even the star-struck George Oppenheimer felt more comfortable with his Eastern compatriots. "Although I attended practically every party to which I was bidden," Oppenheimer reflected, "I never felt at home in Hollywood society. I was happiest in the company of other writers."[166] Authors even tended to frequent the same hotels, restaurants, and neighborhoods. Dave Chasen's on Fairfax Avenue, Lucy's across the street from Paramount's gates, and the Musso and Frank Grill were favorite restaurants. Many writers rented houses in Hollywoodland, the section of the Santa Monica Mountains just north of downtown Hollywood; others rented in West Los Angeles. The Chateau Marmont, the Ambassador, and the Garden of Allah were the preferred residences of Eastern writers on temporary assignment in Hollywood. Much has been written about the legendary Garden of Allah.[167] An enormous Caprean villa, surrounded by a series of two-story bungalows, it was once owned by Alla Nazimova during her reign as a silent screen star. Robert Benchley, Scott Fitzgerald, Robert Sherwood, George S. Kaufman, John O'Hara, Dorothy Parker, Rachel Crothers, and Marc Connelly, among the many writers and actors from New York, all called the Garden home at one time or another during the thirties. There they could sun by the pool, gather at night in each others' apartments, and forget for the moment their trials as screenwriters.

Writers also gathered in the homes of sympathetic friends from the East who were more established in the Hollywood community. George and Lenore Gershwin's house in Beverly Hills became a favorite writers' haunt; Sunday brunch at Charles Brackett's provided another weekly ritual for many a homesick Eastern author. Franchot Tone, an actor in the Group Theater in New York before becoming a major movie star, often invited old friends from Broadway to week-end get-togethers at his estate. "In the afternoon," Harold Clurman recalls, we would chat, mostly about the theater, play badminton, swim in the pool, dine and see a picture in the projection-room, right off the pool. . . . Once, while I lay afloat in the pool, basking lazily in the Sunday sun, Franchot observed me with friendly malice and remarked: "The life of a prostitute is pretty comfortable, isn't it?"[168]

A different group of writers frequented the Stanley Rose Book Shop, conveniently located on Hollywood Boulevard opposite the Writers Guild and adjacent to the Musso and Frank Grille. Although Charles Katz and Carey McWilliams (later the editor of the *Nation)* actually owned the store, Stanley Rose, a hard-drinking, flamboyant Texan managed it. In spite of a fourth-grade education, Rose loved literature and especially writers. He eventually became a literary agent of some note, with William Saroyan as his chief client. Rose befriended many Eastern authors, lent them money and moral support, and introduced those who were interested to his many low-life Hollywood acquaintances. Scott Fitzgerald, Dashiell Hammett, S. J. Perelman, Dorothy Parker, Daniel Fuchs, William Faulkner, Nathanael West, and Budd Schulberg all occasionally visited the Book Shop's backroom, where Rose served jugs of orange wine, and, by unspoken understanding, movie talk was prohibited. The Book Shop was one of those rare places in Hollywood where writers could gather entirely apart from the rigidities of the studios' caste system. Regardless of his meagre salary at a minor studio, Nathanael West, for example, was a respected equal in the company of his fellow writers in Rose's backroom. "In contrast to his position at the studios," Jay Martin suggests, "West was a distinguished man in this group."[169]

All was not unrewarding and unappreciated drudgery even within the studio walls. Studio life did not always strike writers as a mere rat-run of greed, politics, and philistinism. Ben Hecht, for all his loathing of the studio system, remembered with a certain fondness "studios humming with intrigue and happy go-lucky excitements."[170] And James M. Cain, despite his criticisms of the writer's menial status, admitted in 1933 that "I have worked in a number of places in my time, and I have never worked any place where courtesy was more in evidence than on a movie lot, or where daily contacts were more pleasant."[171] Nor were the studios always insensitive to their personal problems and needs of the writers in their employ. George Abbott, for example, while working at Universal, received word that his wife was seriously ill in New York. His brother-in-law called to urge him to return home at once. "I explained the situation to the heads of the studio," Abbott recalls, "and they showed more heart than is generally attributed to large corporations by arranging immediately for me to do the work I owed them in their Long Island studios."[172] Writers' references to such kindnesses appear infrequently in their contemporary and reminiscent accounts of Hollywood, but in sufficient numbers to suggest that hearts of front office executives were not as cold as sometimes pictured.

Similarly while producers as a class were despised, there were a number of individual producers whom writers admired. This handful included those producers who respected the abilities of the writers they hired and thus generally did not interfere with their work. "That type of producer," affirmed Sidney Howard, "though he may impose criticisms and amendments of his own, keeps in the track which has been laid, spares director and writer no end of headaches, and usually turns out fully as good a product as the other [meddling] type."[173] Writers frequently mentioned Samuel Goldwyn, Edwin Knopf, Hunt Stromberg, and Darryl F. Zanuck as producers worthy of their respect. Zanuck, for instance, had begun in movies as a scenarist himself, and greatly valued the writers working for him at Twentieth Century-Fox. Zanuck had a knack for hiring talented writers and, once he had gained confidence in them, allowing them to work with a minimum of interference. Those whom he trusted fully, like Gene Fowler and Nunnally Johnson, did not have to submit outlines or treatments for approval; once agreed upon, they began work immediately on a shooting script. "I consider myself fortunate to have served an apprenticeship as a writer," Zanuck once said "Writers deal, or try to, with the universality of human experience with which motion pictures must deal."[174] Such testimonials were all the more appreciated by writers because of their rarity.

The two producers most admired by Eastern writers were David O. Selznick and Irving Thalberg, although both habitually employed the team-writing concept. Both men kept a tight rein on their writers; both were inveterate story conference callers; both showered their writers with suggestions and orders for script changes; and both rarely hesitated to hire and fire a half-dozen writers to achieve the script they desired. (For instance, at least seven writers worked on *Gone with the Wind,* including Ben Hecht, Scott Fitzgerald and Sidney Howard. Only Howard received screen credit.) Selznick was not bashful about rewriting scripts himself. Yet both men produced such meticulously crafted movies—so far superior to Hollywood's usual output—that they received the respect, if sometimes grudging, of the screenwriting community. Both men eventually came to share writers' loathing for Hollywood's mass production methods and to repudiate the assembly-line system they had helped to create. "When I was at Paramount," Selznick later said of the studio system,

> we made fifty-two pictures a year and our executive judgements and prejudices and attitudes were stamped on every one of them. You can't make top pictures that way. You can't make good pictures by a committee system, filtering them through the minds of half a dozen men.[175]

As early as 1933, Irving Thalberg warned of the dangers of turning out as many as fifty pictures a year to meet the home office's need for product. So many pictures rolled from the studios that not enough time and care could be spent on each one, Thalberg complained:

> To continue the present destructive policy of rushing out pictures poorly made, of destroying stars by robbing them of their glamor and their ability to give distinguished performances, of bewildering the best creative efforts of the best writers through forcing them to work on silly material and rushing them on good material, of loading down good pictures with the production costs and selling expenses of pictures which nobody wants to see—to continue any such suicidal policy is to continue giving the one inescapable answer to the question of why pictures cost so much and invite a condition of public apathy in which there won't be any pictures at all.[176]

Both men firmly believed that the screenplay was the most important creative ingredient in picture making. They agreed with writers that creative control should not be diluted; but, not surprisingly, they felt that control should be vested exclusively in the producer, not the writer. They believed in paying writers well and treating them with respect, although occasionally their practices didn't conform with their beliefs. Both men appreciated the talents of novelists and playwrights even if they didn't often read their works. Thalberg hired more Eastern writers than any other producer in Hollywood. And Selznick, often considered the greatest producer in Hollywood's history, was in fact a frustrated book publisher, having made an ill-fated venture into publishing before he ever went to Hollywood. He carried this frustrated ambition with him for the rest of his life. "I would rather be a fine book publisher," Selznick told H. N. Swanson, then one of his assistant producers, "and have a house like Random House than do what I'm doing."[177]

Yet the cordiality of writers' dealings with even the best movie producers fell short of the warm friendships which existed betweeen many authors and their Eastern publishers and editors. Hollywood, Scott Fitzgerald informed Maxwell Perkins in 1938, was "a strange conglomeration of a few excellent overtired men making the pictures, and as dismal a crowd of fakes and hacks at the bottom as you can imagine." As a result, concluded Fitzgerald: "Every other man is a charlatan, nobody trusts anybody else, and an infinite amount of time is wasted from lack of confidence. Relations have always been so pleasant, not only with you but with Harold [Ober] and with Lorimer's *Saturday Evening Post*, that even working with the pleasantest people in the industry, Eddie Knopf and Hunt Stromberg, I feel this lack of confidence."[178] The writer was still an underling, and something of an adversary, in Hollywood—even when employed by a Stromberg or a Selznick. Moreover, for every producer of quality like Thalberg or Goldwyn, there were, in Ben Hecht's estimation, "fifty nitwits" in the production ranks. "The pain of having to collaborate with such dullards," moaned Hecht, "and to submit myself to their approvals was always acute. Years of experience failed to help. I never became reconciled to taking literary orders from them."[179] Few writers did.

5

Writers' Responses to the Studio System and the Profession of Authorship

Writers did not suffer the indignities of Hollywood lightly or without protest. They responded in a variety of ways, some constructive, some spiteful, and some futile. Most writers tried to defy the system they so despised, even if that defiance meant turning their backs on sizable paychecks. Others tried to work within the system. Still others tried to coopt it. Ultimately though, after almost every attempt to change the system's treatment of writers proved futile, they sought an accommodation, however uneasy, with the film industry.

By the end of the thirties, Eastern writers realized that their problems with Hollywood were not merely temporary and irritating aberrations in the courses of their careers; rather, the studio system anticipated changes occurring in the writer's traditional relationship with the publishing industry and the theater. Much to their dismay, writers slowly came to understand that their Hollywood experience was a harbinger of things to come in New York as the complex, increasingly impersonal and bureaucratic forces of twentieth-century commercial life invaded the literary marketplace.

Most Eastern writers responded to their situation in Hollywood, as Budd Schulberg noted, by "falling into all the familiar ploys of inferior status. First you fib to your producer and then you begin to lie. You play hookey. You rebel in all sorts of little ways that satisfy your immature sense of defiance."[1] Swapping anecdotes laced with malice about producers, Schulberg recalls, became a "favorite form of release therapy for embattled and embarrassed screenwriters."[2] Thus Gene Fowler's habitual reference to MGM's chief executive as "Louis B. Manure." After B. P. Schulberg, then head of production, accused Paramount's writers of disloyalty towards the studio, a contingent of the writers took to composing songs in honor of the studio. Henry Myers composed a Gregorian chant which concluded: "Let us give all our loyalty/And best cooperation/To Paramount Pictures/A Delaware Corporation." Another writer contributed "Fight on for Old B. P.," rousingly sung to the tune of the USC marching song.[3] Such were the tamest kinds of revolt.

Often writers' rebellions were more pointedly directed toward their sense of inferiority in the studios and hostility toward producers. Charles MacArthur, for instance, managed to sneak an illiterate gas station attendant onto the MGM payroll as a contract writer. The gas jockey, alias "Kenneth Woollcott," collected a writer's salary for almost a year before being discovered. Only MacArthur's friendship with Thalberg saved him from the pink slip.[4] Similarly, to protest their cramped quarters in the Selznick Building, Gene Fowler and Ben Hecht transformed their office into a mock-bordello, complete with lurid red velvet curtains, pornographic etchings, and a buxom blonde "secretary" in the foyer.[5]

Fowler's practical jokes were especially savored by his fellow writers. Upon arriving in Hollywood to work for RKO, Fowler knew, of course, that many of the studio's executives had begun in the garment industry. He therefore walked into his first meeting with the studio's top brass carrying his pants over his arm. He threw them on the conference table and ordered: "Cleaned and pressed by tomorrow morning." Then he left before anyone could say a word.[6]

Usually only those writers of considerable value to the studios could get away with such affronts. Fowler was one such writer; Dashiell Hammett, while riding the crest of his popularity in the mid-thirties, was another. "He was one of the many guys," Raymond Chandler commented to a friend in the East,

who couldn't take Hollywood without trying to push God out of the high seat. I recall an incident reported to me when Hammett was occupying a suite at the Beverly-Wilshire Hotel. A party wished to make him a proposition and called late of a morning, was admitted by Hammett's house boy to a living room, and after a very long wait an inner door opened and the great man appeared in it, clad in an expensive lounging robe with a scarf draped tastefully around his neck. He stood in total silence as the man expounded. At the end he said politely "No." He turned and withdrew, the door closed, the house boy ushered the gent out, and the silence fell.[7]

Even less important writers found ways to annoy their studio bosses, often to their ultimate chagrin. For instance, studios occasionally punished troublesome screenwriters by "freezing" them out; such writers would have to report to the studios each working day, but would not be allowed to write. If they violated their contract in any way, the studio could and would cancel it. "This was the humiliation routine," Fox screenwriter Allen Rivkin recalled several years later, "the writer was supposed to get so frustrated that he would... demand that his contract be torn up."[8]

While writers' pranks provided an outlet for their frustrations and hostilities, then, they did nothing to change the screenwriters' basic plight in the studios. Writers were forced to devise other strategies to cope effectively with the studio system. One clear way to beat that Hollywood system was simply to refuse to join it. A handful of Eastern writers—Hemingway, O'Neill, Philip Barry, and Edna Ferber among them—were successful and wealthy enough to resist Hollywood's temptations. They never signed movie contracts. Many more writers, who had at one time signed on as screenwriters, refused further contracts they deemed too trifling. Occasionally writers spurned Hollywood's entreaties because of personal commitments to other writing projects. Paul Green, for one, refused a contract with Paramount in 1936 which could have paid him $100,000 because he was determined to stay in North Carolina and complete a play he was writing.[9]

Far fewer writers, however, actually quit while under contract; most seemed determined to receive weekly paychecks as long as they could. Only three writers I studied actually abrogated contracts. James M. Cain sent back to MGM a check for $10,000 after he found he couldn't write a decent script for *The Duchess of Broadway*.[10] Clifford Odets broke a lucrative writer-director contract in the 1940s to return to New York.[11] Finally, Maxwell Anderson, as mentioned earlier, quit MGM in 1930 in a huff; a decade later he more tactfully asked out of a scripting assignment. His letter to Anatole Litvak, giving his reasons for wanting to quit the project, reveals one writer's justification for such an action:

> Dear Tola—
> You will be wondering why no script has come along to you, and I write in some embarrassment and feeling most apologetic to explain. I had to explain first to myself, and so my story is quite honest.
> It seems to be completely impossible for me to write a good script, or even one I'm not ashamed of for that picture. I tried several times to get it going, each time it was a false start. Now it may be that I'm merely lazy, but I don't think so. The more I consider the matter, the more cetain I become that something inside me doesn't really like that picture—and doesn't want me to do it. At any rate, anything I have turned out so far you wouldn't like anymore than I did. If I drove myself to finish it the result would be uninteresting. If you put it on anyway, poor work would show up and nobody would be happy. It follows that I'd better just give it up. This sort of thing has never happened to me before, and I don't quite know what to make of it, but I assure you that if I thought I could do a job that would please you I would still go ahead. I just don't believe I can.[12]

To Anderson's surprise and great relief, he was released from his contract.

In general, though, writers confronted the studio system rather than ran from it. In almost every case, writers attempted to gain more *control*, either directly or indirectly, over the scripting process and, in some cases, over the actual production itself. Writers employed three principal strategies or gambits to increase their control: insisting on solo assignments; affiliating with an important director or producer; and becoming producers or directors themselves. All of these options were usually available *only* to those writers with some leverage in the studio. Even then, control often remained elusive.

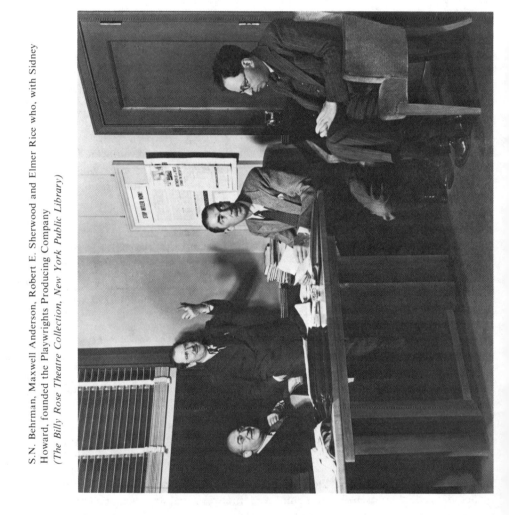

S.N. Behrman, Maxwell Anderson, Robert E. Sherwood and Elmer Rice who, with Sidney Howard, founded the Playwrights Producing Company
(The Billy Rose Theatre Collection, New York Public Library)

The first of these gambits, refusing to collaborate with other writers, was a viable option *only* for those writers whose talents the studios greatly valued. Thus only four writers whose careers I examined successfully insisted on writing without partners on a regular basis: Lillian Hellman, Dudley Nichols, Preston Sturges, and Nunnally Johnson. Darryl F. Zanuck, for instance, allowed Johnson to work alone only after he demanded that his name be removed from any movie whose writing credits listed more than one person. Dudley Nichols wrote without collaborators because his association with director John Ford resulted in a string of highly profitable movies for Twentieth-Century Fox. As we shall see, it was largely Ford's backing which allowed him this privilege. After years as a lowly reader, Lillian Hellman returned to Hollywood in the mid-thirties in the employ of Samuel Goldwyn, who highly regarded her talent. Her first movie for Goldwyn was *Dark Angel,* on which Thornton Wilder also worked. She then wrote a series of successful movies, including *These Three* (1936), *Dead End* (1937), *The Little Foxes* (1941), and *The Searching Wind* (1946), for which she received solo credit. "I like movies," Hellman later explained, "I took them seriously and I liked doing them. I didn't like the ones where I collaborated or where the director or the producer told me what to do."[13] Goldwyn generally left her to her own devices, and thus Hellman's screenwriting experience was, on the whole, satisfying during this period. The trick, as Fitzgerald once said, was to have such a success that the producer couldn't ignore it.[14] If a writer wrote a critically and commercially successful movie, which Nichols, Hellman, and Johnson did with regularity, the front office had less reason to interfere.

Preston Sturges followed a more unlikely path to solo assignments. After working as a dialoguer in New York, and writing an adaptation of *The Invisible Man* for Universal (which was quickly shelved), Sturges wrote an original script in 1933 titled *The Power and the Glory,* an American success story acidly etched, based on the life of Sturges' wife's grandfather, C. W. Post. After peddling it in vain at a number of studios Sturges had the good fortune to sell it finally to Jesse Lasky. Lasky had just been ousted as head of production at Paramount, and he had joined Fox as a line producer when Sturges' story arrived; desperate for his first production to make headlines, the nervous executive ordered Sturges to continue with the project. As Lasky later explained:

> He obviously wasn't wise to the ways of Hollywood in a day when so many original stories were sold in ad-lib form over a luncheon or in a conference before reading the idea instead of listening to it. I knew that if it had any merit I could put a team of two or a half-dozen skilled film writers on it to develop the basic idea in a manner suitable to the film medium.
>
> Preston Sturges went away and wrote his story. And he didn't even know enough about screenwriting to know that the first step is to do a *treatment* or narrative story line. That's what I expected him to bring back, a few pages synopsizing the plot. Instead he brought a

complete screenplay of proper length, complete to every word of dialogue, the action of every scene blueprinted for the director, and including special instructions for the cameramen and all departments.

He told the story in flashback, starting with the death of his subject, an unprecedented screen technique then but later used with powerful effect by Orson Welles and others. The manuscript crackled with its originality of conception and craftsmenship.

I was astounded. It was the most perfect script I'd ever seen. I dispensed with the usual practice of having other writers go over a finished script "with a fresh mind" to make improvements. I wouldn't let anyone touch a word of it.[15]

According to Sturges, he skipped the treatment stage by design rather than out of ignorance. "I felt that proceeding *sans* director, and *sans* teammates gave me an opportunity to show how I thought it should be done," he informed a reporter. Sturges wanted "to wage a sort of one-man battle against conditions I found repellant."[16] Thus Sturges, with his first original script, achieved what many a veteran writer sought in vain his entire career—a movie filmed from his script without substantive changes. If the author thought that *The Power and the Glory*'s success would result in greater control for screenwriters, however, he was sadly mistaken. He learned quickly of the studio system's resistance to change. "I immediately sat down and wrote another shooting script," Sturges later recalled:

It was easily as good as the first and subsequently became much better known. [*The Great McGinty*, 1940] I thought it would take me about two days to sell it. It took me seven years. They said, "No, no, Mr. Sturgeon, you fooled us once but not twice. You'll do your writing just like everyone else does. From some good original story written by another guy, which we will discard later, you will write a rough treatment then a smooth treatment, and then if we like what you've done, maybe we'll let you write the rough screenplay and maybe we won't."[17]

Rather than opening the door to success, *The Power and the Glory* opened a can of worms for Sturges. Directors resented the fact that, for the first time, a writer's name was advertised more prominently than the director's; producers charged that Sturges was destroying the status quo; and some veteran screenwriters grouched that jobs would disappear if only one writer worked on each script. Writing by committee, and on salary or fixed rate, continued as before. Nor did the successes of Hellman, Sturges, Nichols, and Johnson as solo screenwriters insure them against interference; unsympathetic or ambitious directors and stars could, and often did, make changes in their work on the set. Thus the strategy of demanding solo screen assignments was either an option unavailable to most writers, or not completely satisfying for those to whom it was.

A second option did not depend so much on a writer's value to the front office. A handful of writers were able to increase their creative autonomy, or their standing in the studios, by forming an alliance with someone sympathetic to their work and possessing greater power in the studios. The studios' policy of constantly re-assigning personnel precluded most long-term affiliations, consequently, only three of the forty writers I studied—Samson Raphaelson, William Faulkner, and Dudley Nicholas—formed even semi-permanent partnerships with studio higher-ups. And only Raphaelson and Nichols gained an appreciable amount of creative autonomy.

"I did most of my Hollywood work with Lubitsch," Raphaelson recently said, "I did nine pictures with him, and we got along great. Lubitsch was a producer-director and his relationship with me made life in the studios worth living."[18] Among those nine pictures were the highly acclaimed *Trouble in Paradise* (1932), *The Shop Around the Corner* (1940), and *Heaven Can Wait* (1943). "With Lubitsch I never had any problems about changing anything I wrote," Raphaelson continued. "He never used anything I objected to. We had to agree. He never changed anything behind my back—he may have cut some things while editing, but if he wanted to make a change in even one line of dialog, he would call me. Other producers and directors would do any damn thing they felt like."[19]

William Faulkner's well-known association with Howard Hawks, on the other hand, afforded him little opportunity to work on scripts without interference. Rather, it simply allowed Faulkner to continue drawing studio paychecks. Hawks, by reason of his string of box-office hits and ability to bring pictures in on time and under budget, enjoyed an unusually large degree of independence. Even rarer was his use of writers on the set to help improvise scenes. Faulkner harbored few illusions of himself as a master screenwriter; he understood that his principal talent for movie work lay in plot construction and colloquial dialog. But his writing gifts and his personality were tailor-made for Hawk's style of movie making. Faulkner would not have fared as well as he did in Hollywood without the support of Hawks who, on several occasions, insisted that the front office hire him.

Dudley Nichols, like Raphaelson, acquired considerable creative control in the scripting process through his association with a single director. When Nichols arrived at Fox in 1929, its production head, Winfield Sheehan, assigned him to work with one of the studio's better directors, John Ford. Thus began the most successful sustained collaboration of screenwriter and director in Hollywood's history. Ford and Nichols made thirteen films together, beginning with *Men Without Women* (1930), and including *The Lost Patrol* (1934), *The Plough and the Stars* (1937), and *Stagecoach* (1939). Both men worked intermittently with other partners, but neither achieved the same fine results separately that they did together. The quality of Nichols's work with Ford, like Raphaelson's with Lubitsch, indicates that writers *could* collaborate effectively if they were paired with a sympathetic partner and then left alone by the front office. But most collaborations in Hollywood, whether between two writers, or writer and director, were arbitrarily arranged by the front office—shotgun marriages.

Nichols and Ford were seemingly immune to the petty jealousies and ego clashes which plagued most forced collaborations. "We were very close," the director remarked.[20] Ford did not consider his screenwriter a threat or an underling, but rather a truly equal partner. This made him virtually unique among directors in the studios in the thirties. "At the time," Nichols recalled a decade later, "most directors. . . . avoided saying to the scenarist or to anyone in charge of the film that the script was good."[21] Nonetheless Ford lavishly and publicly praised Nichols's very first attempt at a screenplay. Nichols, for his part, believed that a movie's director was, and should be, the dominant force in its making. Writers, he argued, had to recognize and accept this. "Not only is it idle [for writers] to argue the relative importance of writers and directors in films," Nichols observed, "but it is essential that they work in the closest harmony and collaboration."[22] The difficulty lay, Nichols felt, in the hostility of most producers and directors toward writers. The respect necessary for true collaboration was hard to come by in Hollywood:

> Of the manifold diverse talents that are required for the collective job of making a film, no talent has had more grudging admission through the studio gates than that of the writer. . . . The present writer came into the film medium with sound, which meant the word, which also meant confusion; and the writer was suddenly regarded as a necessary nuisance.[23]

Even the long string of commercial and critical successes produced by Ford and Nichols did not exempt them totally from front office interference. Ford was not allowed to edit several of his movies; other directors on the Fox lot demanded Nichols's services; and inappropriate story material was foisted on them both. "It's a constant battle to do something fresh," Ford complained as early as 1936. "First they want you to repeat your last picture. . . . Another time they want you to knock out something *another* studio's gone and cleaned up with."[24]

Occasionally other writers would find compatible directors with whom they would begin promising partnerships. Invariably, though, the front offices' penchant for shifting and re-assigning personnel would nip such collaborations in the bud. Donald Ogden Stewart, for instance, adapted two Philip Barry plays, *Holiday* and *The Philadelphia Story* for MGM. George Cukor directed both. Stewart and Cukor worked well together: "Cukor would always ask me did I like this or that," Stewart remarked to a reporter, "We had a good partnership."[25] Stewart even won an Oscar for his adaptation of *The Philadelphia Story*. Both movies made money for the studio, yet they never worked together again. In the eyes of the front office, Stewart was more valuable as a script doctor, making last-minute revisions on other writers' scripts. In only the rarest cases, then, did long-term partnerships between writers and directors yield any appreciable increase in creative control or studio prestige. The only other team besides Nichols-Ford and Lubitsch-Raphaelson to enjoy long-term success was that of Frank Capra and Robert Riskin at Columbia.

A gambit used more often by Eastern writers in their stuggle for control was to become the producer or director or both, of the movies they wrote. Most often writers who wanted to produce or direct never got the chance. W. R. Burnett, for example, left Warner Brothers after several years as a productive screenwriter over just this issue:

> I got in a beef with Jack Warner because he said that the next thing I buy from you, you produce and direct it; you're not satisfied, you're always yelling, now *you* produce and direct it. So I said fine. Then I sold him a story and he gave it to someone else—and never said a word to me. We had a big fight about it and I eventually left Warners as a result. I'd been there about five years.[26]

And not every writer who *did* produce or direct met with great success. Rachel Crothers, for example, failed miserably. Crothers convinced Samuel Goldwyn in 1935 to allow her not only to write but also to direct a film called *Splendor.* Crothers had successfully staged a number of her plays in New York, but knew little of the workings of a movie set. The result was a turgid movie, reminiscent of the static filmed stage plays the studios had relied on immediately after the introduction of sound. "It was a disaster," recalled George Oppenheimer, then one of Goldwyn's production assistants.[27] Crothers never directed in Hollywood again.

Clifford Odets achieved a more noteworthy directorial debut. The playwright returned to Hollywood in 1942 after having quit the movies in disgust four years earlier. A year later he was hired by RKO to adapt Richard Llewellyn's *None But the Lonely Heart* for the screen. During his first trip to Hollywood Odets had decided that "the only one who can—given the trust of the people who are backing him—the only one in whose hands there is the possibility of something creative is the director."[28] He therefore lobbied RKO to let him direct the picture. They acquiesced. The result was the movie Odets considered his best. John Gassner and Dudley Nichols concurred and named it one of the best films of the year in their movie annual. "The most important fact about *None But the Lonely Heart,*" Nichols suggested, "is that the writer managed to put his personal sign . . . on the work."[29] Odets's movie was praised by the critics, won Ethel Barrymore an Academy Award, and did fairly well at the box-office. *None But the Lonely Heart,* screenwriters suggested, was proof-positive that writers could make commercially viable movies of a higher caliber if given greater creative control. Odets, however, could not capitalize on this initial directorial success. MGM did sign him to a writer-director contract, but the playwright spent a year at the studio without completing a film, and left Hollywood again shortly thereafter. He did not direct another picture until 1960.[30]

Dudley Nichols's achievements as a screenwriter working with Ford qualified him in the eyes of the RKO front office to try his hand at directing. His directorial career was sightly longer, but also less rewarding, than Odets's. Nichols directed three movies for RKO in the 1940s: *Government Girl* (1943), *Sister Kenny* (1946), and *Mourning Becomes Electra* (1947). They were not smashing successes; Nichols was particularly upset with RKO's handling of *Mourning Becomes Electra*. O'Neill had asked specifically that Nichols write and direct the adaptation, and Nichols felt that the studio hadn't allowed him to do justice to the play. *"Electra* was made before our present rage for long films," reflected Nichols in 1958,

> and the studio insisted that I cut an hour out of the rough-cut (which ran 3 1/2 hours). I think the loss was very injurious. But they said they couldn't sell so long a film. Some of the more "shocking" things were dropped, at studio request or demand.[31]

Studio meddling was not the only problem Nichols faced as a director. He decided that he was temperamentally unsuited for the job; a director needed the forcefulness of character to fight the "cut-throat" front office for control. So Nichols returned to writing scripts for directors with enough clout and determination to protect his material. In addition to Ford, Nichols collaborated with Howard Hawks, Fritz Lang, Elia Kazan, Leo McCary, and George Cukor, among others. "I never had the nature it takes to make films," Nichols later remarked. "The temperament of the writer does not lend itself to that; if he is a man of action, he is generally not a good writer, although there are some exceptions."[32]

Preston Sturges was one such exception. After his success with *The Power and the Glory,* Sturges spent the rest of the thirties working on more than a dozen pictures for Paramount, Universal, and MGM, mostly original screenplays. By 1938 he was one of the three highest-paid writers in the industry, Ben Hecht and Robert Riskin being the other two. However, the major studios' refusal to allow him to direct one of his own scripts increasingly frustrated Sturges; in the late thirties, he managed finally to jockey the majors into a bidding war for his writing services. In 1940, Paramount agreed reluctantly to allow Sturges to direct his seven-year-old script, *The Great McGinty*. William LeBaron, himself an ex-writer and then head of production at the studio, insisted that the picture be shot on a very tight budget, $325,000, but allowed Sturges a free hand. *The Great McGinty* proved a tremendous critical and commercial hit, and won Sturges an Academy Award for best original screenplay. For perhaps the first time in Hollywood's history, a writer received not only the major credit for a movie's success, but also the greatest share of its publicity. *The Great McGinty* "was a one-man show," proclaimed *Newsweek,* "and that man is a screenwriter named Preston Sturges."[34] Paramount then gave Sturges a virtual blank-check to write and direct any material he wished, and the writer responded by making eight comedies in the next five years, all money-makers for the studio. In reviewing one of them, *The Miracle of Morgan's Creek* (1944), James Agee praised Sturges as "just the most gifted American working in films."[35] Most movie critics shared Agee's opinion. Hollywood, loving nothing so much as success, lionized Sturges. Alexander King noted in a magazine profile of the writer-director that he was "among the first five celebrities of his community."[36] "At Paramount," John Podeschi notes, "Sturges had nearly the power of the studio's patriarchal film-maker, Cecil B. DeMille."[37]

Thus by the mid-forties Sturges had achieved what most Eastern writers dearly coveted: virtual autonomy over the production of his screenplays. Yet, hoping for even greater success, Sturges left Paramount at the height of his power to form the California Pictures Corporation with Howard Hughes. Sturges was as celebrated for his high-living as his movies, and it may have been that the prospect of untold riches was irresistable. Sturges's professed reason for making the break with Paramount was to strike a blow for artistic independence: he told a reporter that the purpose of the new production was "to invest young writers, directors, and producers with full authority," and that he would "urge them to act on their own initiative."[38] But very little of substance resulted from California Pictures. Sturges did make a great deal of money, but he made only one undistinguished movie before parting company with Hughes. He then signed on with Twentieth Century-Fox as a writer-producer-director, made two mediocre movies, and found himself, by 1949, an outcast in Hollywood. "In twenty-two years," Sturges reasoned, "I had managed to alienate every one of the seven major studios and soon found myself out of work."[39] Sturges's brief reign as one of Hollywood's top movie makers marked the only time an Eastern writer achieved significant automony by asssuming the role of the director. While writers could become directors in theory, then, in practice a screenwriter's chances of establishing himself as a director were negligible.

Screenwriters stood a slightly better chance of joining the ranks of producers, judging from the experiences of the writers I studied. Three of them enjoyed long-term, rewarding careers as producers. Two more, in partnership, met with less success as producer-directors in their own semi-independent production unit. All realized that real creative control lay in the producer's hands; all hoped that by assuming the mantle of the producer they would gain a greater say in the making of the movies they wrote. In each case, their studios let them produce only after they had proved themselves competent commercial screenwriters.

Sidney Buchman's career provides a case in point. Buchman, a playwright, first arrived in Hollywood in 1930 to write the scenario for Cecil B. DeMille's production of *The Sign of the Cross.* Buchman received eight screen credits in his four years at Paramount, an indication that he had learned the screenwriting ropes quickly. In 1934 he signed a long-term contract with Columbia, where he became a valued member of Harry Cohn's scenario department. By 1936 he was the highest paid screenwriter on the Columbia lot. Buchman worked with a variety of partners, performed occasional uncredited "doctoring" assignments, and wrote a number of original screenplays and adaptations without collaborators. In 1939 he wrote an original screenplay, *Mr. Smith Goes to Washington,* for Frank Capra, the studio's best director. The movie was Columbia's biggest hit in years, and Cohn rewarded Buchman by promoting him to producer. In the forties, Buchman became the studio's valued jack-of-all-trades—writing scripts, producing pictures written by others and, on occasion, producing movies from his own scripts. The latter brought him the most satisfaction. Buchman told a reporter in 1950: "I like producing any material that is good, but when I have the time to write *and* produce a story, I'm usually more pleased with the results. That is what every writer in this town would like to do."[40] Buchman continued as one of the stalwarts at Columbia until 1953, when he was blacklisted for contempt of Congress in the midst of the McCarthy frenzy. He then moved to France, and did not return to Hollywood until the mid-sixties.

Charles Brackett was another writer who became one of the industry's top producers. Paramount hired Brackett in 1934 on a six-week contract; he remained with the studio for seventeen years. Like Buchman, Brackett accumulated a substantial number of co-screenwriting credits during his first few years in Hollywood. His career blossomed, however, when he was teamed with Billy Wilder on the script of *Bluebeard's Eighth Wife,* in 1938. The picture was a hit and the two writers got along famously. They worked together for five years on a series of popular movies produced and directed by others, including *Ninotchka* (1939) and *Hold Back the Dawn* (1941). In 1943, when their contracts were up for renewal, Brackett and Wilder demanded that the studio allow the former to produce and the latter direct their own movies from then on. They made this demand, Brackett insisted, "so that we could keep our product pure."[41] Their first effort as a producer-director-writer team, *Five Graves to Cairo* (1943), proved to be an ordinary wartime propaganda movie. Their second project, however, *The Lost Weekend* (1945), received Best Picture and Best Screenplay Oscars. The studio quickly moved Brackett and Wilder from an upstairs office to a first floor suite in the Writers' Building. Brackett and Wilder made two more celebrated movies, *The Emperor Waltz* (1948) and *Sunset Boulevard* (1950), before their partnership dissolved in some bitterness in the early fifties. Brackett continued to produce and co-write several first-class movies for a number of years, but never with the success he had enjoyed with Wilder. "They were," Maurice Zolotow concluded, *"au fond,* two writers, two screenwriters who did not want to be a producer and a director but were drawn into it against their wishes in order to exercise control over their screenplays."[42]

Of all the Eastern writers who became producers, Nunnally Johnson enjoyed the most success. Johnson had impressed Darryl Zanuck while working as a contract writer for the latter's fledgling Twentieth Century Pictures Corporation. When Twentieth Century merged with Fox in 1935, Zanuck made Johnson an associate producer. But Johnson quickly discovered that he was temperamentally "unable to tell other writers how to write."[43] Like many other writers, Johnson hated the thought of tampering with another writer's work. He asked Zanuck to assign him to produce only those properties he had written himself, and Zanuck agreed.

Beginning with *The Man Who Broke the Bank at Monte Carlo* (1935), Johnson wrote and produced nearly thirty movies for Zanuck in the next twenty years. He became Hollywood's premier writer-producer, leading Lawrence van Gelder of *The New York Times* to comment in 1940 that Johnson's was "the most enviable writing job in this movie industry."[44] "The nice thing about it," Johnson himself said that same year, "is that since I'm hired as a producer I can go out on a lot where a director is kicking my script around and say, 'Listen, what we want you to do is make this picture the way it's written here on this paper. Just you stick to this paper.'"[45] For Johnson, then, it was neither the producer's salary nor prestige which attracted him to the job; rather, like Buchman and Brackett, he coveted the power to control the progress of his scripts through the production process.

Ben Hecht and Charles MacArthur were the first Eastern writers afforded the opportunity to both produce and direct their own movies. Their venture into independent production, though begun with the highest of hopes, ended in disappointment. In 1934, after Hecht and MacArthur's screen adaptation of their play, *The Twentieth Century,* had proved enormously popular, Paramount offered the team a multi-picture production deal. Hecht and MacArthur were to produce, write, and direct four movies at Paramount's Long Island facility under the general supervision of Walter Wanger, a literate college-educated executive who promised to keep out of their way. The authors jumped at the chance to work in the East, far removed from front office interference.

By August Hecht-MacArthur Productions occupied a row of offices in the Astoria studio and the two writers, now also co-producers and co-directors, worked on their first project, *Crime Without Passion.* They hired Lee Garmes, a talented veteran cimematographer, and a handful of other key craftsmen to handle technical matters because, as Hecht explained, "neither Charles nor I

Ben Hecht and Charles MacArthur
(Courtesy of the Academy of Motion Picture Arts and Sciences)

had ever spent an hour on a movie set."[46] Nonetheless, they were confident of success since they were convinced that, as Hecht said, "90% percent of the success of a movie (or of its failure) lay in the writing of its script. Producer, director, and stars could add less to a movie script than they could to a stage play."[47] Hecht-MacArthur Productions would prove once and for all, its founders hoped, that the screenwriter made the most important contribution to any movie. *Crime Without Passion* was well-received by the critics but did only modest business at the box office. *The Scoundrel* (1935), loosely based on the life of Horace Liveright and starring Noel Coward in his first screen appearance, provided them a second chance. It won an Oscar as Best Original Screenplay, but fared very poorly at the box office. Their third picture, *Once in a Blue Moon* (1935), proved to be an unmitigated disaster and its release was held up for nearly two years. Hecht later admitted that "our script for *Once in a Blue Moon* was a dud."[48] Hecht-MacArthur Productions' final movie, *Soak the Rich* (1936) was slightly better, but still lost money for Paramount. The studio did not renew its contract with the production unit, and the partners went back to working solely on scripts.

Hecht and McArthur had been convinced that they could make serious, well-crafted movies on small budgets. In this they succeeded. They had hired actors from Broadway who didn't demand large salaries; they had not employed a flock of press agents; they had used existing music rather than hiring high-priced composers; and, most importantly, they had streamlined the production process by cutting the usual number of camera set-ups in half and not insisting on multiple takes. While on the set, they had resisted the temptation to make script changes. Through these measures they had cut production time—and costs—significantly. *Crime Without Passion* cost $180,000 to make; *The Scoundrel* only slightly more. At the time production budgets in Hollywood averaged twice that amount. Although *Crime Without Passion* made a modest profit for Paramount, and *The Scoundrel* eventually broke even, Hecht and MacArthur had been unable to produce the enormous box office hit that would have insured the success of their experiment. Only such a hit could have overcome Paramount's reflexive reluctance to give up control and authority. That Hecht-MacArthur Productions did not succeed does not diminish its importance as a cogent example of Eastern writers' desire to control the fate of their own work, and, in the process, elevate the status of the screenwriter in the film industry.

While many Eastern authors, then, coveted the chance to produce or direct their own material, only those with substantial studio clout were granted the privilege. Of that handful, only a small percentage successfully established themselves as writer-producers or writer-directors. Additionally, of those few writers who *did* become producers or directors, most waited years for the chance. Sturges directed his first movie in 1940, Nichols and Odets in 1943.

Buchman was not promoted to producer until 1939, and Charles Brackett not until 1943. Only Nunnally Johnson established himself as a producer before the late thirties. Moreover, the efforts of these men did little to increase the status and prestige of screenwriters as a group. The assembly-line system of production was far too entrenched, and writing by committee too deeply ingrained in that system, to allow writers such power.

As Eastern writers made little headway within the studio system, they began to contemplate how that system could be modified to improve their position. As we have seen, writers' unfamiliar status as employees in the studios was basic to their dissatisfaction. As the thirties progressed many writers asserted that an end to the practice of hiring writers as salaried employees would ameliorate many of their problems and, by extension, improve not only the quality of Hollywood's product but also the efficiency of studio operations. Sidney Howard, for one, believed "that the whole system of the writer-employee is basically an unsound one."[49] Howard and others asserted that under the existing system in Hollywood, writers prolonged assignments in order to collect extra week's salary. There was a built-in disincentive to work quickly and well. Not surprisingly, these writers looked to the literary marketplace in New York for a more appropriate model of compensation. "If movie producers offered writers royalty arrangements like those in the theater and in publishing instead of straight salary," S. N. Behrman argued in 1936, "both writers and producer would be much happier. Producers would find their writers more attentive to their work, and writers would have a stake in doing the best job they possibly could."[50] Sidney Howard made exactly the same point when he claimed:

> The screen will get the most from its writers, and the writers most from the screen, when motion-picture bookkeeping and business methods have been so revised that the author of a picture is paid a royalty on its gross receipts and not a salary while he is writing it. Why I should be paid a salary while I am adapting a novel to the screen and a royalty when I dramatize the same novel for the stage I do not understand. I do know, however, that in the studio I am through on receipt of my last salary check, whereas in the theater I am at work up to the last moment before opening night, because, being human, I know that my reward is still to come and depends on my doing my very utmost.[51]

In the mid-thirties a group of playwrights, including Howard, Robert E. Sherwood, Maxwell Anderson, Lawrence Stallings, and Philip Barry, so favored this idea that they demanded royalty payments for screen work as part of a proposed scheme whereby Paramount would invest in theater production in return for their services as screenwriters. The plan was abandoned, however, when the playwrights could not agree on some of the legal arrangements. Another group of Eastern writers, including Rachel Crothers, Zoe Akins, George S. Kaufman, and Donald Ogden Stewart, wrote a joint letter to *Variety* in 1935 announcing their resolve to seek just such a royalty arrangement in their future contracts.[52] This proposal, like virtually all others to the same effect, fell on deaf ears in Hollywood. The status of the writer as an employee was too crucial to the producers' control over the scripting and production process for it to be abandoned. Only one writer I studied ever was paid on a royalty basis during the thirties: Jesse Lasky agreed to pay Preston Sturges $17,500 plus a percentage of the film's gross for the screenplay of *The Power and the Glory.* When he did, the other studios and even the other producers on the Fox lot, according to Sturges, accused Lasky and Sturges of "undermining the very foundation of the industry."[53] On his next picture, Sturges returned to straight salary.

As Eastern writers came to realize that the studio system was virtually impervious to individual assault from without *and* from within, they faced a formidable dilemma. It was simply impossible to be a writer in the traditional Eastern sense in Hollywood without destroying that which made them writers in the first place. How could they retain their self-images as writers while continuing to work in Hollywood? Not every writer found the same solution to this dilemma. Some found no solution at all. But most came to accept the necessity of conforming to Hollywood's expectations and accordingly readjusted their conception of what the writer was and did.

Writers could no longer afford to bury their heads in the sand and pretend that Hollywood's way of doing business did not exist; nor could they realistically expect that Hollywood would meet them on their own terms. "However secondary the writer's function in the making of pictures may be," Sidney Howard concluded in 1938, "two facts should at once be conceded: that so long as writers earn their living by writing they are economic nitwits not to earn at least some of it where the pay is both high and certain, and that to the very vast majority of the international public, the screen has superceded both plays and novels."[54] It would help a writer arriving in Hollywood, James M. Cain advised, "to have a clear idea of what his function is, and to discharge that function, instead of aspiring to functions which simply are not there."[55] When Clifford Odets returned to Hollywood in the 1940s he heeded Cain's advice and, for one, resolved not to fight the studio system. "Hollywood can have me if it wants me," he told a reporter for the *New York Times.* "From now on I'll do things conventionally, stay on speaking terms with the bosses, collect a well-rounded weekly salary and get a good sun-tan."[56]

Instead of fighting their status as employees, writers came to accept it. "After all," S. J. Perelman said later, "it was no worse than playing the piano in a whorehouse."[57] "The way I see it," Faulkner concurred, "it's like chopping cotton or picking potato bugs off plants; you know damn well it's not painting the Sistine Chapel or winning the Kentucky Derby. But a man likes the feel of some money in his pocket."[58] James M. Cain finally concluded after three years as a screenwriter that "there are worse trades than confecting entertainment."[59]

The secret to retaining sanity in Hollywood, writers came to realize, lay in drawing a distinct line between movie work and serious writing. Eastern writers became, in a sense, literary schizophrenics, acting out one identity when working on that which mattered to them and another when in the studios. One indication of how completely some writers subscribed to this dichotomy was John O'Hara's habit of segregating his Hollywood earnings from his "honest" money.[60] If the studios insisted on treating writers as hired hands, then they would abandon temporaily their identities as "writers" and act like hired hands, giving a day's work for wages but no more. Investing their sense of artistic integrity and purposefulness in movie work only led to unhappiness. "One of the first things you had to learn," Donald Ogden Stewart advised, "was not to let them break your heart because if you really put yourself into a script and began creating and cared terribly about it, then the producer, director, and the star would go to work on it and they could break your heart with what they could do to something you were very proud of."[61] Nathanael West explained clearly the distinction writers made between movie work and their other writing when he told Budd Schulberg:

> I don't mind doing those C movies at Republic. I watch my friends struggling to get their social messages into their million-dollar situation comedies and it seems to me it takes too much out of them—that is, if they hope to have anything left for their own work. The higher you get on the screenwriting ladder the more they expect of you. This way I can write, "Pardner, when you say that, smile," and "You dot dot dot mean?" and it's relatively painless. . . . This way I give them a fair day's work and can still concentrate on what I want to write for myself.[62]

By making this distinction between screenwriting and serious writing, some authors effectively shielded their self-images from Hollywood's threats, while at the same time gaining a sizeable weekly paycheck. "I work a few weeks a year, and collect the main part of my living expenses," wrote James M. Cain from Hollywood to *New Yorker* writer Wolcott Gibbs in 1938, "which leaves me free to do my other work without having to worry about the rent. I don't go nuts."[63] In this way, writers could justify their status as employees, as workers rather than independent free agents. "It's a trade, screenwriting," W. R. Burnett asserted, "you have to learn it, and it's not like writing novels."[64] Similarly, when an interviewer asked Nunnally Johnson whether he thought of himself as a craftsman rather than as an artist, he replied:

> Absolutely. An artist to me is the one who does it by himself, alone. Nobody helps him. What I'm doing, have done, and have never thought of myself any different, is I developed. . . . an ability, say, to convert a piece of property, as we call stories, from an original form into a moving picture form. I'm like a first-rate cabinet maker.[65]

Dudley Nichols, in contrast, once defined the writer (in the traditional sense) as "the dreamer, the imaginer, the shaper. He works in loneliness, with nebulous materials, with nothing more tangible than paper and a pot of ink, and his theater is written in the mind."[66] By considering screenwriting less a matter of dreaming than of crafting, authors could look upon it as honest work. Clifford Odets, for one, professed no guilt over the movies he wrote: "Let them stand for what they are. They are technically very adept. I have learned a great deal from making and shaping these scripts.... It's professional work; I'm a professional writer. And I am never ashamed of the professional competence which is in these scripts."[67] Budd Schulberg, for another, argued that Hollywood "isn't a hell from which you can't escape. The challenge of doing a good movie, of doing a good piece of work, isn't something to be ashamed of.... There were people who went there and met it on its own terms and beat it."[68]

The danger, as writers came to see it, lay not in the work itself, but in letting the lure of Hollywood money coopt their literary aspirations. "The only thing to be ashamed of," Schulberg warned, "is to be sucked in and let yourself be dependent on that contract and paycheck. That's when you're lost."[69] And that was when writers lost their sense of themselves as real writers. The trick, as S. J. Perelman explained it, was to accommodate Hollywood, collect your salary, and then get out.[70]

William Faulkner was also frequently concerned with the effect Hollywood had on his serious writing. "I have turned out three short stories since I quit the movies," he informed a friend after he returned to Oxford from his first trip to Hollywood in 1933, "so I have not forgotten how to write during my sojourn downriver."[71] After returning from another stint in the studios more than a decade later, Faulkner similarly reported to a friend, "It took me about a week to get Hollywood out of my lungs, but I am still writing all right, I believe."[72] Faulkner later explained why he had been able to work in Hollywood without damaging his ability to work on his serious writing:

> There's [sic] some people who are writers who believed they had talent, they believed in the dream of perfection, they get offers to go to Hollywood where they can make a lot of money, and they can't quit their jobs because they have got to continue to own that swimming pool and the imported cars. There are others with the same dream of perfection, the same belief that they can match it, that go there and resist the money without becoming a slave to it ... it is going to be difficult to go completely against the grain or current of a culture. But you can compromise without selling your individuality completely to it. You've got to compromise because it makes things easier.[73]

For Eastern writers in Hollywood, that compromise involved accepting their new status as workers with all the limitations on their traditonal prerogatives it entailed.

Moreover, in the 1940s authors in and out of Hollywood began to realize that the forces of large-scale industrial production at work in the studios were inevitably overwhelming the literary marketplace as well. "The cinema is still a giant in chains and a giant who has not yet even stood up and shaken those chains," Dudley Nichols wrote in 1943. "Those chains are censorship, commercialism, monopoly, and specialization—*all faults that are indigenous to industrial society and are not just characteristics of the cinema.*"[74] As the institutions of the literary marketplace began to cultivate the same mass audience as the motion picture industry, writers throughout the country noted with regret that while the economic benefits of professional authorship had inceased tremendously, writers had come to serve those institutions rather than the reverse. The much-publicized experiences of Eastern screenwriters, authors believed in the 1940s, both anticipated and fostered the increasing bureaucratization—to use their own favorite word—of the writer in the marketplace generally. No longer could most writers expect to be independent and autonomous free agents.

Articles filled the pages of literary journals and magazines in the forties both recognizing and deploring, as William Barrett wrote in the *Partisan Review* in 1946, "the enormous shifts which have occurred from the situation of the twenties to that of the forties" for the professional author.[75] R. P. Blackmur perhaps best summed up the crucial dilemma facing writers in the forties when, in 1946, he asked: "Can contemporary artists in any possible society permit themselves the pride, or the waste, as the case may be, of the traditional role of the artist?"[76] Barrett, for one, clearly believed not. He bitterly complained that writers were now "manipulated and strategically disposed like factory hands on an assembly line."[77] The Hollywood studios, the publications of the Luce empire, and the radio networks "carry the bureaucratization of the writer furthest in this country," Barrett continued, but they were not the only culprits:

> Publishers now strive to "catch up with and surpass" Hollywood in the wholesale manufacture of best-sellers from prefabricated parts and prearranged designs, precisely as Metro-Goldwyn-Mayer calculates in advance just what plots and stars will register at the box office. Following Hollywood, publishers know they can sell absolutely any book—even a dull religious novel—by the millions through the pressures of social imitation induced by high-pressure advertising.[78]

In such a situation, many writers nostalgically looked back to the more hospitable days of the twenties. "Ours was a lucky generation," Malcolm Cowley decided in 1945,

> and I am speaking of the writers who came of age during or shortly after the First World War.... We were lucky to have started writing at a time when it was comparatively easy to break into the magazines and when the public was hospitable to new writers.... Those

writers who came after us were not so lucky. They started their careers at a time when the public wasn't buying books, when several publishing houses were bankrupt, when magazines were getting thinner and finally dying of malnutrition, and when it was almost impossible for young men to earn their livings as free-lance writers. They had to find jobs somehow, and the jobs were likely to be in Hollywood or with the Luce magazines, which had continued to prosper, or else with the Federal Writers' Project; in all these cases the young men were attached to bureaucratic organizations which had a tendency to discourage their taking personal risks. [79]

In sum, the difficulties Eastern writers encountered in Hollywood had much to do with the constraints the studio system placed upon the authors' traditional independence and creative automony. Some authors rebelled against the system; others tried to increase their own power within it by assuming the duties of the producer and director. In neither case were writers able to improve *substantially* their lot in Hollywood. Ultimately, Eastern writers realized that if that system would not accommodate them, they would have to accommodate it.

Finally, by the 1940s writers in and out of Hollywood concluded that the writers' predicament in Hollywood merely foreshadowed a change in their professional situation generally, as the institutions of the literary marketplace—publishing houses, theatrical production companies, and magazine editorial offices—sought to tap the mass audience in America. As the economic stakes of publishing and theatrical production increased dramatically after World War Two, neither publisher nor producers could always afford the writer the same privileges and deference he had enjoyed in the twenties. If writers as individuals were rarely destroyed in Hollywood, then, the profession of authorship as they knew it certainly was under attack. This was the true significance of the Eastern writer's experience in Hollywood in the 1930s.

Appendix A

Eastern Writers in Hollywood, 1927-1940

*Abbott, George
Ade, George
*Akins, Zoe
*Anderson, Maxwell

Balderston, John
Baldwin, Faith
*Behrman, S.N.
*Benchley, Robert
*Benét, Stephen Vincent
Bolton, Guy
*Brackett, Charles
Bright, John
Brooks, George S.
*Buchman, Sidney
Burnet, Dana
*Burnett, W. R.
Busch, Niven

Caesar, Arthur
*Cain, James M.
Carpenter, Edward Childs
Carson, Robert
Caspary, Vera
Chodorov, Edward
Chodorov, Jerome
Colton, John
Connell, Richard
*Connelly, Marc
Cormack, Bartlett
*Cram, Mildred
Craven, Frank
*Crothers, Rachel
Crouse, Russell
Croy, Homer
Curwood, James Oliver

Davis, Owen Sr.
Delmar, Vina
*Dos Passos, John

Endore, Guy

Fante, John
Faragoh, Francis
*Faulkner, William
Fessier, Michael
Fields, Joseph
*Fitzgerald, F. Scott
Flavin, Martin
Ford, Corey
*Fowler, Gene
Franken, Rose
*Fuchs, Daniel

Gallico, Paul
Goodrich, Frances
*Green, Paul

Hackett, Albert
Hart, Moss
*Hammett, Dashiell
*Hecht, Ben
*Hellman, Lillian
*Hoffenstein, Samuel
*Howard, Sidney

Jennings, Talbot
*Johnson, Nunnally

Kandel, Aben
Kandel, Judith
*Kaufman, George S.
Kelly, George
Kennedy, Margaret

Kenyon, Charles
Kober, Arthur
Krasna, Norman
Kummer, Clare

Lamb, Harold
Latimer, Jonathan
Lawrence, Vincent
Lawson, John Howard
Lederer, Charles
Lindsay, Howard

*MacArthur, Charles
McCoy, Horace
McDonald, Philip
McGuire, William Anthony
Mankiewicz, Herman
March, Joseph Moncure
Mayer, Edward Justice
Murney, R. J.

Nash, Ogden
*Nichols, Dudley
Nicholson, Kenyon
Nugent, Eliot
Nugent, J. C.

*Odets, Clifford
*O'Hara, John
O'Neil, George
*Oppenheimer, George
Ornitz, Samuel

Pagano, Jo
*Parker, Dorothy
Patrick, John
*Perelman, S.J.

Raine, Norman Reilly
*Raphaelson, Samson
Richman, Arthur
Riggs, Lynn
Riskin, Robert

Rubin, Daniel
Runyan, Damon
Ryskind, Morris

St. Joseph, Ellis
Sale, Richard
Sanford, John
Saunders, John Monk
Sayre, Joel
Schiller, Fred
*Schulberg, Budd
Scott, Alan
Segall, Harry
Shaw, Irwin
*Sherwood, Robert E.
Spevak, Bella
Spevak, Samuel
Stallings, Lawrence
Starling, Lynn
*Stewart, Donald Ogden
*Sturges, Preston
Swerling, Jo

Tarkington, Booth
Taylor, Dwight
Thomas, A. E.
Totheroh, Daniel
Tully, Jim

Wallace, Francis
Watkins, Maurice
Wead, Frank
Weaver, John V. A.
Weitzenkorn, Louis
*West, Nathanael
*Wilder, Thornton
Wylie, Phillip

Yellen, Jack

*Denotes study group member

Appendix B

Study Group Members in the Studios, 1928-1940

1928

Fox—Behrman*
MGM-Howard*
Paramount—Abbott*, Hecht

1929

Fox—Nichols*, Raphaelson
MGM—Anderson, Howard
Paramount—Hecht
United Artists—Benét*
Universal—Abbott, Anderson*, Raphaelson*
Sam Goldwyn (ind.)—Howard

1930

Fox—Behrman, Nichols, Raphaelson
MGM—Anderson, Cram*
Paramount—Hammett*, Sturges*
RKO—Behrman
United Artists—Benét
Universal—Abbott
Warner Brothers—Burnett*

1931

Columbia—Abbott
Fox—Nichols
MGM—Akins*, Cram, Crothers*, Behrman, Fitzgerald
Paramount—Abbott, Cain*, Hammett, Raphaelson
RKO—Sherwood*, Fowler*
United Artists—Hecht, Sherwood
Universal—Sherwood, Sturge

Warner Brothers—Burnett
Howard Hughes (ind.)—Sherwood

1932

Columbia—Cain
Fox—Green, Nichols, Sherwood
MGM—Akins, Behrman, Cram, Crothers, Faulkner*, Fitzgerald, Sherwood, Stewart
Paramount—Brackett*, Hammett, Green, Johnson*, Raphaelson, Stewart
United Arts—Hecht, Sherwood
Universal—Akins, Crother
Warner Brothers—Burnett, Green*, Hammett

1933

Columbia—West*
Fox—Behrman, Hoffenstein*, Johnson, Nichols, Sturges
MGM—Anderson, Behrman, Benchley, Cram, Hecht, MacArthur*, Sherwood, Stewart
Paramount—Brackett, Parker*, Raphaelson
RKO—Benchley
United Artists—Hecht, Sherwood
Warner Brothers—Burnett, Green
S. Goldwyn (ind.)—Kaufman*, Oppenheimer*, Sherwood

1934

Columbia—Hecht
Fox—Hecht, Johnson, Nichols
MGM—Behrman, Benchley, Cain, Hammett, Hecht, MacArthur, Parker, Sherwood, Stewart
Paramount—Brackett, Dos Passos*, Hecht, MacArthur, O'Hara*, Raphaelson, Sturges
United Artists—Sturges
Universal—Faulkner, Sturges
Warner Brothers—Burnett, Hecht
S. Goldwyn (ind.)—Oppenheimer, Sturges

1935

Columbia—Buchman*
MGM—Akins, Behrman, Benchley, Connelly, Hoffenstein, Kaufman, MacArthur, Parker,
    Perelman, Oppenheimer, Stewart
Paramount—Brackett, Hammett, Odets*, Raphaelson
RKO—Nichols
Twentieth Century-Fox—Johnson, Nichols, Faulkner, Raphaelson
United Artists—Hecht
Universal—Hammett, Sturges
Warner Brothers—Burnett, Hammett

1936

Columbia—Buchman*
MGM—Akins, Behrman, Benchley, Connelly, Hoffenstein, Parker, Oppenheimer, Stewart
Paramount—Brackett, Hecht, MacArthur
RKO—Nichols
Twentieth Century-Fox—Johnson, Nichols, Faulkner, Raphaelson
United Artists—Hecht
Universal—Hammett, Sturges
Warner Brothers—Burnett, Hammett

1937

Columbia—Buchman, Oppenheimer
MGM—Akins, Benchley, Fitzgerald, Fowler, Hecht, Hoffenstein, MacArthur, Oppenheimer,
     Parker, Sherwood, Stewart
Paramount—Brackett, Sturges
RKO—Nichols
Twentieth Century-Fox—Faulkner, Johnson
United Artists—Hecht
Universal—Cram
Warner Brothers—Burnett, Connelly, Odets
S. Goldwyn—Hellman, Sherwood
D. Selznick—Howard, Schulberg

1938

Columbia—Buchman
MGM—Behrman, Benchley, Fitzgerald, Fowler, Hecht, Hoffenstein, Oppenheimer, Parker,
     Perelman, Schulberg
Paramount—Brackett, Sturges
RKO—Fuchs*, Hecht, West
Twentieth Century-Fox—Johnson
United Artists—Hecht, Sherwood
Warner Brothers—Burnett
S. Goldwyn (ind.)—Hellman
D. Selznick (ind.)—Parker

1939

Columbia—Buchman, Hecht
MGM—Benchley, Crothers, Fitzgerald, Fowler, Hoffenstein, Oppenheimer, MacArthur, Parker
     Perelman, Sherwood, Schulberg, Stewart
Paramount—Brackett, Sturges
RKO—O'Hara
Twentieth Century-Fox—Johnson
Universal—West
Warner Brothers—Burnett
S. Goldwyn (ind.)—Hecht
D. Selznick—Sherwood

*Denotes first Hollywood assignment

Notes

Introduction

1. Benét to Nannine Joseph, 20 February 1930, in Benét, *Selected Letters of Stephen Vincent Benét*, ed. Charles A. Fenton (New Haven: Yale University Press, 1960), p. 204.

2. George Jean Nathan, *The Entertainment of a Nation* (New York: Alfred A. Knopf, 1942), p. 85.

3. Nathan, "Theater," *Scribner's Magazine*, 102, no. 5 (November 1937), p. 66.

4. "Theater," pp. 66-68

5. "Theater," p. 68.

6. Wilson, *The Boys in the Back Room* (San Francisco: Colt Press, 1941), p.5.

7. Wilson, p. 56. My emphasis.

8. "S.J. Perelman," in *Writers at Work: The Paris Review Interviews, Second Series,* ed. George Plimpton (New York: The Viking Press, 1963), p. 251.

9. Quoted in Joseph Blotner, "Faulkner in Hollywood," in *Man and the Movies,* ed. W.R. Robinson (Baton Rouge: Louisiana State University Press, 1967), p. 293.

10. Sherwood, "Footnote to a Preface," *Saturday Review,* no. 32 (6 August 1949), p. 134.

11. Marx, "The Last Writes of the 'Eminent Authors'," *Los Angeles Times,* 12 March 1977, p. 3.

12. Matthew J. Bruccoli, *Some Sort of Epic Grandeur: The Life of F. Scott Fitzgerald* (New York: Harcourt Brace and Jovanovich, 1981), p. 259.

13. *Epic Grandeur,* p. 259.

14. Fitzgerald, *The Letters of F. Scott Fitzgerald,* ed. Andrew Turnbull. (New York: Scribners, 1963), p. 33.

15. Fitzgerald to Alice Robertson, 29 July 1940, in *Letters,* p. 603.

16. John Carmody, "Jim Cain: Master Teller of Hoary Old Hollywood Tales," *Los Angeles Times Calendar,* 2 February 1969, p. 8. For other portraits of Fitzgerald in Hollywood, see Arthur Mizener, *The Far Side of Paradise* (Boston: Houghton Mifflin, 1951), pp. 299-338; Andrew Turnbull, *Scott Fitzgerald* (New York: Scribners, 1962), pp. 294-333 and Bruccoli, *Some Sort of Epic Grandeur,* pp. 423-43, 454-74.

17. See Sheilah Graham with Gerold Frank, *Beloved Infidel* (New York: Holt, Rinehart and Winston, 1958); Graham, *The Rest of the Story* (New York: Coward-McCann, 1964); and most recently Graham's *The Real F. Scott Fitzgerald* (New York: Grosset and Dunlap, 1976).

18. Latham, *Crazy Sundays: F. Scott Fitzgerald in Hollywood* (New York: The Viking Press, 1970), p. 273.

19. See Schulberg's novel, *The Disenchanted* (New York: Random House, 1950); and "Old Scott: The Mask, the Myth and the Man," *Esquire* (January 1961), pp. 97-101. Schulberg expanded this essay in a later collection, *The Four Seasons of Success* (Garden City: Doubleday & Co., 1972), itself revised and re-issued in 1983 by Stein and Day as *Writers in America*. Yet another retelling should occur in the next volume of Schulberg's memoirs, following *Moving Pictures* (New York: Stein and Day, 1981).

20. *Four Seasons of Success*, p. 114.

21. André LeVot, *F. Scott Fitzgerald: A Biography*, trans. William Byron (Garden City: Doubleday & Co., 1983), p. 342.

22. Sherwood, "Renaissance in Hollywood," *American Mercury*, (April 1929), p. 434.

23. Sarris, "Preface," in Richard Corliss, *Talking Pictures* (Woodstock, N.Y.: The Overlook Press, 1974), p. xxi.

24. Vidal, "Who Makes the Movies," *New York Review of Books*, 25 Novembers 1976, p. 35.

25. Quoted in John Carroll, "Let Us Make You a Star," *Village Voice*, 28 July 1975, p. 8.

26. McMurtay, "On James Baldwin and the Movies," rev. of *The Devil Finds Work* by James Baldwin, *American Film*, (August 1976), p. 75.

27. Cain, "Camera Obscura," *American Mercury*, 30, no. 118 (October 1933), p. 139.

28. Shaw quoted in *Variety*, 2 December 1975, p. 23.

29. Shaw quoted in William Tuohy, "Author Irwin Shaw's Career Survives Day of the Critic," *Los Angeles Times*, 25 February 1973, p. 14.

30. Quoted in Stan Swinton, "Faulkner Hits Writers' Alibis," *Hollywood Citizen News*, 8 March 1953, p.18.

31. Letter to author from Daniel Fuchs, 21 October 1977.

32. Ben Hecht, *A Child of the Century* (New York: Simon and Schuster, 1954), pp. 466, 516.

33. Kael, "Raising Kane," in *The Citizen Kane Book* (Boston: Little, Brown Co., 1971), p. 19.

34. Kirsch, "Hollywood 'Hacks' Reconsidered," rev. of *Some Time in the Sun* by Tom Dardis, *Los Angeles Times*, 25 July 1976, p. 8.

35. Schultheiss, "A Study of the 'Eastern' Writer in Hollywood in the 1930s," Diss. USC 1973.

36. Dardis, *Some Time in the Sun* (New York: Scribners, 1976), A lesser book dealing with writers in Hollywood is Fred Lawrence Guiles's, *Hanging on in Paradise* (New York: McGraw-Hill, 1975.)

37. Dardis, p. 139.

38. Schultheiss, pp. 329-30.

39. Dardis, p. 128.

40. One of the major frustrations in trying to uncover Hollywood's history is the fact that most books in the field are second-rate. Despite the intense interest in American movies over the past twenty years, the most substantive and balanced accounts of the film industry are now at least thirty-five years old: Benjamin B. Hampton's *A History of the Movies* (1931); Lewis Jacobs's *The Rise of the American Film* (1939); and Leo Rosten's *Hollywood: The Movie Colony and the Movie Makers* (1941). These three books remain unsurpassed in accuracy, scope, and insight.

41. Among those who have written extensively about the Eastern writer in Hollywood, only Schultheiss makes an effort to define what he means by "Eastern." He is "concerned with those writers who had their literary origins and developed their reputations in *non-movie* fields.... The term "Eastern" writer is used in recognition of the fact that the Eastern seaboard, particularly New York and Boston, has been traditionally thought of as metonymical representation of America's literary establishment." (p. 2) I would supplement Schultheiss's definition by asserting that these writers' ties with the East were more than symbolic. They were the result of very real encounters with the businesses of the literary marketplace headquartered in New York.

42. "MGM," *Fortune* 6, no. 6 (December 1932), p. 54. Irving Thalberg was the boy-wonder supervisor of production at MGM at the time.

43. "Where are the Playwrights of Yesteryear?," *Literary Digest*, 3 October 1931, p. 21.

44. Marx, "Last Writes," p. 3.

45. The expatriate community in particular was ill-defined. There exists only a thin line between those writers who travelled extensively in Europe in the twenties and those who were genuinely committed to a life outside the United States. Literary groups of this kind are generally incohesive and rarely discrete.

46. By this definition, writers like Budd Schulberg and Sidney Howard, both Californians by birth and early upbringing, may be considered Eastern. They both came in contact with the literary establishment in New York before accepting their first screenwriting assignment. Schulberg had been schooled at Dartmouth and published a number of stories in New York magazines. Howard had supervised the production of several of his plays on Broadway and taken an active part in New York's literary affairs.

47. This list was compiled by comparing publication lists and theatrical credits from 1920-1938 with screenplay credit lists, studio directories, and motion picture almanacs from the 1930s. The list is definitely incomplete: there is no reliable source of information on those writers who worked for independent producers, for example, or for those who worked on short-term contracts and did not receive screen credit for their work. The 138 writers listed in Appendix A are those whose involvement in New York and Hollywood has been verified.

48. Rosten, *Hollywood: The Movie Colony and the Movie Makers* (New York: Harcourt, Brace and Co., 1941), p. 363.

49. The study group was chosen according to three criteria: first, that they conform to the definition of "Eastern" mentioned earlier; second, that they arrived in Hollywood for the first time between late 1927 and 1938; and finally, that they left some record which indicates their reaction to working in the studios. Many of the 138 writers listed in Appendix A left no such record; consequently, the study group is not a scientific or random sample of the larger group and its members are more likely to have been successful than those who were omitted.

50. Priestley, *Midnight on the Desert* (New York: Harper Brothers, 1937), pp. 175-76.

51. Goodenough, "Cultural Anthropology and Lingusitics," in *Report of the Seventh Annual Round Table Meeting on Linguistics and Language Study,* ed. P. L. Garvin (Washington, D.C.: Georgetown University Press, 1957), p. 167. Goodenough elaborates: "A society's culture consists of whatever it is one has to know or believe in order to operate in a manner acceptable to its members, and to do so in any role that they accept for any of themselves.... By this definition, we should note that culture is not a material phenomenon; it does not consist of things, people, behavior, or emotions. It is rather an organization of these things. It is the forms of things that people have in mind, their models for perceiving, relating, and otherwise interpreting them." (p.167)

52. Jay Martin, *Nathanael West: The Art of His Life* (New York: Hayden Book Company, 1970), p. 205.

53. See, for instance, George Bluestone, *Novels into Film* (Berkeley: University of California Press, 1957); and Robert Richardson, *Literature and Film* (Bloomington: Indiana University Press, 1969).

54. Carolyn See, "The Hollywood Novel: An Historical and Critical Study," Diss. UCLA 1963; Jonas Spatz, *Hollywood in Fiction* (The Hague: Mouton Press, 1969); and Walter Wells, *Tycoons and Locusts* (Carbondale: Southern Illinois Univeristy Press, 1973). For a bibliography of Hollywood novels, refer to Carolyn see, "The Hollywood Novel: A Partial Bibliography," Bulletin of Bibliography, *Bulletin of Bibliography* 24, no .9 (1966), 208-16.

Chapter 1

1. Kazin quoted in Susan Edminston and Linda D. Cirino, *Literary New York* (Boston: Houghton-Mifflin Co., 1976), p. ix.

2. Howells, *Literature and Life* (New York: Harper & Brothers, 1902), p. 179. For further information on the growth of New York as a publishing center, see John Tebbell, *A History of Book Publishing in the United States, vol. 2,* (New York: R. R. Bowker, 1975), pp. 78-94, 114-16; and Hellmut Lehman-Haupt's *The Book in America* (New York: R. R. Bowker, 1939), pp. 212-34.

3. Alfred Bernheim, *The Business of the Theatre: An Economic History of the American Theatre 1790-1932* (New York: Benjamin Blom, 1932), pp. 26-43. A broader study of the commercial theater is Jack Poggi's *The Theater in America: The Impact of Economic Forces 1870-1967* (Ithaca: Cornell Univesity Press, 1966). For information on the growth of the theater in New York, see Mary C. Henderson, *The City and the Theater* (Clifton, N.J.: James T. White & Co., 1973).

    Of the combination system's impact on New York, Bernheim writes:
    > Where decentralization was the keynote of the stock system, centralization became the outstanding feature of the combination regime. This centralization had two manifestations. In the first place, it made New York the producing center for the entire country. Where New York, due to its wealth, its size, its more immediate contact with the old world, and its general prestige as the great metropolis of the nation, had already become the principal theatrical city, its influence over the rest of the country in matters theatrical was mainly that of a leader of fashion and taste. Its direct contact with other communities was limited to the tours of the stars, which generally originated in New York, and to the occasional tours of its own stock companies. Now, however, it actually became the feeder for virtually all the theaters that adopted the combination system, for New York, in addition to the advantages named above, was the only city where all the plays could be cast and mounted that were needed to supply the theaters throughout the country. (p. 33).

4.   Van Doren, "First Day in New York," *Three Worlds* (New York: The Viking Press), p. 58.

5.   Benchley to John Reed, 8 October 1912, John Reed Papers, Houghton Library, Harvard University, Cambridge, Massachusetts.

6.   Benchley to John Reed, 8 October 1912, Reed Papers.

7.   Abbott, *Mister Abbott* (New York: Random House, 1963), p. 73.

8.   Scott Fitzgerald to Zelda Sayre, 19 February 1919, in Fitzgerald, *The Correspondence of F. Scott Fitzgerald*, eds. Matthew J. Bruccoli and Margaret M. Duggan (New York: Random House, 1980), p. 38.

9.   O'Hara to Robert Simonds, 25 March 1925, in O'Hara, *Selected Letters of John O'Hara*, ed. Matthew J. Bruccoli (New York: Random House, 1978), p. 14.

10.   O'Hara to Simonds, Spring 1928, in *Letters of John O'Hara*, p. 34.

11.   Ben Hecht, *Child of the Century*, p. 372. Pascal Covici was a Chicago publisher very much interested in avant-garde writing, who moved to New York shortly after Hecht.

12.   Maxwell Anderson to Alvin Johnson, 17 November 1918, Maxwell Anderson Papers, Humanities Research Center, University of Texas, Austin, Texas.

13.   Anderson to Harold Munro, 3 June 1920, Anderson Papers.

14.   Anderson to W.S. Braithewaite, n.d., W. S. Braithewaite Papers, Houghton Library, Harvard University, Cambridge, Mass.

15.   Statistics culled from Burns Mantle, *The Best Plays of 1919-20 to 1929-30*, 11 volumes (New York: Dodd, Mead and Co., 1920-30); and Otis L. Guernsey, Jr., ed., *The Best Plays of 1970-1 to 1977-8*, 8 volumes (New York: Dodd, Mead and Co., 1970-78).

16.   Charles Madison, *Book Publishing in America* (New York: Random House, 1966), pp. 470-74.

17.   Cowley quoted in Allen Churchill, *The Literary Decade* (Englewood Cliffs: Prentice-Hall, 1971), p. 219.

18.   Van Wyck Brooks, *Days of the Phoenix: The 1920s I Remember* (New York: E. P. Dutton, 1957), p. 5.

19.   Madison, pp. 470-71; Tebbell, pp. 212-30.

20.   Walker Gilmer, *Horace Liveright* (New York: David Lewis, 1970), pp. 60-80.

21.   Louis Kronenberger, "Gambler in Publishing: Horace Liveright," *Atlantic Monthly* 215, no. 1 (January 1965), p. 94.

22.   Hellman, *An Unfinished Woman* (Boston: Little, Brown Co., 1969), p. 28.

23.   Gilmer, p. 24.

24.   Kronenberger, p. 98.

25.   Hellman, p. 30.

26.   Kronenberger, p. 99.

27.   Liveright quoted in "The House of Boni & Liveright," *Literary Digest*, 2 (August 1924), 686. My emphasis.

28.   Liveright to Eugene O'Neill, 28 July 1930, quoted in Gilmer, p. 224.

29.   Hellman, p. 40.

30.   Roger Burlingame, *Of Making Many Books* (New York: Charles Scribner's Sons, 1946), p. 107. See also Malcolm Cowley, *The Literary Situation* (New York: Viking Press, 1954), pp. 174-76.

31.   Burlingame, p. 63.

32.   John Farrar, "Securing the Manuscript," in Chandler Grannis, ed., *What Happens in Book Publishing* (New York: Columbia University Press, 1957), p. 33.

33.   "A Canfield-Knopf Dialogue," *Saturday Review*, 10 August 1974, p. 46.

34.   H. S. Latham to William Rose Benét, 30 August 1920, William Rose Benét Papers, Beinecke Library, Yale University, New Haven, Connecticut.

35.   William Charvat, *The Profession of Authorship in the United States* (Columbus: Ohio State University Press, 1968), pp. 292-93.

36.   Walter Hines Page, *Confessions of a Publisher* (New York: Doubleday, Page and Co., 1905), p. 14.

37.   Henry Holt, "The Commercialization of Literature," *Atlantic Monthly*, 96, no. 5 (November 1905), p. 73.

38.   Richard Harding Davis to Charles Scribner, 11 May 1892, quoted in Burlingame, p. 5.

39.   Benét to John Farrar, 28 December 1927, in *Letters of Stephen Vincent Benét*, p. 149.

40.   Fitzgerald to Maxwell Perkins, 1 June 1925, in *Dear Scott/Dear Max: The Fitzgerald-Perkins Correspondence*, eds. John Kuehl and Jackson Bryer (New York: Scribner's, 1971), p. 273.

41.   Fitzgerald to Perkins, 1 June 1925, in *Dear Scott/Dear Max*, p. 107.

42.   Perkins to Fitzgerald, 13 June 1925, in *Dear Scott/Dear Max*, p. 115.

43.   Cheney, pp. 131-32.

44.   Tebbell, p. 132.

45.   Tebbell, p. 136.

46.   On the formation of the Authors' League, see Lehman-Haupt, pp. 240-45; and Tebbell, 138-48.

47.   Lehman-Haupt, pp. 103-5.

48.   "Are Your Book Contracts Satisfactory?" *Authors' League Bulletin* 6, no. 11 (February 1919), pp. 6-7.

49.   Cheney, p. 136.

50.   Perkins quoted in Scott Berg, *Maxwell Perkins* (New York: E. P. Dutton, 1978), p. 4.

51.   For a history of authors' compensation in the marketplace, see Tebbell, pp. 138-44. Fitzgerald's royalty figure from *As Ever, Scott Fitz-*, ed. Matthew J. Bruccoli (Philadelphia: J. B. Lippincott Co., 1972), p. xviii.

52.   "Are Your Book Contracts Satisfactory?" p. 7.

53. Cheney, p. 138.

54. Cheney, p. 131.

55. "Are Your Book Contracts Satisfactory?" p. 6.

56. "Canfield-Knopf Dialogue," p. 44.

57. Perkins quoted in Berg, p. 6.

58. Perkins to Marjorie Kinnan Rawlings, 26 March 1936, quoted in Berg, pp. 298-99. My emphasis.

59. Bernheim, p. 115.

60. Sherwood quoted in Brown, p. 236.

61. Oppenheimer, *The View from the Sixties* (New York: David McKay Company, 1966), p. 73.

62. Hellman, p. 30.

63. Edminston and Cirino, *Literary New York*, pp. 184-85.

64. Brown, pp. 151-52.

65. Schulberg, *Four Seasons of Success*, p. 3.

66. Connelly, *Voices Offstage* (New York: Holt, Rinehart and Winston, 1968), pp. 80-81.

67. Brooks, *Days of the Phoenix*, p. 164.

68. Personal interview with W. R. Burnett, 31 October 1977, Los Angeles, California.

69. Personal interview with W. R. Burnett, 31 October 1977, Los Angeles, California.

70. Sculley Bradley to Maxwell Anderson, 12 December 1950; Samuel Berger to Anderson, 6 April 1928; and Arlene Francis to Anderson, n.d.; all Maxwell Anderson Papers.

Chapter 2

1. Lewis Jacobs, *The Rise of the American Film* (New York: Teachers College Press, 1939), p. 287.

2. Benjamin Hampton, *A History of the Movies* (New York: Covici, Friede, 1931), p. 30.

3. Hampton, p. 43.

4. Jacobs, p. 82. For more on the MPPC and the trust war, see Gordon Henricks, *The Edison Motion Picture Myth* (Berkeley: University of California Press, 1961). Hampton's *A History of the Movies*, pp. 64-145, remains an essential source.

5. McWilliams, *Southern California: An Island on the Land* (1946; rpt. Santa Barbara: Peregrine Smith, 1973), p. 331.

6. Robert Sklar, *Movie-Made America* (New York: Random House, 1975), pp. 67-68. Sklar, who effectively demolishes the tents-in-the-night theory, writes: "Los Angeles was well-known at the time—though no Hollywood memoir chooses to recall it—as the nation's leading open-shop, nonunion city. A constant inflow of new residents, buying inexpensive bungalows and seeking work, maintained a surplus of settled laborers and kept wages low, from a fifth to a third below the prevailing rates in San Francisco, and in some cases half the wage levels of New York." (68).

7. Hampton, p. 362.

8. Jacobs, pp. 129-31.

9. Jacobs, p. 130.

10. Jacobs, p. 131.

11. "Famous Authors With Universal," *The Moving Picture World,* 5 September 1914, p. 17.

12. "$100,000 For Photoplay Ideas," *Theatre Magazine,* August 1916, p. 88.

13. Hampton, p. 193.

14. Philip French, *The Movie Moguls* (London: Penguin, 1971), p. 173. See also Arthur Marx, *Goldwyn* (New York: W. W. Norton, 1976), pp. 37-39.

15. French, p. 173; also Marx, pp. 69-71.

16. Tom Stempel, "Interview With Nunnally Johnson," unpublished transcription, American Film Institute Library, American Film Institute, Beverly Hills, California.

17. Oppenheimer, *View From the Sixties,* p. 96.

18. Goldwyn, *Behind the Screen* (New York: George Doran Company, 1923), p. 235.

19. Goldwyn, p. 100.

20. *Movie Mirror,* October 1919, p. 33.

21. *Photoplay,* June 1921, p. 42.

22. "The Author and the Film," *Mentor* 9, no. 6 (July 1921), p. 31.

23. Marx, pp. 103-6; Goldwyn's version is in *Behind the Screen,* pp. 251-53.

24. Goldwyn, p. 243.

25. Goldwyn, p. 243.

26. Rinehart, *My Story* (New York: Farrar and Rinehart, 1931), p. 292.

27. Rinehart, pp. 292-93, 297.

28. Rinehart, p. 294.

29. Rinehart, pp. 292, 297.

30. Elinor Glyn, *Romantic Adventure* (New York: E. P. Dutton, 1937), p. 292.

31. Glyn, p. 291.

32. Glyn, p. 295.

33. Glyn, p. 296.

34. Rinehart, pp. 292-93.

35. Rice, *Minority Report* (New York: Simon and Schuster, 1963), p. 170.

36. Rice, p. 170.

37. Rice, p. 173.

38. Rice, p. 179.

39. Rice, p. 179.

40. Rice, p. 185.

41. Rice, pp. 179-80.

42. Rice, pp. 179-80. My emphasis.

43. Will Hays, *The Memoirs of Will H. Hays* (Garden City: Doubleday and Co., 1955), p. 324. See also Garth Jowett, *Film: The Democratic Art* (Boston: Little, Brown and Co., 1976), pp. 160-71.

44. Quoted in Edward H. Smith, "Dreiser—After Twenty Years," *Bookman*, 53 (March 1921), p. 34.

45. Quoted in Edith Millicent Ryan, "Cruel Words—Theodore Dreiser," *Los Angeles Times*, 27 September 1922, p. 15.

46. Dreiser, "Hollywood Now," *McCall's Magazine*, 47, no. 8 (Sept. 1921), pp. 18, 54; and "Hollywood: Its Manners and Morals," which appeared in several issues of *Shadowland* and included: "I. The Struggle on the Threshold of Motion Pictures" (November 1921), pp. 37, 61-63; The Commonplace Tale of a Thousand Endings" (December 1921), pp. 51, 61; "III. The Beginner's Thousand-to-One Change" (January 1922) pp. 43, 67; and "IV. The Extra's Fight to Exist" (February 1922), pp. 53, 66. See also Neil Leonard, "Theodore Dreiser and the Film," *Film Heritage* (Fall, 1966), pp. 7-16; and A. W. Swanberg, *Dreiser* (New York: Charles Scribner's Sons, 1965), pp. 249-63, 372-77.

47. Sherwood quoted in Brown, p. 175.

48. Sherwood quoted in Brown, p. 176.

49. Van Vechten's articles were published in *Vanity Fair*, 28, under the titles, "Fabulous Hollywood" (May 1927), p. 54; "Hollywood Parties" (June 1927),pp. 47, 86, 90; "Hollywood Royalty" (July 1921), pp. 38, 86; and "Understanding Hollywood" (August 1927), pp. 45, 78. See also Bruce Kellner, *Carl Van Vechten and the Irreverent Decades* (Norman, Oklahoma: University of Oklahoma Press, 1968).

50. "Understanding Hollywood," p. 45.

51. "Understanding Hollywood," p. 78.

52. "RKO Press Biography of Herman J. Mankiewicz," 1936, Herman Mankiewicz File, Academy of Motion Picture Arts and Sciences Library, Beverly Hills, California.

53. Richard Meryman, *Mank: The Wit, World and Life of Herman Mankiewicz* (New York: William Morrow and Company, 1978), pp. 38-62.

54. Meryman, p. 90.

55. Meryman, p. 123.

56. Meryman, p. 121.

57. Meryman, p. 137.

58. Hecht, *A Child of the Century*, p. 272.

59. "Gene Fowler's Hollywood," *Hollywood Reporter*, 14 July 1949, p. 3.

60. Quoted in Meryman, p. 173.

61. Johnson quoted in Guiles, *Hanging on in Paradise,* p. 189.

62. Kael, *The Citizen Kane Book,* pp. 48, 51-52.

63. Schulberg, *Four Seasons of Success,* p. 98.

64. Stempel, "Interview With Nunnally Johnson," pp. 190-91.

65. Personal interview with W. R. Burnett, 31 October 1977, Los Angeles, California.

66. Hecht, *A Child of the Century,* pp. 393-94.

67. Quoted in Ben Hecht, *Charlie* (New York: Harper Brothers, 1957), p. 97.

68. *Child of the Century,* p. 471.

69. Lawrence Stallings to Charles MacArthur, 22 June 1928, Theater Arts Collection, Humanities Research Center, University of Texas, Austin, Texas.

70. *Child of the Century,* p. 466.

71. Bauer, "The Movies Tackle Literature," *The American Mercury,* 14 (July 1928), pp. 293-94.

72. Bauer, p. 294.

73. Dreiser quoted by H. S. Kraft, "Forward," in Borden Deal, *The Tobacco Men* (New York: Holt, Rinehart and Winston, 1965), p. 11.

74. Rosten, p. 167.

75. Connelly, *Voices Offstage,* photo following p. 150.

76. Clurman, *The Fervent Years* (New York: Alfred A. Knopf, 1945), p. 170.

Chapter 3

1. *Film Daily,* 6 August 1926, p. 1. For more information on the introduction of sound, see Harry M. Geduld, *The Birth of the Talkies: From Edison to Jolson* (Bloomington: Indiana University Press, 1975), and J. Douglas Gomery, "The Coming of the Talkies: Invention, Innovation, and Diffusion," in Tino Balio, ed., *The American Film Industry* (Madison: University of Wisconsin Press, 1976), pp. 193-210.

2. *Los Angeles Times,* 19 October 1928, p. 5.

3. Jacobs, *The Rise of the American Film,* p. 435.

4. Sherwood, "Renaissance in Hollywood," *American Mercury* 16, no. 64 (April 1929), p. 432.

5. "Renaissance in Hollywood," p. 433.

6. Letter to author from S. N. Behrman, 5 April 1976.

7. Behrman, *People in a Diary* (Boston: Little, Brown, 1972), p. 131.

8. James Curtis, *Between Flops: A Biography of Preston Sturges* (New York: Harcourt, Brace, Jovanovich, 1982), pp. 73-5.

9. Stewart, "Writing for the Movies," *Focus on Film,* (Winter 1970), p. 50.

10. Abbott, *Mister Abbott,* p. 130.

11. Cheney, *Economic Survey of the Book Industry,* p. 14. A number of writers did lose heavily on Black Friday. George S. Kaufman and Samson Raphaelson, for instance, had invested a large portion of their play royalties in the market.

12. Helmut Lehman-Haupt, *The Book in America*, pp. 320-21; Eugene Exman *The House of Harper* (New York: Harper and Row, 1967), p. 248; and Berg, *Max Perkins* p. 207.

13. Elmer Davis, "Some Aspects of the Economics of Authorship," *Bowker Lectures on Book Publishing* (New York: The Typophiles, 1945), p. 8.

14. Mantle, *Best Plays of 1930-1*, p. v. For an account of Broadway during the Depression, see Cabell Phillips, *From the Crash to the Blitz* (New York: MacMillan, 1969), p. 365.

15. Mantle, *The Best Plays of 1932-3*, p. 10.

16. Clurman, *The Fervent Years* (1945; rpt. New York: Harcourt, Brace, and Jovanovich, 1975), p. 113.

17. See Appendix B.

18. See Charles A. Fenton, *Stephen Vincent Benét* (New Haven: Yale University Press, 1957), pp. 231-41.

19. John Considine to Stephen Vincent Benét, 18 November 1929, Benét Papers.

20. Stephen Vincent Benét to John Considine, 19 November 1929, Benét Papers.

21. Fenton, *Stephen Vincent Benét*, p. 233.

22. Personal interview with W. R. Burnett, 31 October 1977, Los Angeles, California.

23. Stempel, "Interview with Nunnally Johnson," pp. 13-14.

24. Rosten, p. 62.

25. Daniel Bertrand, *The Motion Picture Industry* (Washington, D. C.: Temporary National Economic Committee, 1941), p. 12.

26. Rosten, p. 61.

27. Balio, *The American Film Industry*, p. 247. The best business history of the movies in the 1930s remains Mae D. Huettig, *Economic Control of the Motion Picture Industry* (Philadelphia: University of Pennsylvania Press, 1944). See also the more recent Douglas Gomery and Robert C. Allen, eds., "Economic and Technological History," *Cinema Journal* 18 (Spring 1979); and Jeanne Thomas Allen, ed., "Economic and Industry History of the American Film," *The Journal of the University Film Association* 31 (Spring 1979).

28. West worked for Republic Studios, one of a number of smaller production companies in Hollywood surviving on the remnants of the market left by the majors.

29. Balio, p. 238.

30. Sklar, *Movie-Made America*, p. 230.

31. Rosten identifies seven basic types of producers: The executive head of a studio; the executive in charge of production: independent producers; the producer in charge of A pictures; the producer in charge of B pictures; the associate producer; and the producer-director. (pp. 260-64).

32. Bosley Crowther, *The Lion's Share* (New York: E. P. Dutton, 1957), p. 131.

33. Rosten, p. 238.

34. Jesse Lasky with Don Weldon, *I Blow My Own Horn* (Garden City: Doubleday and Co., 1957), p. 89.

35. "An Analysis of the Motion Picture Industry," *Report to the Screen Directors Guild,* 18 July 1938, pp. 1-2, 4-5. Unpublished document located in the Academy of Motion Picture Arts and Sciences Library, Beverly Hills, California.

36. Sklar, p. 230.

37. Sklar, p. 239.

38. Sklar, p. 239.

39. Crowther, *The Lion's Share,* p. 182.

40. About the Production Code Administration, see Raymond Moley's flattering *The Hays Office* (New York: Bobbs-Merrill, 1945); Richard Randall's more considered *Censorship in the Movies* (Madison: University of Wisconsin Press, 1968); and, from Hays himself, *The Memoirs of Will H. Hays* (Garden City: Doubleday and Co., 1955).

41. Moley, p. 245.

42. Moley, p. 242.

43. Stewart, "Writing for Hollywood," p. 53.

44. Joan Crawford, for instance, reportedly threw Scott Fitzgerald off the set of one of her movies.

45. Blotner, "Faulkner in Hollywood," pp. 294-303.

46. For a detailed history of United Artists, see Tino Balio, *United Artists: The Company Built By the Stars* (Madison: University of Wisconsin Press, 1976). This is by far the best history of any of the studios. It is incisive and meticulously documented.

47. For a more detailed narrative of Universal's growth, see I. G. Edmunds, *Big U: Universal in the Silent Days* (New York: A. S. Barnes, 1977).

48. For more information about Columbia, see Rochelle Larkin's slight *Hail, Columbia!* (New Rochelle: Arlington House, 1975). A more detailed look at the studio is given in Bob Thomas, *King Cohn: The Life and Times of Harry Cohn* (New York: G. P. Putnam's, 1967).

49. Frank Capra, *The Name Above the Title* (New York: MacMillan, 1971), p. 81.

50. Capra, p. 82.

51. Charles Higham, *Warner Brothers* (New York: Charles Scribner's Sons, 1975), p. 45. See also Clive Hirschhorn, *The Warner Brothers Story* (New York: Crown Publishers, 1979).

52. Rosten, p. 174.

53. Personal interview with W. R. Burnett, 31 October 1977, Los Angeles, California.

54. For an examination of Fox's career, see Hampton, pp. 329-41; and "The Case of William Fox," *Fortune,* 1 (May 1930), pp. 48-49.

55. About Twentieth Century Pictures and its founders, see "Twentieth Century-Fox," *Fortune,* 12 (December 1935), pp. 85-93; and Mel Gussow, *Don't Say Yes Until I Finish Talking: A Biography of Darryl F. Zanuck* (Garden City: Doubleday and Co., 1971).

56. See John Davis, "RKO: A Studio Chronology," *Velvet Light Trap,* 10 (Fall 1973), pp. 6-12; and the more extensive Richard Jewell and Vernon Harbin, *The RKO Story* (New Rochelle: Arlington House, 1982).

57. For a more detailed look at Paramount, see both Will Irvin, *The House That Shadows Built* (Garden City: Doubleday and Co., 1928); and "Paramount Pictures," *Fortune* 15 (March 1937), pp. 87-96.

58. "Metro-Goldwyn-Mayer," *Fortune* 6 (December 1932), p. 51. For more on MGM, see John Douglas Eames, *The MGM Story: The Complete History of Fifty Roaring Years* (New York: Octopus, 1975).

59. Crowther, *The Lion's Share*, p. 43.

60. Rosten, p. 243; *The Lion's Share*, p. 71.

61. "Metro-Goldwyn-Mayer," p. 53.

62. "Metro-Goldwyn-Mayer," p. 54.

63. Powdermaker, *Hollywood: The Dream Factory*, p. 85.

64. Sklar, pp. 231-32.

65. Before the Screen Writers Guild agreement in 1941, producers could suspend writers without pay, and often did, if there was no current project for them to work on.

66. Bob Nero, "Interview with H. N. Swanson," unpublished transcription of interviews conducted December 1974-March 1975, American Film Institute Library, American Film Institute, Beverly Hills, California, p. 80.

67. Rosten, p. 323.

68. Dardis, *Some Time in the Sun*, p. 115.

69. Rosten, p. 381.

70. Personal interview with W. R. Burnett, 31 October 1977, Los Angeles, California.

71. Nero, "Interview with H. N. Swanson," p. 78.

72. Personal interview with Samson Raphaelson, 21 June 1979, New York, New York; letter from S. N. Behrman, 5 April 1979; Diane Johnson, *Dashiell Hammett: A Life* (New York: Random House, 1983), p. 119.

Chapter 4

1. Benét to Rosemary Benét, December 1929, *Selected Letters*, p. 192.

2. Benét to Rosemary Benét, December 1929, *Selected Letters*, p. 192.

3. Benét to Rosemary Benét, December 1929, *Selected Letters*, pp. 192-93.

4. Benét to Rosemary Benét, December 1929, *Selected Letters*, p. 193.

5. Benét to Rosemary Benét, December 1929, *Selected Letters*, p. 194.

6. Benét to John Farrar, December-January 1929-30, Stephen Vincent Benét Papers, Beinecke Library, Yale University, New Haven, Connecticut.

7. Benét to Rosemary Benét, December 1929, *Selected Letters*, pp. 194-95.

8. Benét to Frieda Lubelle, December 1929, *Selected Letters*, p. 196.

9. Benét to John Farrar, December-January 1929-30, Benét Papers.

10.   Benét to Rosemary Benét, December 1929, *Selected Letters,* p. 198.

11.   Quoted in Charles A. Fenton, *Stephen Vincent Benét* (New Haven: Yale University Press, 1958), pp. 237-38.

12.   Benét to Rosemary Benét, 23 January 1930, *Selected Letters,* pp. 202-3.

13.   Benét to Carl Brandt, 23 January 1930, *Selected Letters,* pp. 200-201. William A. Brady, Sr. was a New York theatrical producer.

14.   *Variety,* 29 January 1930, p. 11.

15.   Benét to Carl Brandt, 3 February 1930, *Selected Letters,* p. 203.

16.   Memorandum, Harry Brand to John W. Considine, 5 February 1930, Benét Papers.

17.   Brand to Considine, 5 February 1930, Benét Papers.

18.   John W. Considine to James Starr, 4 February 1930, Benét Papers.

19.   Considine to Starr, 4 February 1930, Benét Papers.

20.   Benét to Rosemary Benét, 8 February 1930, quoted in Fenton, p. 240.

21.   Benét to William Rose Benét, January 1930, *Selected Letters,* p. 200.

22.   Benét to Rosemary Benét, December 1929, *Selected Letters,* p. 193.

23.   John Dos Passos, *The Best Times: An Informal Memoir* (New York: New American Library, 1966), p. 205.

24.   John Dos Passos, *The Fourteenth Chronicle: The Letters and Diaries of John Dos Passos,* ed. Townsend Ludington (Boston: Gambit, Inc., 1973), p. 437.

25.   Dos Passos to Edmund Wilson, quoted in Townsend Ludington, *John Dos Passos: A Twentieth Century Odyssey* (New York: E. P. Dutton, 1980), p. 330.

26.   Quoted in Joseph Blotner, *Faulkner: A Biography* (New York: Random House, 1974), p. 727. Hal Smith was one of Faulkner's publishers.

27.   Blotner, *Faulkner,* p. 768.

28.   Dorothy Parker to Alexander Woollcott, n.d., Alexander Woollcott Papers, Houghton Library, Harvard University, Cambridge, Massachusetts.

29.   "Are Film Writers Workers?" *Pacific Weekly,* 4, no. 6 (29 June 1939), 371.

30.   Quoted in John Mason Brown, *Robert E. Sherwood* (New York: Harper & Row, 1962), p. 263.

31.   Brown, p. 263.

32.   Wilder to Rosemary Ames, 24 July 1934, Thorton Wilder Papers, Beinecke Library, Yale University, New Haven, Connecticut. By stipulation of the Wilder estate, his unpublished writings may not be quoted directly.

33.   John O'Hara, *Selected Letters of John O'Hara,* ed. Matthew J. Bruccoli (New York: Random House, 1978), p. 80.

34.   Matthew Bruccoli, *The O'Hara Concern* (New York: Random House, 1975), p. 105.

35.   O'Hara, *Letters,* pp. 93-94.

36. O'Hara, *Letters,* p. 95.

37. O'Hara, *Letters,* p. 109.

38. O'Hara, *Letters,* p. 122.

39. O'Hara, *Letters,* p. 122.

40. *New York Herald Tribune,* 11 May 1941, p. 11.

41. For example, Nathanael West, John Dos Passos, John O'Hara, and Budd Schulberg all viewed Hollywood as grist for their fiction mills.

42. Quoted in Jay Martin, *Nathanael West: The Art of His Life,* (New York: Farrar, Straus and Giroux, 1970), p. 205.

43. Dorothy Parker to Alexander Woollcott, n.d., Woollcott Papers, Houghton Library, Harvard University, Cambridge, Massachusetts.

44. George Oppenheimer, *The View From the Sixties* (New York: David McKay Co., 1966), pp. 104, 123.

45. Melford Spiro, for instance, described social systems as "characterized by a configuration of reciprocal roles that are shared by the members of the social group and are acquired from a previous generation." "Cognition in Culture and Personality," in James Spradley, ed., *Culture and Cognition* (San Francisco: Chandler Publishing Co., 1972), p. 103. Each role, or identity relationship, is comprised of a set of right and duty interactions. Ward Goodenough defined an important aspect of social interaction when he observed, "We tend to think of duties as things we owe to individual alters, but in reality we owe them to their social identities." "Rethinking 'Status' and 'Role,'" in *The Relevance of Models for Social Anthropology,* Ass. Soc. Anthropologists Monograph, 1965, no. 1, p. 4. In short, the interaction of any given writer and producer was governed by each's perception of what a "writer" and a "producer" was.

46. Abbott, *Mister Abbott,* p. 207.

47. "Hollywood Wit," *New York Herald Tribune,* 23 January 1940, p. 19.

48. "Kaufman Returns From the West," *Broadway Notes,* 15 March 1938, p. 4.

49. Howard, "The Story Gets a Treatment," in *We Make the Movies,* ed. Nancy Naumberg (New York: W. W. Norton, 1937), p. 44.

50. Benét to Carl Brandt, 23 January 1930, *Selected Letters,* p. 201.

51. "Interview with S.J. Perelman," in *Writers at Work: The Paris Review Interviews,* Second Series, ed. George Plimpton (New York: The Viking Press, 1963), p. 251.

52. Hecht, *Bohemia,* pp. 47-48. Sam Zimbalist was a producer at MGM.

53. Marx, "Last Writes," p. 3.

54. Lincoln Barnett, "The Happiest Couple of Them All," *Life,* 11 December 1944, pp. 101-2.

55. Dos Passos to F. Scott Fitzgerald, 19 October 1934, in Dos Passos, *The Fourteenth Chronicle,* p. 445.

56. Cram, "Author in Hollywood," in *The American Spectator Yearbook,* ed. George Jean Nathan (New York: Stokes Publishing Co., 1934), pp. 176-77.

57. Schulberg, *Four Seasons of Success,* p. 99.

58. Blotner, "Faulkner in Hollywood," p. 268.

59. Latham, *Crazy Sundays*, p. 6.

60. Blotner, "Faulkner in Hollywood," p. 282.

61. Hecht, *Bohemia*, p. 41.

62. Hecht, *Bohemia*, p. 43.

63. Hecht, *Bohemia*, pp. 43-44.

64. Schulberg, *Four Seasons of Success*, p. 113.

65. Stewart quoted in Nancy Schwartz, *The Hollywood Writers' Wars* (New York: Alfred A. Knopf, 1982), p. 20.

66. Fuchs, "Hollywood Diary," *The New Yorker*, (6 August 1938), p. 23.

67. Personal interview with W. R. Burnett, 31 October 1977, Los Angeles, Ca.

68. Abbott, *Mister Abbott*, pp. 205-6.

69. Hellman, *An Unfinished Woman* (Boston: Little-Brown, 1969), p. 49.

70. Rosten, *Hollywood*, p. 40.

71. Fuchs, "Hollywood Diary," p. 26.

72. Hellman, *Unfinished Woman*, p. 48.

73. Schulberg quoted in Robert Van Gelder, "An Interview with Budd Schulberg," *New York Times Book Review*, 46 (10 August 1941), p. 2.

74. Howard, "The Story Gets a Treatment," p. 35.

75. Schulberg quoted in Van Gelder, p. 2.

76. Schulberg, "Poor Scott: The Mask, the Myth and the Man," *Esquire*, 55 (January 1961), p. 98.

77. Hellman, *An Unfinished Woman*, p. 52.

78. Bruccoli, *Epic Grandeur*, p. 426.

79. "Screenwriters Speak Out," *Los Angeles Times*, 11 November 1937, p. 3.

80. Donald Ogden Stewart, "Writing for the Movies," *Focus on Film*, 5 (Winter 1970), p. 52.

81. Letter to author from Nunnally Johnson, 21 January 1975.

82. Quoted in Schwartz, p. 12.

83. Howard, "The Story Gets a Treatment," p. 44.

84. Hecht, *Child of the Century*, p. 473.

85. "Hollywood Wit," p.19.

86. Benét to Carl Brandt, 23 January 1930, *Selected Letters*, p. 201.

87. Personal interview with W. R. Burnett, 31 October 1977, Los Angeles, Ca.

88. Buchman quoted in *Hollywood Citizen News*, 11 February 1947, p. 17.

89.   Dorothy Parker to Alexander Woollcott, n.d., Woollcott Papers, Houghton Library, Harvard University, Cambridge, Massachusetts.

90.   Howard, "The Story Gets a Treatment," pp. 35-36.

91.   Howard, "The Story Gets a Treatment," p. 33.

92.   "Kaufman's Return," *The New York Times,* 30 January 1938, p. 23.

93.   Schulberg, *The Four Seasons of Success,* p.7.

94.   Roy Hoopes, *Cain: The Biography of James M. Cain* (New York: Holt, Rinehart and Winston, 1982), p. 220-21.

95.   Fuchs, "A Hollywood Diary," p. 23.

96.   S. N. Behrman to Alexander Woollcott, 15 May 1933, Woollcott Papers, Houghton Library, Harvard University, Cambridge, Massachusetts.

97.   Personal interview with W. R. Burnett, 31 October 1977, Los Angeles, Ca.

98.   Blotner, "Faulkner in Hollywood," p. 267.

99.   Behrman, *People in a Diary,* p. 158. Gene Fowler expressed sympathy for the producer's point of view on this matter. "They appreciate industry out here," he told a reporter in 1940, "a lot of writers who come to Hollywood don't realize that and hold up pictures that should be made fast." "Gene Fowler Tells of His Writing Plans," *New York Times,* 15 September 1940, p. 3.

100.   Cram, "Author in Hollywood," pp. 178-79.

101.   Quoted in Martin, *Nathanael West,* p. 205.

102.   Hecht, *Child of the Century,* p. 487.

103.   Dos Passos, *Fourteenth Chronicle,* p. 443.

104.   Schulberg quoted in Van Gelder, p. 2.

105.   Quoted in Tom Stempel, "Interview with Nunnally Johnson," p. 17.

106.   Howard, "The Story Gets a Treatment," p. 44.

107.   Personal interview with Samson Raphaelson, 21 June 1979, New York, New York.

108.   Fitzgerald, *Letters,* pp. 558-60.

109.   Fitzgerald, *Letters,* p. 563.

110.   Fitzgerald, *Letters,* p. 564.

111.   Schulberg, *Four Seasons,* p. 98.

112.   Hecht, *Charlie,* p. 161.

113.   Johnson to Edgar Watson Howe, 9 July 1933, Houghton Library, Harvard University, Cambridge, Massachusetts.

114.   Anderson to George A. Volck, 16 June 1930, Anderson Papers, Humanities Research Center, University of Texas, Austin, Texas.

115.   "Going Their Own Way Now," *New York Times,* 27 August 1944, p. 17.

116.   Schulberg, *Four Seasons,* p. 26.

117. Stempel, "Interview with Nunnally Johnson," p. 16.

118. Personal interview with W. R. Burnett, 31 October 1977, Los Angeles, California.

119. Barnett, "Happiest Couple," p. 103.

120. Stewart, "Writing for Hollywood," p. 52.

121. "Interview with S.J. Perelman," *Writers at Work*, p. 254.

122. Schulberg, *Four Seasons*, p. 108.

123. Hecht, *Child of the Century*, p. 474.

124. Anderson to John Mason Brown, 18 May 1949, in *Dramatist in America: Letters of Maxwell Anderson, 1912-1958*, ed. Laurence G. Avery (Chapel Hill: University of North Carolina Press, 1977), p. 231.

125. Anderson, "Cut Is the Branch That Might Have Grown Full Straight," *Off Broadway* (New York: William Sloan, 1947), p. 71.

126. Cain, "Camera Obscura," *American Mercury*, 30 (October 1933), p. 144.

127. Brackett, "But What Do You Do?" *Hollywood Reporter*, 8 October 1940, p. 3.

128. Howard, "The Story Gets a Treatment," p. 32.

129. Fitzgerald, *Letters*, p. 284.

130. Hecht, *Child of the Century*, p. 476. My emphasis.

131. Cram, "Author in Hollywood," p. 175.

132. Quoted in Nathaniel Benchley, *Robert Benchley* (New York: McGraw-Hill Book Company, 1955), p. 17.

133. Faulkner, *Letters*, p. 101.

134. Faulkner, *Letters*, p. 199.

135. Cain, "Camera Obscura," p. 138.

136. Dos Passos, *Fourteenth Chronicle*, p. 444.

137. Quoted in Blotner, *Faulkner*, p. 818.

138. Odets to John Mason Brown, 16 December 1935, John Mason Brown Papers, Houghton Library, Harvard University, Cambridge, Massachusetts.

139. Anderson, "Cut Is The Branch," p. 73.

140. This version from Nunnally Johnson to E. W. Howe, 9 July 1933, Houghton Library, Harvard University, Cambridge, Massachusetts.

141. Hecht, *Charlie*, p. 159.

142. Quoted in H. Allen Smith, *The Life and Legend of Gene Fowler* (New York: William Marrow and Co., 1977), p. 235.

143. Schulberg, *Four Seasons*, p. 129.

144. Deutsch to Mab Maynard, 3 June 1940, Maxwell Anderson Papers, Humanities Research Center, University of Texas, Austin, Texas.

145.   Deutsch to Maynard, 17 September 1940, Anderson Papers.

146.   Deutsch to Maynard, 30 October 1940, Anderson Papers.

147.   Deutsch to Maynard, 17 April 1941, Anderson Papers.

148.   Deutsch to Maynard, 4 November 1941, Anderson Papers.

149.   Deutsch to Maynard, 3 February 1942, Anderson Papers.

150.   Frank MacShane, "Raymond Chandler in Hollywood," *American Film* (April 1976), p. 62. See also MacShane, *The Life of Raymond Chandler* (New York: E. P. Dutton, 1976).

151.   MacShane, "Raymond Chandler in Hollywood," p. 67.

152.   Chandler to Charles Morton, 21 September 1944, in *Raymond Chandler Speaking,* eds. Dorothy Gardiner and Kathrine Sorley Walker (Boston: Houghton-Mifflin, 1977), p. 115.

153.   Chandler, "Writers in Hollywood," *Atlantic Monthly,* 176 (November 1945), p. 50.

154.   "Writers in Hollywood," pp. 50, 52.

155.   "Writers in Hollywood," p. 51.

156.   "Writers in Hollywood," p. 52.

157.   "Writers in Hollywood," p. 51.

158.   "Writers in Hollywood," p. 54.

159.   "Writers in Hollywood," p. 57.

160.   "Writers in Hollywood," p. 51.

161.   "Writers in Hollywood," pp. 51, 53.

162.   *Raymond Chandler Speaking,* p. 125.

163.   Hecht, *Bohemia,* p. 40.

164.   Connelly, *Voices Offstage,* p. 219.

165.   Behrman, *People in a Diary,* p. 153.

166.   Oppenheimer, *View From the Sixties,* p. 133.

167.   See, for example, Sheilah Graham, *The Garden of Allah* (New York: Crown Publishers, 1970).

168.   Clurman, *The Fervent Years* (New York: Alfred A. Knopf, 1945), pp. 200-201.

169.   Martin, *Nathanael West,* p. 271.

170.   Hecht, *Child of the Century,* p. 481.

171.   Cain, "Camera Obscura," p. 139.

172.   Abbott, *Mister Abbott,* p. 135.

173.   Howard, "The Story Gets a Treatment," p. 44.

174.   Quoted in Norman Zierold, *The Moguls* (New York: Coward-McCann, Inc., 1969), p. 266.

175.   Quoted in French, *The Movie Moguls,* p. 89.

176.   "Why Motion Pictures Cost So Much," *Saturday Evening Post,* 4 November 1933, p. 74.

177.   Bob Nero, "Interview with H. N. Swanson," December 1974-March 1975, American Film Institute manuscript, Beverly Hills, California.

178.   Fitzgerald, *Letters*, p. 278.

179.   Hecht, *Child of the Century*, p. 476.

Chapter 5

1.   Schulberg, *Four Seasons*, p. 108.

2.   Schulberg, *Four Seasons*, p. 105.

3.   Carmody, "Jim Cain," p. 8.

4.   Hecht, *Charlie*, p. 172.

5.   Hecht, *Bohemia*, p. 41.

6.   Smith, *Life and Legend of Gene Fowler*, p. 218. Story repeated to me, in slightly different form, by W. R. Burnett and Nunnally Johnson.

7.   Raymond Chandler, *Selected Letters of Raymond Chandler*, ed. Frank MacShane (New York: Columbia University Press, 1981), pp. 53-54.

8.   Allen Rivkin and Laura Kerr, *Hello Hollywood!* (Garden City: Doubleday and Co., 1962), p. 65.

9.   Walter Lazenby, *Paul Green* (Austin: Steck-Vaughn Co., 1970), p. 32.

10.   Marx, "Last Writes," p. 3.

11.   Edward Murray, *Clifford Odets: The Thirties and After* (New York: Frederick Unger, 1968), p. 106.

12.   Anderson to Anatole Litvak, 28 July 1942, Maxwell Anderson Papers, Humanties Research Center, University of Texas, Austin, Texas.

13.   Quoted in Wayne Warga, "From Hollywood to HUAC with Hellman," *Los Angeles Times West View*, 10 June 1976, p. 3.

14.   Schulberg, *Four Seasons*, p. 132.

15.   Lasky, *I Blow My Own Horn*, p. 246.

16.   Quoted in Noel Busch, "Preston Sturges," *Life*, 20, no. 1 (7 January 1946), p. 86. For a fuller account of *The Power and the Glory*, see James Curtis, *Between Flops: A Biography of Preston Sturges* (New York: Harcourt Brace Jovanovich, 1982), pp. 80-88.

17.   Quoted in Busch, p. 86.

18.   Personal interview with Samson Raphaelson, 21 June 1979, New York, New York.

19.   Personal interview with Samson Raphaelson, 21 June 1979, New York, New York.

20.   Quoted in George J. Mitchell, "Ford on Ford," *Films in Review*, 15, no. 6 (June-July 1964), p. 325.

21.   Quoted in John Podeschi, "The Writer in Hollywood," Diss. University of Illinois 1971, p. 185.

22. Nichols, "Writer, Director and Film," in John Gassner and Dudley Nichols, ed., *Best Film Plays of 1943-44* (New York: Crown Publishers, 1945), p. xxii.

23. Nichols, "Film Writing," *Theatre Arts Monthly*, 26, no. 12 (December 1942), 770-71.

24. Quoted in Emanuel Eisenberg, "John Ford: Fighting Irish," *New Theatre* (April 1936), p. 67.

25. Stewart, "Writing for Hollywood," p. 52.

26. Personal interview with W. R. Burnett, 31 October 1977, Los Angeles, California.

27. Oppenheimer, *View from the Sixties*, p. 96.

28. Quoted in Michael J. Mendelsohn, "Odets at Center Stage," *Theatre Arts Monthly*, 47, no. 6 (June 1963), p. 28.

29. Nichols, "Introduction," in John Gassner and Dudley Nichols, eds., *Best Film Plays—1945* (New York: Crown Publishers, 1946), p. xviii.

30. The reason Odets did not make a movie for MGM is unclear. As the author tells it: "After I finished *None But the Lonely Heart*, MGM signed me to a fantastic deal to write and direct. For over a year I did nothing. I sat in the basement of my big house and did little watercolors which were costing MGM about $500 a painting. Finally, I told my agent to cancel the deal, which would still have paid me $250,000 or $300,000." (Quoted in Murray, *Clifford Odets*, pp. 106-7.) The studio, however, claimed that Odets did submit story ideas and outlines, none of which it deemed commercially viable.

31. Nichols, "Mourning Becomes Electra," *Films in Review*, 9, no. 7 (Aug-Sept 1958), p. 409.

32. Quoted in Podeschi, p. 194.

33. Curtis, p. 125.

34. "Paramount's One-Man Show: Sturges Writes, Then Directs Film on American Politics," *Newsweek*, 16, no. 8 (19 August 1940), p. 44.

35. *Agee on Film: Volume I* (New York: MacDowell, Obelensky, Inc., 1958), p. 73.

36. King, "Preston Sturges," *Vogue*, 104, no. 3 (15 August 1944), p. 179.

37. Podeschi, p. 58. See also Curtis, 194-95, for evidence of friction between the two men.

38. "Cinemaschluss," *Time*, 43, no. 19 (6 March 1944), p. 94. For more information on California Pictures, see Curtis, pp. 200-28.

39. Quoted in Alicia L. Carey, "Then and Now," *New York Times Magazine*, 2 December 1956, p. 94.

40. *Motion Picture Herald*, 14 March 1950, p. 11.

41. Quoted in Barnett, "The Happiest Couple in Hollywood," p. 75.

42. Maurice Zolotow, *Billy Wilder in Hollywood* (New York: G. P. Putnam's Sons, 1977), p. 170.

43. Stempel, "Interview with Nunnally Johnson," p. 1.

44. Robert van Gelder, "This Business of Writing for the Movies," *New York Times*, 1 September 1940, p. 2.

45. Johnson quoted in van Gelder, p. 2.

46. Hecht, *Charlie*, p. 185.

47. Hecht, *Charlie*, p. 185.

48. Hecht, *Charlie*, p. 189.

49. Howard, "The Story Gets a Treatment," p. 48.

50. *Motion Picture Herald*, 7 May 1936, p.7.

51. Howard, "The Story Gets a Treatment," p. 50.

52. *Variety*, 4 February 1935, p. 14.

53. Sturges quoted by Busch, p. 86. In 1948, Samuel Goldwyn made a similar proposal for a profit-sharing system, claiming that writers should not "sacrifice their artistic aspirations for the security of a weekly paycheck." (*The Screen Writer* [April 1948], p. 34). Writers then replied that such a scheme would only work if the producer, too, put his salary into the capital fund; if writers and producers then lived on modest drawing accounts from the capital fund; and if rights to the property then reverted to the writer. Nothing came of Goldwyn's offer.

54. Howard, "The Story Gets a Treatment," p. 47.

55. Cain, "Camera Obscura," p. 146.

56. "Going Their Own Way," *New York Times*, 27 August 1944, p. 31.

57. "Interview with S.J. Perelman," *Writers at Work*, p. 253.

58. Faulkner quoted in Blotner, "Faulkner in Hollywood," p. 294.

59. Cain, "Camera Obscura," p. 146.

60. Bruccoli, *The O'Hara Concern*, p. 153.

61. Stewart, "Writing for Hollywood," p. 52.

62. West quoted in Schulberg, *Four Seasons*, pp. 157-58.

63. James M. Cain to Wolcott Gibbs, 16 April 1938, quoted in Hoopes, pp. 189-90.

64. Personal interview with W. R. Burnett, 31 October 1977, Los Angeles, California.

65. Stempel, "Interview with Nunnally Johnson," p. 220.

66. Nichols, "The Writer and the Film," in *Twenty Best Film Plays*, p. xl.

67. Odets quoted in Mendelsohn, p. 29.

68. Schulberg quoted in Harvey Breit, "A Talk with Mr. Schulberg," *New York Times Book Review*, 5 November 1950, p. 28.

69. Schulberg quoted in Breit, p. 28.

70. "Interview with S.J. Perelman," p. 252.

71. Quoted in Blotner, "Faulkner in Hollywood," p. 272.

72. Quoted in Blotner, "Faulkner in Hollywood," p. 297.

73. Quoted in Blotner, "Faulkner in Hollywood," p. 303.

74. Nichols, "The Writer and the Film," p. xl. My emphasis.

75.   Barrett, "The Resistance," *Partisan Review*, 13 (1946), p. 479.

76.   Blackmur, "The Economy of the American Writer," *Sewanee Review*, 40 (1945), p. 185.

77.   Barrett, p. 483.

78.   Barrett, p. 483.

79.   Cowley, "For the Postwar Writers," *New Republic*, 113 (3 December 1945), pp. 751-52.

Bibliography

New York and the Literary Marketplace

"A Canfield-Knopf Dialog," *Saturday Review*, 10 August 1974, pp. 44-47.

Adams, Franklin P. *Diary of Our Own Samuel Pepys*. New York: Simon and Schuster, 1935.

Barrett, William. "The Resistance," *Partisan Review* 13 (1946): 479-88.

Berg, A. Scott. *Max Perkins: Editor of Genius*. New York: E. P. Dutton & Co., 1978.

Bernheim, Alfred L. *The Business of the Theatre: An Economic History of the American Theatre 1790-1932*. New York: Benjamin Blom, 1932.

Blackmur, R. P. "The Economy of the American Writer." *Sewanee Review* 55 (1945): 175-85.

Boyer, Paul S. *Purity in Print: The Vice Society Movement and Book Censorship in America*. New York: Charles Scribner's Sons, 1968.

Brooks, Van Wyck. *Days of the Phoenix: The 1920s I Remember*. New York: E. P. Dutton & Co., 1957.

_____. *The Writer in America*. New York: E. P. Dutton & Co., 1953.

Burlingame, Roger. *Of Making Many Books: A Hundred Years of Reading, Writing and Publishing*. New York: Charles Scribner's Sons, 1946.

Case, Frank. *Tales of a Wayward Inn*. Garden City: Doubleday & Co., 1940.

Cerf, Bennett. *At Random*. New York: Random House, 1977.

Charvat, William. *The Profession of Authorship in the United States*. Columbus, Ohio: Ohio State University Press, 1968.

Cheney, Orion H. *Economic Survey of the Book Industry: 1930-31*. New York: National Association of Book Publishers, 1931.

Clurman, Harold. *The Fervent Years: The Story of the Group Theater and the Thirties*. New York: Alfred A. Knopf, 1945.

Cowley, Malcolm. *Exile's Return: A Literary Odyssey of the 1920s*. New York: The Viking Press, 1951.

_____. *The Literary Situation*. New York: The Viking Press. 1947.

_____. "For the Post War Writers." *New Republic* 113 (1945): 751-52.

Dallman, John. *The Art of Play Production*. New York: Harper and Brothers, 1928.

Davis, Elmer. "Some Aspects of the Economics of Authorship." *Bowker Lectures on Book Publishing*. New York: The Typophiles, 1945.

Earnest, Ernest. *Expatriates and Patriots*. Durham: Duke University Press, 1968.

_____. *The Single Vision: The Alienation of American Intellectuals 1910-1930*. New York: New York University Press. 1971.

Edminston, Susan and Cirino, Linda D. *Literary New York*. Boston: Houghton Mifflin Co., 1976.

Exman, Eugene. *The House of Harper*. New York: Harper and Row, 1967.

Frick, Constance. *The Dramatic Criticism of George Jean Nathan.* Ithaca: Cornell University Press, 1943.

Gilmer, Walker. *Horace Liveright: Publisher of the Twenties.* New York: David Lewis, 1970.

Grannis, Chandler P. *What Happens in Book Publishing.* New York: Columbia University Press, 1957.

Henderson, Mary C. *The City and the Theater.* Clifton, New Jersey: James T. White & Co., 1973.

Hepburn, James. *The Author's Empty Purse and the Rise of the Literary Agent.* London: Oxford University Press, 1968.

Hoffman, Frederick J. *The Twenties: American Writing in the Post War Decade.* New York: The Viking Press, 1949.

Jovanovich, William. *Now, Barabbas.* New York: Harper and Row, 1964.

Kronenberger, Louis. "Gambler in Publishing: Horace Liveright." *Atlantic Monthly,* January 1965, pp. 94-107.

Kujoth, Jean Speakman, ed. *Book Publishing: Inside Views.* Metuchen, New Jersey: The Scarecrow Press, Inc., 1971.

Lehmann-Haupt, Hellmut. *The Book in America.* New York: R. R. Bowker, 1939.

Madison, Charles A. *Irving to Irving: Author-Publisher Relations 1800-1974.* New York: R. R. Bowker, 1974.

Miller, William. *The Book Industry.* New York: Columbia University Press, 1949.

Mott, Frank Luther. *American Journalism: A History 1690-1960.* 3rd ed. New York: The MacMillan Co., 1962.

Nathan, George Jean. *Entertainment of a Nation.* New York: Alfred A. Knopf, 1938.

———. "Theater." *Scribner's Magazine,* November 1937, pp. 66-68.

Phillips, Cabell. *From the Crash to the Blitz.* New York: The MacMillan Co., 1969.

Poggi, Jack. *Theater in America: The Impact of Economic Forces 1870-1967.* Ithaca: Cornell University Press, 1966.

Ross, Isabel. *The Expatriates.* New York: Thomas Y. Crowell Co., 1970.

Schultheiss, John. "George Jean Nathan and the Dramatist in Hollywood." *Literature/Film Quarterly* 4 (1976), 13-27.

Tebbel, John. *A History of Book Publishing in the United States.* 4 vols. New York: R. R. Bowker, 1975-1981.

Van Doren, Carl. "First Day in New York." In *Carl Van Doren.* New York: The Viking Press, 1945. pp. 58-65.

Wharton, John F. *Life Among the Playwrights.* New York: The New York Times Book Co., 1974.

"Where Are the Playwrights of Yesteryear?" *The Literary Digest.* 3 October 1931, p. 21.

Wincor, Richard. *Literary Property.* New York: Clarkson N. Potter, Inc., 1967.

Hollywood and the Studio System

Agee, James. *Agee on Film.* 2 vols. New York: McDowell, Obelensky, Co., 1958.

Allen, Jeanne Thomas, eds. "Economic and Industrial History of the American Film." *The Journal of the University Film Association,* 31 (Spring 1979).

Balio, Tino. *United Artists: The Company Built by the Stars.* Madison: University of Wisconsin Press, 1976.

———, ed. *The American Film Industry.* Madison: University of Wisconsin Press, 1976.

Bauer, Leda V. "The Movies Tackle Literature." *American Mercury,* July 1928, pp. 288-94.

Behlmer, Rudy, ed. *Memo From David O. Selznick.* New York: The Viking Press, 1972.

Bluestone, George. *Novels into Film: The Metamorphosis of Fiction into Cinema.* Berkeley: The University of California Press, 1957.

Capra, Frank. *The Name Above the Title.* New York: The MacMillan Co., 1971.

Cohen, Keith. *Film and Fiction: The Dynamics of Exchange.* New Haven: Yale University Press, 1979.

Corliss, Richard. *The Hollywood Screenwriters.* New York: Discuss Books, 1972.

_____. *Talking Pictures.* Woodstock, New York: The Overlook Press, 1974.

Crowther, Bosley. *Hollywood Rajah: The Life and Times of Louis B. Mayer.* New York: Holt, Rinehart and Winston, 1960.

_____. *The Lion's Share: The Story of an Entertainment Empire.* New York: E. P. Dutton, 1957.

Eames, John Douglas. *The MGM Story: The Complete History of Fifty Roaring Years.* New York: Octopus, 1975.

Easton, Carol. *The Search for Sam Goldwyn.* New York: William Morrow, 1976.

Edmunds, I. G. *Big U: Universal in the Silent Days.* New York: A. S. Barnes and Co., 1977.

Eisenberg, Emanuel. "John Ford: Fighting Irish." *New Theatre,* April 1936, pp. 66-69.

"Famous Authors with Universal." *The Moving Picture World.* 5 September 1914, p. 1356.

French, Philip. *The Movie Moguls.* London: Weidenfield and Nicholson, 1969.

Geduld, Harry M. *The Birth of the Talkies: From Edison to Jolson.* Bloomington: Indiana University Press, 1975.

Goldwyn, Samuel. *Behind the Screen.* New York: George Doran Co., 1923.

Gomery, Douglas, and Robert C. Allen, eds. "Economic and Technological History." *Cinema Journal,* 18 (Spring 1979).

Griffith, Richard. *Samuel Goldwyn: The Producer and His Films.* New York: Museum of Modern Art Library, 1956.

Gussow, Mel. *Don't Say Yes Until I Finish Talking: A Biography of Darryl F. Zanuck.* Garden City: Doubleday & Co., 1971.

Hampton, Benjamin B. *History of the American Film Industry: From its Beginnings to 1931.* 1932; rpt. New York: Dover Publications, 1970.

Harrington, John. *Film and/as Literature.* Englewood Cliffs: Prentice-Hall, 1977.

Hirschhorn, Clive. *The Warner Brothers Story.* New York: Crown Publishers, 1979.

Huettig, Mae D. *Economic Control of the Motion Picture Industry.* Philadelphia: University of Pennsylvania Press, 1944.

Irwin, Will. *The House That Shadows Built.* Garden City: Doubleday, Doran and Co., 1928.

Jacobs, Lewis. *The Rise of the American Film: A Critical Study.* New York: Teachers College Press, 1939.

Jewell, Richard with Vernon Harbin. *The RKO Story.* New Rochelle: Arlington House, 1982.

Kael, Pauline. "Raising Kane." In *The Citizen Kane Book,* ed., Pauline Kael. Boston: Little, Brown & Co., 1971.

Lahue, Kalton C. *Dreams for Sale: The Rise and Fall of The Triangle Film Corporation.* New York: A. S. Barnes & Co., 1971.

Larkin, Rochelle. *Hail, Columbia!* New Rochelle: Arlington House, 1975.

Lasky, Jesse L. with Don Weldon. *I Blow My Own Horn.* Garden City: Doubleday & Co., 1957.

McWilliams, Carey. *Southern California: An Island on the Land.* 1946; rpt. Santa Barbara: Peregrine Smith, 1973.

Marx, Samuel. "The Last Writes of the 'Eminent Authors'." *Los Angeles Times,* 12 March 1977, p. 3.

_____. *Mayer and Thalberg: The Make-Believe Saints.* New York: Random House, 1975.

Mast, Gerald. *A Short History of the Movies.* Indianapolis: The Bobb-Merrill Co., 1976.

Naumberg, Nancy, ed. *We Make the Movies.* New York: W. W. Norton Co., 1937.

North, Joseph H. *The Early Development of the Motion Picture (1887-1909).* New York: Arno Press, 1973.

O'Hara, Kenneth. "The Life of Thomas H. Ince." *Photoplay,* June 1917, pp. 34-47.

"100,000 For Photoplay Ideas." *The Theater,* August 1916, p. 12.

Podeschi, John. "The Writer in Hollywood." Diss. University of Illinois at Champagne-Urbana 1971.

Powdermaker, Hortense. *Hollywood: The Dream Factory.* Boston: Little, Brown and Co., 1950.

Priestley, J. B. *Midnight on the Desert.* New York: Harper & Brothers, 1937.

Richardson, Robert. *Literature and Film.* Bloomington: Indiana University Press, 1969.

Rivkin, Allen, and Kerr, Laura. *Hello, Hollywood!* Garden City: Doubleday & co., 1962.

Robinson, W. R., ed. *Man and the Movies.* Baton Rouge: Louisiana State University Press, 1967.

Ross, Lillian. *Picture.* New York: Rinehart & Co., 1952.

Ross, Murray. *Stars and Strikes: The Unionization of Hollywood.* New York: Columbia University Press, 1941.

Rosten, Leo. *Hollywood: The Movie Colony and the Movie Makers.* New York: Harcourt, Brace & Co., 1941.

Sarris, Andrew. "Notes on the Auteur Theory in 1962." *Film Culture,* No. 27 (1962/3), pp. 1-8.

Schwartz, Nancy Lynn completed by Sheila Schwartz. *The Hollywood Writers' Wars.* New York: Alfred A. Knopf, 1982.

See, Carolyn. "The Hollywood Novel: An Historical and Critical Study." Diss. University of California, Los Angeles, 1963.

Sklar, Robert. *Movie-Made America: A Social History of American Movies.* New York: Random House, 1975.

Spatz, Jonas. *Hollywood in Fiction.* The Hague: Mouton Press, 1969.

Thomas, Bob. *King Cohn: The Life and Times of Harry Cohn.* New York: G. P. Putnam's Sons, 1967.

————. *Selznick.* New York: Pocket Books. 1972.

————. *Thalberg: Life and Legend.* Garden City: Doubleday & Co., 1969.

Vidal, Gore. "Who Makes the Movies?" *New York Review of Books,* 25 November 1976, pp. 35-39.

Wanger, Walter. "Hollywood and the Intellectual." *Saturday Review,* 5 December 1942, pp. 6, 40.

Warner, Jack L. *My First Hundred Years in Hollywood.* New York: Random House, 1964.

Wells, Walter. *Tycoons and Locusts.* Carbondale, Illinois: Southern Illinois University Press, 1973.

Wheaton, Christopher. "A History of the Screen Writers Guild (1920-1942)." Diss. University of Southern California, 1974.

Zierold, Norman. *The Moguls.* New York: Coward-McCann, Inc., 1969.

Writers

Abbe, George. *Stephen Vincent Benét on Writing.* Brattleboro, Vt.: The Stephen Greene Press, 1964.

Algren, Nelson. "Hollywood Dijun." *The Nation,* 25 July 1953, pp. 68-70.

Anderson, Maxwell. "Cut is the Branch That Might Have Grown Full Straight." In *Off Broadway,* ed., Maxwell Anderson. New York: William Sloan, 1947, pp. 67-74.

————. *Dramatist in America: Letters of Maxwell Anderson, 1912-1958.* Ed. Laurence G. Avery. Chapel Hill: University of North Carolina Press, 1977.

"Are Film Writers Workers?" *Pacific Weekly,* 29 June 1936, p. 371.

Austin, Texas. Humanities Research Center. Maxwell Anderson Collection.

Barnett, Lincoln. "The Happiest Couple of Them All." *Life,* 11 December 1944, pp. 100-106.

Basso, Hamilton. "William Faulkner: Man and Writer." *Saturday Review,* 28 July 1962, pp. 11-14.

Beach, Rex. "The Author and the Film." *The Mentor,* 1 July 1921, p. 31.

Behrman, S.N. *People in a Diary.* Boston: Little, Brown & Co., 1972.

Benchley, Nathaniel. *Robert Benchley.* New York: McGraw-Hill Book Co., 1955.

Benét, Stephen Vincent. *Selected Letters of Stephen Vincent Benet.* Ed. Charles A. Fenton. New Haven: Yale University Press, 1960.

Bishop, John Peale. "Their Royal Highnesses of Hollywood." *Vanity Fair*, April 1927, p. 70.

Blotner, Joseph. *Faulkner: A Biography. 2 vols.* New York: Random House, 1974.

Breit, Harvey. "A Talk With Mr. Schulberg." *New York Times Book Review*, 5 November 1950, p. 28.

Brenman-Wilson, Margaret. *Clifford Odets, American Playwright: The Years From 1906-1940.* New York: Atheneum, 1981.

Brown, John Mason. *The Worlds of Robert E. Sherwood: Mirror to His Times.* New York: Harper & Row, 1965.

Bruccoli, Matthew J. *The O'Hara Concern: A Biography of John O'Hara.* New York: Random House, 1975.

_____. *Some Sort of Epic Grandeur: The Life of F. Scott Fitzgerald.* New York: Harcourt, Brace and Jovanovich, 1981.

Cain, James M. "Camera Obscura." *American Mercury*, October 1933, pp. 138-46.

Cambridge, Massachusetts. Houghton Library. W. S. Braithewaite Papers.

_____. Houghton Library. John Mason Brown Papers.

_____. Houghton Library. Edgar Watson Howe Papers.

_____. Houghton Library. John Reed Papers.

_____. Houghton Library. Alexander Woollcott Papers.

Carey, Gary. "The Many Voices of Donald Ogden Stewart." *Film Comment*, Winter 1970, pp. 74-79.

Carmody, John. "Jim Cain: Master Teller of Hoary Old Hollywood Tales." *Los Angeles Times Calendar*, 2 February 1969, p. 8.

Carr, Gary Lee. "The Screen Writing Career of John Howard Lawson 1928-1947: Playwright at Work in Hollywood." Diss. University of Texas at Austin 1975.

Chandler, Raymond. "Oscar Night in Hollywood." *Atlantic Monthly*, March 1948, pp. 24-27.

_____. *Selected Letters of Raymond Chandler.* Ed. Frank MacShane. New York: Columbia University Press, 1981.

_____. "Writers in Hollywood." *Atlantic Monthly*, November 1945, pp. 50-54.

Connelly, Marc. *Voices Offstage.* New York: Holt, Rinehart & Winston, 1968.

Cowley, Malcolm. *Exile's Return: A Literary Odyssey of the 1920s.* New York: The Viking Press, Viking Press, 1957.

Cram, Mildred. "Author in Hollywood." *The American Spectator Yearbook.* Ed. George Jean Nathan, et. al. New York: Stokes Publishing Co., 1934.

Curtis, James. *Between Flops: A Biography of Preston Sturges.* New York: Harcourt, Brace and Jovanovich, 1982.

Dardis, Tom. *Some Time in the Sun: The Hollywood Years of Fitzgerald, Faulkner, Nathanael West, Aldous Huxley and James Agee.* New York: Charles Scribner's Sons, 1976.

Dos Passos, John. *The Best Times: An Informal Memoir.* New York American Library, 1966.

_____. *The Fourteenth Chronicle: Letters and Diaries of John Dos Passos.* Ed. Townsend Ludington. Boston: Gambit, Inc., 1973.

Dreiser, Theodore. "Myself and the Movies." *Esquire*, July 1943, pp. 43-44.

Dunne, Philip. "An Essay on Dignity." *The Screenwriter*, December 1945, pp. 31-38.

Farrell, James T. *The League of Frightened Philistines.* New York: The Vanguard Press, 1945.

Faulkner, William. *Faulkner's MGM Screenplays.* Ed. Bruce F. Kawin. Knoxville: University of Tennessee Press, 1982.

_____. *Selected Letters of William Faulkner.* Ed. Joseph Blotner. New York: Random House, 1977.

Fenton, Charles A. *Stephen Vincent Benét.* New Haven: Yale University Press, 1958.

Fitzgerald, F. Scott. *As Ever, Scott Fitz-.* Ed. Matthew J. Bruccoli. Philadelphia: J. B. Lippincott Co., 1972.

————. *Correspondence of F. Scott Fitzgerald.* Eds. Matthew J. Bruccoli and Margaret M. Duggan. New York: Random House, 1980.

————. *Letters of F. Scott Fitzgerald.* Ed. *Andrew Turnbull.* New York: Charles Scribner's Sons, 1963.

————. *The Last Tycoon.* New York: Charles Scribner's Sons, 1941.

————. *The Pat Hobby Stories.* New York: Charles Scribner's Sons, 1962.

Fowler, Douglas. *S. J. Perelman.* Boston: Twayne, 1983.

Fowler, Gene. "Confessions of a Celluloid-Eater." *Show Business Illustrated,* 2 January 1962, pp.14-18.

Freeman, Everett. *"Hollywood and The New Yorker." The Screenwriter,* June-July 1948, pp. 30-33.

Fuchs, Daniel. "A Hollywood Diary." *The New Yorker,* 6 August 1938, pp. 22-26.

————. "Days in the Gardens of Hollywood." *New York Times Book Review,* 28 July 1971, p.3.

Glyn, Anthony. *Elinor Glyn.* Garden City: Doubleday & Co., 1937.

Glyn, Elinor. *Romantic Adventure.* New York: E. P. Dutton & Co., 1937.

Goldstone, Richard. *Thornton Wilder: An Intimate Portrait.* New York: E. P. Dutton & Co., 1975.

Gottlieb, Lois. *Rachel Crothers.* Boston: Twayne, 1979.

Graham, Sheilah, with Gerold Frank. *Beloved Infidel.* New York: Holt, Rinehart & Winston, 1958.

————. *The Real F. Scott Fitzgerald.* New York: Grosset & Dunlop, 1976.

————. *The Rest of the Story.* New York: Coward-McCann, 1964.

Guiles, Fred Lawrence. *Hanging On in Paradise.* New York: McGraw-Hill Book Co., 1975.

Harriman, Margaret Case. "Miss Lilly of New Orleans." *The New Yorker,* 8 November 1941, pp. 22-32.

Hecht, Ben. *Charlie: The Improbable Life and Times of Charles MacArthur.* New York: Harper & Bros., 1957.

————. *A Child of the Century.* New York: Simon and Schuster, 1954.

————. *Letters From Bohemia.* Garden City: Doubleday & Co., 1964.

————. "My Testiment to the Movies." *Theater,* June 1929, pp. 31-35.

Hellman, Lillian. *Pentimento.* Boston: Little, Brown & Co., 1973.

————. *An Unfinished Woman.* Boston: Little, Brown & Co., 1969.

Hoopes, Roy. *Cain: The Biography of James M. Cain.* New York: Holt, Rinehart and Winston, 1982.

Hughes, Rupert. "Fiction Writers and Scenarios." *The Mentor,* 1 July 1921, p. 29.

Jones, Henry Arthur. "The Dramatist and the Photoplay." *The Mentor,* 1 July 1921, p. 29.

Johnson, Diane. *Dashiell Hammett: A Life.* New York: Random House, 1983.

Johnson, Nunnally. *The Letters of Nunnally Johnson.* Ed. Dorris Johnson and Ellen Leventhal. New York: Alfred A. Knopf, 1981.

Keats, John. *You Might As Well Live: The Life of Dorothy Parker.* New York: New York: Simon and Schuster, 1970.

Kellner, Bruce. *Carl Van Vechten and the Irreverent Decades.* Norman, Oklahoma: University of Oklahoma Press, 1968.

Kenny, Vincent S. *Paul Green.* New York: Twayne Publishers, 1971.

Kinney, Arthur F. *Dorothy Parker.* Boston: Twayne, 1978.

Kuehl, John and Bryer, Jackson, eds. *Dear Scott/Dear Max: The Fitzgerald-Perkins Correspondence.* New York: Charles Scribner's Sons, 1971.

Latham, Aaron. *Crazy Sundays: F. Scott Fitzgerald in Hollywood.* New York: The Viking Press, 1970.

Lazenby, Walter. *Paul Green.* Austin, Texas: Steck-Vaughn Co., 1970.

LeVot, Andre. *F. Scott Fitzgerald: A Biography.* Trans. William Byron. Garden City: Doubleday & Co., 1983.

Ludington, Townsend. *John Dos Passos: A Twentieth Century Odyssey.* New York: E. P. Dutton, 1980.

Luhr, William. *Raymond Chandler and Film.* New York: Frederick Ungar Publshing Co., 1982.

MacShane, Frank. *The Life of Raymond Chandler.* New York: E. P. Dutton & Co., 1976.

Madden, David. *James M. Cain.* New York: Twayne Publishers, 1970.

Martin, Jay. *Nathanael West: The Art of His Life.* New York: Farrar, Straus & Giroux, 1970.

Maugham, W. Somerset. "On Writing for Films." *North American Review,* May 1921, pp. 670-78.

Meryman, Richard. *Mank: The Wit, World and Life of Herman Mankiewicz.* New York: William Morrow & Co., 1978.

Miller, Gabriel. "Daniel Fuchs: A Creed Grows in Brooklyn." *Los Angeles Times Calendar,* 17 April 1977, p. 3.

Mizener, Arthur. *The Far Side of Paradise.* Boston: Houghton-Mifflin Co., 1951.

Moody, Richard. *Lillian Hellman: Playwright.* Indianapolis: Bobbs-Merrill Co., 1972.

New Haven, Connecticut. Beinecke Library. Stephen Vincent Benét Papers.

———. Beinecke Library. William Rose Benét Papers.

———. Beinecke Library. Thornton Wilder Papers.

Nolan, Paul T. *Marc Connelly.* New York: Twayne Publishers, 1969.

Nolan, William F. *Dashiell Hammett: A Casebook.* Santa Barbara: McNally & Loflin, Publishers, 1969.

Odets, Clifford. "How a Playwright Triumphs." *Harper's Magazine,* September 1966, pp. 64-75.

O'Hara, John. *Selected Letters of John O'Hara.* Ed. Matthew J. Bruccoli. New York: Random House, 1978.

Oppenheimer, George. *The View from the Sixties: Memoirs of a Life Spent.* New York: David McKay Co., 1966.

Parker, Sir Gilbert. "The Author and the Motion Picture." *The Mentor,* 1 July 1921, p. 14.

Perelman, S. J. "Moonstruck at Sunset." *The New Yorker,* 16 August 1964, pp. 28-31.

Plimpton, George, ed. *Writers at Work: The Paris Review Interviews.* 2nd ser. New York: The Viking Press, 1963.

Raphaelson, Samson. "Freundschraft." *The New Yorker,* 11 May 1981, pp. 38-66.

Reed, Kennth. *S. N. Behrman.* Boston: G. K. Hall & Co., 1975.

Rice, Elmer. *Minority Report: An Autobiography.* New York: Simon and Schuster, 1963.

Rinehart, Mary Roberts. *My Story.* New York: Farrar and Rinehart, 1931.

Rosmond, Babette. *Robert Benchley: His Life and Good Times.* Garden City: Doubleday & Co., 1970.

Ryan, Edith Millicent. "Cruel Words, Theodore Dreiser." *Los Angeles Times,* 27 September 1922, p. 14.

Sanderson, Elizabeth. "Ex-Detective Hammett." *The Bookman,* January-February 1932, p. 232.

Schulberg, Budd. *The Disenchanted.* New York: Random House, 1950.

———. *The Four Seasons of Success.* Garden City: Doubleday & Co., 1972.

———. *Moving Pictures: Memories of a Hollywood Prince.* New York: Stein and Day, 1981.

———. *What Makes Sammy Run?* New York: Random House, 1941.

Schultheiss, John. "A Study of the 'Eastern' Writer in Hollywood in the 1930s." Diss. University of Southern California, 1973.

Sherwood, Robert E. "Footnote to a Preface." *Saturday Review,* 6 August 1949, p. 134.

———. "Renaissance in Hollywood." *American Mercury,* April 1929, pp. 431-37.

Shivers, Alfred S. *The Life of Maxwell Anderson.* New York: Stein and Day, 1983.

Sidney, George. "Faulkner in Hollywood: His Career as a Scenarist." Diss. University of New Mexico 1959.

Simon, Linda. *Thornton Wilder: His World*. Garden City: Doubleday & Co., 1979.

Smith, Edward. "Dreiser—After Twenty Years." *The Bookman*, March 1931, p. 276-92.

Smith, H. Allen. *The Life and Legend of Gene Fowler*. New York: William Marrow & Co., 1977.

Stempel, Tom. "Interview with Nunnally Johnson." 9 October 1968 - 5 February 1969. American Film Institute, Beverly Hills, California.

————. *Screenwriter: The Life and Times of Nunnally Johnson*. New York: A. S. Barnes & Co., 1980.

Stewart, Donald Ogden. *By a Stroke of Luck: An Autobiography*. New York: Paddington Press, 1975.

————. "Writing for the Movies." *Focus on Film*, November-December 1970, pp. 49-57.

Teichman, Howard. "The Man Who Hated Hollywood." *New York Times Book Review*, 30 April 1972, p. 11.

Townsend, Dorothy. "The Queen of Wisecracks Marshalls Her Subjects." *Los Angeles Times*, 18 June 1962, p. 17.

Turnbull, Andrew. *Scott Fitzgerald*. New York: Charles Scribner's Sons, 1962.

van Gelder, Robert. *Writers and Writing*. New York: Charles Scribner's Sons, 1946.

Van Vechten, Carl. "Fabulous Hollywood." *Vanity Fair*, May 1927, p. 54.

————. "Hollywood Parties." *Vanity Fair*, June 1927, pp. 47, 86, 90.

————. "Hollywood Royalty." *Vanity Fair*, July 1927, pp. 38, 86.

————. "Understanding Hollywood." *Vanity Fair*, August 1927, pp. 45, 78.

Viertal, Salka. *The Kindness of Strangers*. New York: Holt, Rinehart & Winston, 1969.

Warga, Wayne. "From Hollywood to HUAC with Hellman." *Los Angeles Times Calendar*, 10 June 1976, p. 3.

Weales, Gerald. *Clifford Odets: Playwright*. New York: Pegasus Publishers, 1971.

West, Nathanael. *The Day of the Locust*. 1939; rpt. New York: New Directions Paperback, 1962.

Wilson, Edmund. *The Boys in the Backroom*. San Francisco: Colt Press, 1941.

Wylie, Philip. "Writing for the Movies." *Harper's Magazine*, November, 1933, pp. 715-26.

Zolotow, Maurice. *Billy Wilder in Hollywood*. New York: G. P. Putnam's Sons, 1977.

Index